Hanover and Great Britain 1740–1760

Gerlach Adolph von Münchhausen (1688–1770). *Schrader, courtesy Historisches Museum, Hanover.*

Hanover and Great Britain 1740–1760

Diplomacy and survival

Uriel Dann

Leicester University Press
(a division of Pinter Publishers)
Leicester, London

First published in Great Britain in 1991 by Leicester University Press
(a division of Pinter Publishers Limited)

Editorial offices
Fielding Johnson Building University of Leicester
University Road, Leicester, LE1 7RH

Trade and other enquiries
25 Floral Street, London, WC2E 9DS and P.O. Box 157, Irvington, New York.

British Library Cataloguing in Publication Data
A CIP cataloguing record for this book is available
from the British Library
ISBN 0-7185-1352-5

Library of Congress Cataloguing-in-Publication Data
Dann, Uriel, 1922–
Hanover and Great Britain, 1740–1760: diplomacy and survival / Uriel Dann.
p. cm.
Includes bibliographical references and index.
ISBN 0-7185-1352-5
1. Great Britain—Foreign relations—1727-1760. 2. Great Britain—Foreign relations — Germany (West) — Hannover (Province) 3. Hannover (Germany : Province)—Foreign relations—Great Britain. 4. Hanover, House of. I. Title.
DA498.D36 1991
941.07—dc20 90-23110 CIP

Typeset by Koinonia Ltd, Bury, Lancashire
Printed and bound in Great Britain by Biddles Ltd., Guildford and Kings Lynn

In Memory of My Parents
Margot and Alfred Dann

Contents

Preface

George I and George II never ceased to feel as Hanoverians. Their devotion to the land of their birth made the Hanoverian connection a factor of consequence to Britain; it made the British connection the major factor of political life for Hanover. Largely for this reason, between 1740 and 1760—from the accession of Frederick II to the throne of Prussia until the death of George II—Hanover was exposed to dangers which appeared to threaten her survival and which therefore gave the British connection a new poignancy.

Though this is a political history, economic and cultural aspects cannot be entirely disregarded. Apart from their innate significance they bear on our understanding of events, at the very least. The bulk of the study is narrative-analytical which ought not to need an apology.

My most important source is the Hanoverian office in London between 1714 and 1837, styled the Deutsche Kanzlei. Without detracting from the interest of the other material used, 'Hann. 92', the Deutsche Kanzlei files now in the state archives at Hanover, are the skeleton which gives my story cohesion. In quotations from German I have modernized spelling and punctuation. I have left quotation marks whenever I translated direct speech into English. Dates in Britain before September 1752 (and in Russia throughout) are Old Style, unless denoted otherwise. The year always starts with 1 January.

This study originated in 1980 as an Oxford D. Phil. thesis, supervised by Dr. Paul Langford. It was published in 1986 in German by Verlag August Lax, Hildesheim, under the auspices of the Historischer Verein für Niedersachsen. Both the German and the present editions have benefited from criticism of the earlier versions and from recent research. I am particularly indebted to Professor Walther Mediger for his continuing concern. Professor Ragnhild Hatton and Dr. John B. Owen put at my disposal their views of my thesis.

Her Majesty the Queen has graciously permitted me to use the Royal Archives at Windsor. Also, I am obliged to H.R.H. the Prince of Hanover and to Freiherr Siegfried von Cramm for access to their house archives.

The staffs of the Niedersächsisches Hauptstaatsarchiv, of the British Library and of the other depositories utilized were invariably helpful. The Gerda Henkel Stiftung assisted me with a generous grant. The cooperation of the Moshe Dayan Centre, Tel-Aviv University, was invaluable—the more so, as the relations between Hanover and Great Britain 1740–1760 do not normally come within its purview; my special gratitude goes to Mrs. Lydia Gareh. Professor Aubrey N. Newman made the present edition possible by the active interest he showed in its publication. At Leicester University Press I owe thanks, above all, to Mr. Alec McAulay, the publisher, and Ms. Jane Evans, the production editor of my work. My daughter Naomi served as rear headquarters during the gestation period of the thesis, an inconspicuous but essential charge.

My wife identified with the task since its beginnings in 1974. She lived to know that the English revision had been accepted for publication and she was pleased.

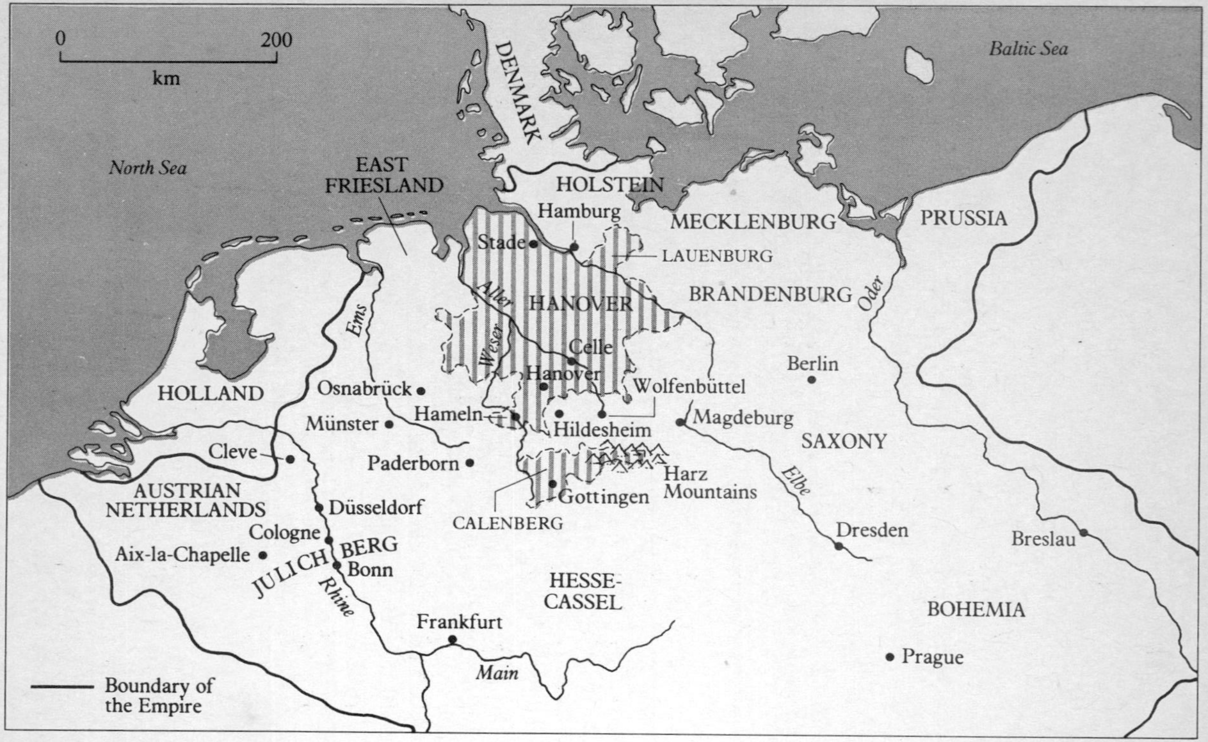
0
200
km
North Sea
Baltic Sea
DENMARK
EAST
FRIESLAND
HOLSTEIN
Hamburg
Stade
LAUENBURG
MECKLENBURG
PRUSSIA
BRANDENBURG
Oder
HANOVER
Aller
Weser
Ems
Celle
Hanover
Berlin
HOLLAND
Osnabrück
Wolfenbüttel
Hameln
Hildesheim
Magdeburg
Münster
SAXONY
Cleve
Paderborn
Harz
Mountains
Elbe
AUSTRIAN
NETHERLANDS
Düsseldorf
Gottingen
CALENBERG
Cologne
Dresden
Breslau
BERG
Aix-la-Chapelle
JULICH
Bonn
Rhine
HESSE-
CASSEL
Frankfurt
BOHEMIA
Prague
Main
Boundary of
the Empire

Introduction
Hanover in the mid-eighteenth century

In 1740 the 'Electorate of Hanover', as it was commonly called,[1] comprised an area of about 26,000 sq. km (roughly 10,000 English sq. miles) and 700,000 inhabitants. The area was fairly compact; its smaller southern part, with Göttingen and a portion of the Hartz, was separated from the bulk of the state by a strip of Brunswick-Wolfenbüttel to which—as the 'elder line of the Guelph house'—Hanover was closely allied dynastically. The capital Hanover was with its 14,000 inhabitants by far the most considerable town in the electorate.

These facts place Hanover in the Empire far behind the Habsburg lands in Germany, and Prussia. Hanover could put forward a somewhat ambitious claim to be considered on a par with the electorates of Saxony and Bavaria, and she was clearly superior to all the other German states. This classification does not allow for Hanover's connection with Britain nor, for that matter, Saxony's with Poland.[2] Both connections are imponderables; the former is the theme of the present work.

Topographically the electorate was almost entirely part of the flat or slightly undulating North German plain. To the north of the city of Hanover the soil was generally poor—heather and moors, with strips of rich, converted marshes; to the south there was much good clay. The hill country of central Germany protruded into the south of the electorate—still densely wooded then, and alive with deer and boar. The Hartz mountains in the south-east, though only moderately high, were wild and strange; their economy and their population set them apart from the rest of the state. The entire electorate fell within the river systems of the Weser and Elbe, both of which empty into the North Sea.

The people were Germans of Lower Saxon stock, and *plattdeutsch* was universally spoken. Exceptions were Upper Saxon mining communities in the Hartz and remnants of the earlier Slavonic population along the Elbe—the 'Wenden'. Popular assessment of character portrayed the lower Saxon as stolid, conservative and unenterprising; stubborn and litigious at the parish-pump level; and, above that level, as unpolitical and steadfast in his loyalties; a hard fighter; uncommunicative; unintellectual but not unintelligent. The vagueness of these generalizations and the danger of turning them into emotive slogans need no emphasis. Still, an accumulation of observable detail suggests that they contain as much truth as can be expected from their nature.

The population derived its living from an agriculture notably stagnant in technique. Sheep-rearing and horse-breeding took second place to field crops. Even the burghers of the many tiny towns were *Ackerbürger*, peasants with the social and legal status of townsmen, more often than craftsmen, shopkeepers or professionals. 'Industries' dependent on agriculture—clothmaking and tanning, beekeeping, brewing and distilling—were important chiefly for the home market. If anything, economic activity in terms of cash earning was on the decline. The salt springs of

Lüneburg and the metal ores of the Hartz, of first rank in the economy of Europe in the sixteenth century, had lost much of their importance by the mid-eighteenth century. Though the electorate had a sea coast, it had no seagoing ships.

Then again, in spite of its favourable location in the heart of Europe the electorate played no significant part in transcontinental communications. It had no metalled roads until about 1770.[3] The trade between the British Isles and Holland on the one side, and Poland and Russia on the other, went by sea, via the old-established ports on the Baltic. Neither the mouth of the Elbe nor that of the Weser was Hanoverian territory. The Elbe, in any case, was only marginally a Hanoverian river. The Weser was better placed to serve Hanover, and the great lock at Hameln still bears evidence of the care of Gerlach Adolph von Münchhausen.[4] Even so, the authorities looked on this riverway mainly as a source of transit tolls—like other governments of the day—to the detriment of commercial enterprise. One practical advantage which the location of Hanover offered was to the mail riders who travelled across north Germany with their light burdens and relative indifference to the state of roads. It was a boon to British intelligence, thanks to the efficiency of Hanoverian interception services.

The most remarkable facet of the economy of the electorate was its stagnancy; it was also its most persistent. The political leaders of Hanover between 1714 and 1866 were deeply suspicious of economic advance, whether as understood by mercantilists or by *laissez-faire* capitalists. No fundamental difference in outlook emerged in this respect from the *Geheime Räte*, from the post-Napoleonic *Staats- und Kabinettsminister* who ruled Hanover for George IV and William IV, or from kings Ernest Augustus and George V, who again reigned at Hanover. Together they kept the electorate far beneath its probable economic potential. Their attitude was consonant with the consensus of Hanoverian society. It is only since the Prussian annexation of 1866 that Hanover has entered the modern industrial and commercial age.

It was not only the economy of Hanover that was backward, by applicable standards of comparison and potential in the reign of George II, for the same can be said of the society as a whole. The arable land was mostly owned by the crown, by the nobility, and by the ecclesiastical institutions that had survived the Reformation. Tenure was in the main in the hands of the peasants, who held their land by *Meierrecht*: they were personally free, and given hereditary possession that was reasonably secure, but subject to manifold and heavy imposts due to the landlord as well as to the central government. Still, in Hanover the peasant was no worse off than in most other German states, and much better off than, say, in Poland, Hungary or Ireland. The landowning nobility was decidedly the backbone of the social and political order; its position enhanced by the usual absence of the elector. It was of immemorial lineage, whose members rarely intermarried with other ranks, and kept up an enormous self-respect. It formed the one effective component of the *Landschaften* (see below). It enjoyed far-reaching immunity from taxation, but it was not rich. The landed estates were small when compared to those in many other parts of Germany, and the economy was too primitive to provide high monetary incomes. Hence the nobility was accustomed to look to the crown for suitable employment, and by the reign of George II it had come to corner most of the influential, prestigious and lucrative offices of the electorate. However, the nobility was neither absentee nor parasitic, and its identification with the family seat was as complete as that with the state. It recognized obligations as well as rights—though this juxtaposition would not have made much sense to most of their order. Townspeople and peasantry—and the clergy, for that matter—knew their station. One of the most pervasive impressions the student of history receives is the absence in the electorate of 'revolutionary tension'. (The mining communities of the Hartz may be considered a marginal exception.)

The established church was Lutheran (*evangelisch*); politically it was entirely subservient to the authorities. Calvinists (*Reformierte*), Catholics and Jews, in all a tiny fraction of the population, were fundamentally strangers in the society—Calvinists least so, Jews most. They all received a degree of official toleration, rather grudgingly measured out to each minority, with the central government more liberal by and large than either local authorities or popular attitudes—a picture presented in the eighteenth century throughout Europe.

The standards of schooling in Hanover were as good as anywhere in Germany, and far higher than in contemporary England. Elementary education had been compulsory for generations, though in practice such stipulations were not fulfilled to the letter. However, every considerable village had its schoolmaster—supervised by the local pastor—who taught reading and, with less emphasis, writing and arithmetic. A fair number of towns and some religious institutions maintained grammar schools, some of which had an excellent reputation. The University of Göttingen was not merely new but 'modern' in purpose with its stress on the 'cameral sciences'.

Considering the size of its population, Hanover in 1740 had a considerable standing army—about 20,000 strong.[5] By the standards of the time it was well equipped: its muskets were produced in a state-owned factory at Herzberg in the Hartz region. The army had a good reputation, and it had reliably proved its worth against Louis XIV and the Turks on the side of the Emperor. It was very dear to George II, an enthusiastic amateur soldier. And yet Hanover was anything but militaristic. The ruling aristocracy did not consider soldiering the finest career open to its sons, and an appreciable part of the officer corps were commoners. All three commanders-in-chief between 1740 and 1760 came of non-Hanoverian families. Recruiting was genuinely voluntary on the whole. Even at the height of the Seven Years War, when there was conscription, we find an occasional readiness in the Privy Council at Hanover to excuse the unwillingness of the population to submit. Furthermore, the primacy of the civilian power over the military was never in doubt.

The electoral revenues amounted in the years of peace prior to 1756 to about 4 million thaler, (some £700,000) p.a.[6] The largest income was provided by the domains, the Hartz ore workings and the Lüneburg salt pans, all of which were treated as the elector's freehold. These revenues paid for the court and the electoral administration. The item second in importance was the *Licent*, an excise duty on a wide range of consumption goods, which was collected through the *Landschaften* (see below), whose consent was needed for changes in rates and incidence. The *Licent* was supposed to cover the cost of the army in peacetime. (An analogy with the contemporary British dualism of Civil List versus Parliament-controlled budgeting is tempting, but does not lead far.) River and road tolls and custom duties played only a secondary role in the sluggish economy of Hanover. In times of war throughout the eighteenth century the army, and indeed the state household, relied on foreign subsidies. Royal remittances from London, though regular and involving considerable sums (see below, p. 128), cannot properly be classified as 'electoral revenues'. They went to the Privy Purse (*Schatulle*) or the War Treasury (*Kriegsgewölbe*), and until the Seven Years War they entered circulation only in rare cases. Direct taxation was not entirely unknown, but it counted for little.

Like most states of the *ancien régime*, Hanover could not be considered a unit either historically or constitutionally. It was a conglomerate, under a common hereditary ruler, of a rough dozen of duchies, principalities and counties each with its own traditions and privileges. Six or seven of their number (depending on whether Bremen[7] and Verden are treated as one or two) still had their *Landschaften*, their provincial assemblies. There the three estates, of prelates (emphatically not co-terminous with 'the clergy'), nobles (strictly, the owners of 'noble' estates—who might be commoners in rare cases), and burgesses met to discuss grievances, vote *new* taxes, and dispense patronage.[8] In effect these activities were carried out in committee—the *Ausschüsse* which were noble preserves to all intents and purposes. However, for the purposes of political history these sturdy remnants of past divisions can and should be disregarded. When they came to consider Hanover's part on the European stage, George II and his advisers deliberated with as little concern for Grubenhagen or Lauenburg as historical entities as ever Frederick II did respecting Neumark or Halberstadt.

* * *

Since the present work is a political history, the formal, constitutional, rules which provided the framework for George II and his Hanoverian advisers must be examined in closer detail. Special attention, moreover, must be given to those rules which applied to the governing of the country in the absence of the elector—and his absence was the norm after 1714 when Elector George Louis succeeded to the British throne as George I. Also, since the theme is Hanoverian relations with Britain, comparisons must be drawn with relevant British constitutional practices of the time.

Though the electorate was not a limited monarchy in the British sense, it was not 'governed despotically from Hanover' either, as British historians have tended to think.[9] It had its Custom of the Constitution which owed much of its evolution to the century that preceded 1740—as in England. The fundamental difference is that, unlike in England, the evolution in Hanover was initiated and steered from above, with no convulsions to, or from, the body politic. It is a very German phenomenon.

The basic constitutional document which concerns the history of Hanover during the personal union with Britain is the *Regierungsreglement* which Duke Ernest Augustus of Brunswick-Lüneburg promulgated for his principalities of Calenberg and Grubenhagen in 1680.[10]

Ernest Augustus deserves the main credit for the upswing of Guelph fortunes in the latter half of the seventeenth century. His beginnings were not particularly propitious, however: the youngest of four brothers, in 1662 he became the Protestant lay Bishop of Osnabrück under the terms of the Westphalian Peace which 'alternated' that see between a bishop elected by the catholic chapter, and a lay prince chosen by the Duke of Brunswick-Lüneburg. It looked like a dead end. But Ernest Augustus was a baroque ruler of the better stamp. He was clear-sighted, single-minded and unscrupulous. He was also lucky. The death of two elder brothers, the one childless, the other without sons, secured him in 1680 the hereditary principalities of Calenberg (capital, Hanover) and Grubenhagen in the first place. Subsequently he obtained the expectancy of his eldest surviving brother George William's duchy of Celle. In due course he enforced the rule of primogeniture; the custom of partition had been the bane of the Guelphs for nearly 500 years. Then, in 1692, he obtained from the

Emperor for his own and his brother's territories the coveted dignity of electorship—not for those of his cousins at Wolfenbüttel.[11] It was the ninth *Kur*.[12]

Ernest Augustus's elevation sealed an Imperial concept of the first rank. It spelled the mission of the new electorate to stand guard in the Protestant north of the Empire against the soaring advance of Hohenzollern Brandenburg-Prussia—a mission which Ernest Augustus, his son and his grandson, never forgot.

The greatest stroke of Ernest Augustus was his marriage to the Princess Sophia of the Palatinate in 1658, though he could not have known it at the time. By 1689 Sophia with her children had become the only Protestant survivor among the descendants of James I of England, apart from the daughters of James II. When Ernest Augustus died in 1698, his first-born son and successor George Louis stood a fair chance of perpetuating through his person not merely a greatly augmented electorate of Brunswick-Lüneburg, but also the Protestant settlement in England and Scotland.

The *Regierungsreglement* of 1680 consolidated rather than changed existing constitutional forms. But its clarity and directness, and the consistency with which it was to be applied in both letter and spirit, make it the key to an understanding of the Hanoverian polity for more than a century.

The government of Calenberg and Grubenhagen was vested in four Colleges (*Collegia*): the Privy Council (*Geheime Ratsstube, Geheimes Ratskollegium* and *Geheimer Rat*; these terms are used interchangeably, though the last, being ambiguous, is the least frequent); the Board (*Kammer*); the Chancery (*Justizkanzlei*); and the Consistory (*Konsistorium*). The existence of two further bodies directly subject to the ruler is implied in the *Reglement*, though evidently they were not part of the 'government': they are the *Hofmarschallamt* in charge of the ducal household, and the army establishment. A fifth college, the War Chancery (*Kriegskanzlei*), was set up by Ernest Augustus before his death, both to relieve the Privy Council of part of its enormous burden and to ensure greater efficiency in military matters at a time when Hanover was becoming ever more involved in the crises which convulsed Europe. The members of all Colleges, as well as the higher charges in army and *Hofmarschallamt*, were appointed by the ruler and held office during his pleasure; this point is not explicitly made in the *Reglement*, since it was self-evident to contemporaries.

Chief among the Colleges was the Privy Council, though in accordance with the collegiate principle it exercised no formal jurisdiction over its compeers. The *Reglement* describes its character and competences as they basically were to remain until 1837. Its members alone were *Geheime Räte*, *sans phrase*.[13] It dealt with foreign affairs, army administration, police matters and what would today be called 'internal security', and with all that touched upon 'privileges': feudal tenure, charters, religious endowments and, above all, the *Landschaften*. In addition, the *Reglement* entrusted the Privy Council with supervisory and co-ordinating functions of great significance. The three remaining Colleges were enjoined to bring affairs 'of special importance' before the Privy Council for comment and approval, though the Privy Council could not enforce its own view if it diverged from that of the other body. If discussion *in pleno* did not lead to agreement, or a vote taken among the members of both Colleges concerned showed no majority, then the issue was to be left to the ruler. In practice, however, the pre-eminence of the Privy Council was facilitated by provisions in the *Reglement* which gave the chair of each College (except, most of the time, the Consistory) to a Privy Councillor.

Within the Privy Council each member took charge of a particular field—whether a department subject immediately to the Privy Council or to one of the other Colleges at which he doubled, or with regard to matters of continuous import not functionally organized. When a member presented the issue under his care together with his vote, his colleagues in Council voted in reverse order of seniority; the resolution was by majority.[14] Thus the chairman—the senior member of the Privy Council—was merely convener and co-ordinator, so far as the constitution was concerned. He derived what power and influence he had within the Council from his personal qualities, and from his standing with the ruler; the two factors often coincided, not always. The *Reglement* did not make clear the working relationship between the Privy Council and the ruler. Obviously they were his servants, and their *raison d'être* lay in facilitating a rule as autocratic as circumstances permitted. But on the same reckoning they had to be efficient, and the *Reglement* explicitly allowed them to act on their own responsibility whenever speed was imperative, or public danger was to be averted.

The remaining Colleges can be dismissed briefly, for the present purpose. The Board was to administer the domains—in Hanover, as everywhere in Germany, still the main source of 'state' revenue. (Taxation concerned the *Landschaften* whose dealings were with the Privy Council, as mentioned above). The Board also checked the accounts of the court. The Chancery administered justice; the Consistory, church affairs and education—again, with the limitations in favour of the Privy Council mentioned above. The *Reglement* also concerned itself with the smooth working of the Colleges by briefing *Geheim*-secretaries, stressing the need for orderly minutes, and regulating reports to the ruler, both written and oral.

* * *

When Elector George Louis prepared to assume his British crown in August 1714 his foremost concern was the welfare and administration of Hanover in his absence. Therefore, on 29 August he promulgated his own *Regierungsreglement*, explicitly based on his father's *Reglement* of 1680.[15] For this reason, and through the circumstances that occasioned it, *Reglement II* was evidently conceived as an *ad hoc* set of instructions rather than a constitution. However, its longevity—it survived until the French occupation of 1803—its thoroughness, which dealt with every significant contingency and, above all, its incisive common sense make it in the context of the present study a document of great importance.

They key to *Reglement II* is the last sentence of paragraph 9: '... Our Privy Councillors who stay at home shall ... make it their foremost concern [*vornehmstes Absehen*] that our lands and people may live in peace and quiet; and they shall also keep up, so far as possible, a good understanding with the neighbours so that no unnecessary consequences may arise.' All else is mere application of this guiding principle. Even so the details are of great significance in themselves for the light they throw on the relationship between the elector and his Privy Council (and indeed, his political public in general); and, since the elector's absence became the norm, for the pattern they laid for the future. The problem which exercised the elector above all was security: the chance of war and invasion; troop movements and concentrations along the borders; demands for military passage through Hanoverian territory—in brief, man-made perils of every description. Here the guideline of *Reglement II*, apart from the overriding principle of taking such immediate action as the situation might demand, including 'violence for violence', was constant consultation between the

Privy Council and the ranking army officer. When no particular danger threatened, the Privy Council was to treat 'matters of peace and war' *ad referendum* until the elector's pleasure could be taken—but it was the Privy Council's express responsibility to determine what constituted 'danger'. The diplomatic representatives of Hanover were to report to the Privy Council, with duplicate reports despatched to London; the exception was the legation at the Imperial Diet at Ratisbon, which need not send to London more than 'brief summaries'—an interesting reflection on the state and prestige of the Empire. Ordinances and other edicts which ordinarily were signed by the elector were to be signed *ad mandatum* by the Privy Councillor departmentally in charge. (The vote, as distinct from the signature, was taken in collegiate form; see above.) However, edicts 'of some importance'—no elaboration was offered—were to be sent to London to ascertain the elector's pleasure.

Reglement II is more precise in financial matters than was its predecessor. The Privy Council might indeed, when necessary, authorize expenditure not budgeted for in advance; but if such expenditure exceeded fifty thaler, all the Privy Councillors had to sign the assignation.[16] Appointments to vacancies in any College or its dependent agencies, above a rather inferior grade, were to be referred to the elector through the Privy Council, which presumably vetted recommendations. Clemency and the remission of sentences remained the prerogative of the elector. However, the Privy Council had a negative say, since it might order sentences, including capital sentences, to be carried out unless it decided to refer the case to London. 'A person of quality' (*eine vornehme Person*) was to have special status; on sufficient evidence he (or she) might be arrested and brought to court, but no sentence was to be carried out without the elector's order.

The collegiate character of the Privy Council is brought into relief by the directive that every report to the elector is to be signed by every privy councillor. The privy councillors were empowered to sign letters of enfeoffment. By 1714 this was a matter of mostly formal importance. However, the relevant commission as stylized in *Reglement II* introduces the title by which Hanoverian privy councillors were addressed, with minor variations, until the French occupation of 1803: *Königlich Grossbritannische zur Kurfürstlich Braunschweig-Lüneburgischen Regierung verordnete Geheime Räte.*

The last paragraph of *Reglement II*, despite its horribly involuted style, is evidently more than a flourish. It can be sensibly paraphrased as 'So long as I trust you, you may trust me'. By and large it is the *Leitmotiv* of the relations between three generations of Hanoverian kings in Britain and their German ministries.

The two documents annotated so far are valid as expressions of the elector's authority. A third document is derived from a different source, and it carries authority of another kind.

When Bernhard Christoph von Behr, a senior Hanoverian diplomatist, was appointed to the Privy Council in 1754, Münchhausen wrote for him an 'Instruction concerning the Brunswick-Lüneburgian Privy Council and Board'.[17] Nobody could have been better qualified for this task than Münchhausen. His pre-eminence in the ministry had by then been established for long, though he was not formally to become 'Premier minister' for another eleven years, and he had in him a strong didactic strain. What could be expected of him was not an analytical critique but a level-headed description of constitutional practice as it then stood, and this is what he gave. The following points attract the historian's attention:

1. The *Reglements* of 1680 and 1714 were much alive in 1754. Münchhausen not merely cites them as fundamental to the constitution, but his narrative makes it clear that few amendments had been made—none of them of incisive importance. There is no hint that the *Reglements* might be outmoded or in any way opposed to the good of the country. There is also no hint that any of the provisions were inoperative in practice or ought to be treated as such.

2. On the other hand, the *Instruction* is full of suggestions, subtle and perhaps not wholly conscious, which enhance the importance of the ministry *vis-à-vis* the elector, the other Colleges, the army command, the public. No new rules are invented, but the emphases are different: the ministry's role as channel between the country and its prince; the desirability of not burdening the elector—or even the mails—with trivia; the ministry's powers when dealing with the *Landschaften*; the ministry's obligation to protect 'the subjects' against possible excesses of the militia; improper petitioning of the elector to the prejudice of justice, order and, of course, the ministers' standing. It all somehow assumes a larger dimension than in either of the two *Reglements*. Consultations between the ministry and the ranking army officer in times of danger, which play such a prominent part in *Reglement II*, find no mention in the *Instruction*, though in fact they did take place.

3. Münchhausen does full justice to his reputation as a pedant. His *Instruction* goes into incredible detail. (Who of us knew that it takes 1,200 sheep one night to provide manure for one *Morgen*?) In mitigation it can be said that this fussiness was not alien to the spirit of the times—the *Zopfzeit*—in much of Europe; that none of it is in itself stupid, and most of it is interesting; and lastly, that the *Instruction* does after all deal with all the significant matters clearly and competently.

* * *

It is instructive to compare the Hanoverian decrees regarding the government of the electorate in the elector's absence with those which George I and George II issued as kings of Great Britain whenever they went to Hanover.[18] Even at first glance the similarities hit the eye, while the dissimilarities are easily explained as technicalities. The period was the same, the sovereigns were the same. The fundamental objective was the same: to ensure security and continuity; to delegate power without forgoing control. Indeed, there was no institutional parallel in Britain to the *Geheimes Ratskollegium*; the British Privy Council of the eighteenth century bore no resemblance to the 'Privy Council' at Hanover, whatever the legal position of the former may have been at the time.

But by 1740 (and indeed one or two generations earlier) a Cabinet Council had evolved in Britain that bears comparison with the Hanoverian ministry in important respects: in social class—it was overwhelmingly composed of the landowning nobility; in organization—departmental functions developing on a collegiate basis; in numbers—twelve to twenty in Britain, as against the customary seven to nine *Geheime Räte*. And just as the Hanoverian ministry had no chief, though it had a senior member who was not necessarily its *de facto* leader,[19] so the British Cabinet Council member who led in precedence, the Archbishop of Canterbury, certainly did not lead in consequence. And since twelve to twenty men without an institutionally recognized chief, most of whom had their distinct offices which did not bear on the political governance of the realm and who were, moreover, often uninterested in politics, cannot effectively govern—an 'inner' or 'effective cabinet' of five or six members had developed within the Cabinet Council, 'those Lords whom His Majesty was pleased to direct should be consulted in his most secret affairs'. Something comparable had occurred in Hanover, where two or three *Geheime Räte* would habitually consult on important affairs before the *Collegium* as a whole would issue its memoranda with their impressive array of signatures.

The last comparison that can be made between the two 'ministries' (in the British case either the Cabinet Council or the inner cabinet) is strictly functional: both were chiefly concerned with foreign policy; eighteenth century government dealt with few of the domestic concerns which take up most of government energy in our own time, and in the middle of the eighteenth century the governments of Britain and Hanover were even less active in this field than most others in Europe—though for different reasons. Also, both ministries shared the problem of how to arrogate to themselves a fair share of influence in foreign policy, while foreign policy was still regarded as in the decision sphere of the sovereign in a special sense, even in the 'limited monarchy' of Britain. But here the exercise in approximation must cease: by 1740 it was the chief function of the inner cabinet, 'constitutional' in the English meaning of the term, to bridge between the king and the House of Commons. While the *Geheimes Ratskollegium* did have its occasional vexations with the *Landschaften*, this was another world altogether: Hanover had no national parliament.

All in all, it is a fundamental parallel to the Hanoverian solution that in Britain the members of the Cabinet Council, for all their as yet undefined status, were commissioned as 'Guardians and Justices of the Kingdom' the moment the king embarked for Hanover, or 'Lords Justices', as their working appellation went. It is not surprising that the competences of the British Lords Justices resembled—*mutatis mutandis*—those of the Hanoverian *Geheime Räte*. By and large limitations on the former seem more pronounced, though not substantially so. After all, the king's dignity in Britain was a more tender plant than the elector's in Hanover—at least, it is obvious that George II thought so. As to emergencies, Hanover lay more exposed to sudden invasion than Britain, and after 1740 this contingency became a terrifying danger, as we shall see. Hence the discretionary powers accorded to the Hanoverian ministers in this field make more poignant reading, though in legal analysis they did not differ from what the British regents might do in a similar case. Then there was Parliament: the king could not delegate his authority to the Lords Justices, as he did to the *Geheime Räte* with respect to the various *Landschaften*. (Parliament did not sit while the king was abroad; it was not to be dissolved unless by his order.) 'That you [the Lords Justices] may be the better enabled to discharge the great trust We have reposed in you', the king would not accept petitions for the redress of oppression which had not first been addressed to the regents. The Hanoverian equivalent was stricter. There, petitions to London were practically prohibited altogether. However, the king made one formal concession which as elector he admitted merely in practice: the Lords Justices were expressly permitted to suspend the execution of any royal order which they thought impracticable, pending clarification.

Like the Hanoverian *Reglement* of 1714, the 'Instructions' to the Lords Justices paid attention to the burning issues of the hour. Thus the 'Instructions' of 1748 referred in some detail to France, which had acceded to the preliminary peace of Aix-la-Chapelle, and to Spain, which as yet had not. In their relations with the armed forces the British regents seem to have had more express authority than the

Hanoverian ministry; there certainly was no difference in practice.

One divergence deserves at least passing notice. The British instructions to the regents usually open with an injunction 'in a particular manner' to have regard for religion as 'the surest foundation for a nation's happiness'. Nothing of the kind appears as a preamble to either *Reglement*, or indeed in any directive of the elector to his Hanoverian ministers. And yet the Whig nobles were often free-thinkers, whereas their Hanoverian counterparts were all of them, so far as we can sense, deeply religious. The historian who is unversed in psychology can merely register the facts.

Liaison worked in similar ways at Herrenhausen—the electoral summer residence near Hanover—and in London. One member of the Hanoverian ministry permanently attended on George II in London, and a Council member (normally the secretary of state for the Northern Department) went with the king to Hanover. (George I had occasionally kept two Hanoverian ministers by his side in London, and both secretaries of state in Hanover. Serious inconveniences arose.) In each case skeleton secretariats developed. That in London—the *Deutsche Kanzlei* or 'German Chancery' housed in St James's Palace—naturally was permanent and hence more elaborate. Even so it seem to have been strangely starved of personnel, considering its load.[20] After 1714 no British representation in Hanover was considered necessary, whether diplomatic or consular. In London the head of the German Chancery ranked officially as the Hanoverian minister-resident.

It is no constitutional monarchy in the British tradition that emerges from the Hanoverian documents. The *Reglements* of 1680 and 1714 emanated from the ruler's will alone. They did not represent a political nation, in our sense or even in the English, contemporaneous sense. They are in the spirit of the absolutist state, and they mirror its reality to no small extent. But this is only part of the truth. These decrees amount to a fundamental law; they intricately order the polity to which they apply. They might have been repealed—but they never were repealed until that polity was shattered from without. Moreover, when this fundamental law was promulgated, the polity was still largely pre-absolutist, and the conditions created in 1714 ensured that absolutism receded rather than advanced. The elector accepted the situation. He would manipulate; he rarely coerced. It begs the question to argue that he had no need to act with harshness. And last not least, both decrees assume that the foremost servants of the state are men with a stake in the country, not *novi homines* or paid officials only: conservative indeed, but active, knowledgeable and with a habit of responsibility; possessed of a loyalty that went to the land as well as to the prince—in a word, patriots. (That, as the century advanced, the preponderance of the old nobility in the Hanoverian establishment became more, rather than less, pronounced merely underlines the principle.) Münchhausen's *Instruction* of 1754 confirms these conclusions.

A case can be made, and has been made, that their standing orders induced the ministers to play safe and inundate their absent master with tedious requests for inconsequential decisions, in a sustained effort to evade responsibility. The sheer weight of official correspondence that left Hanover for London twice a week at least lends *prima facie* support to this contention. The opposite thesis—that the ministers ruled Hanover much as they saw fit—derives support from the opportunities offered by the elector's absence from Hanover; from the class interest of the ministers that did not always match the interest of the ruler, or that of the state as understood by the ruler; and of course from the purposive elasticity of the two *Reglements*. George

II's character comes into such an assessment too: unlike his father he could be led by those who knew their way about him. By and large the *Instruction* of 1754 strengthens the thesis that the ministers were essentially autonomous; Münchhausen would have made nonsense of his self-appointed task if his exposition had differed radically from practice. Observation supplies a host of instances pointing in either direction, depending on a kaleidoscope of circumstance and personalities. What makes a hard-and-fast rule particularly difficult in the present case is the fact that George II and his noble Hanoverian ministers held so much in common—much, but not everything. When we also allow for the deferential manners of the period (which the Hanoverian ministers shared with their British colleagues) the argument for the ministers' essential self-reliance is stronger than that for their subservience.

* * *

Having said all this, the nature of the position and responsibilities of the Hanoverian ministers, and of their peculiar relationship with the British polity, makes it imperative to enquire into their probity in the narrower sense. Did they derive material benefits that were secret or at least discreet by virtue of their position? In other words, were they tainted with 'corruption'?

Once, late in 1758, George II wrote to them of a rumour that 'many of them were at the disposal of the French ministry'. Would they explain themselves? They did, singly and collectively, with spirit and dignity. The king, by return of mail, declared himself fully satisfied.[21] We may do likewise.

Then, the Hanoverian ministers might have been in the pay of the British government. The Secret Service funds were tailor-made for such disbursements. Also, some of the British ministers were rich enough and possessed of enough public spirit—or vanity—to indulge in such expenditure out of their own pockets; Newcastle comes to mind. The morality of accepting favours like these is not easy to determine: Britain was no 'enemy' of Hanover, though the interests of both countries were by no means identical. Even the Hanoverian ministers' oath of office might be interpreted so as not to exclude British money from official sources: their master and that of the British ministers was one and the same person, after all.[22] The known facts are meagre. Philip von Münchhausen received a Secret Service pension of £1,000 p.a. towards the end of George II's reign. But Philip, as head of the German Chancery in London a virtual absentee from Hanover, is a special case; nothing is known of pensions paid to Hanoverian ministers at Hanover, who were policy-makers in a sense that their London colleague was not.[23]. It would be important to know whether Gerlach von Münchhausen, the virtual chief minister, derived material advantage from his English connections. Generations of researchers have found no evidence that he did.

Then George II might reward Hanoverian favourites from his British income on his own initiative and responsibility. An obvious case is the wealth acquired by Lady Yarmouth, his Hanoverian mistress and after Queen Caroline's death his common-law wife in all but name. Another is a pension of £300 p.a. on the Irish revenue, granted in 1743 to Madame von Steinberg, wife of the then head of the German Chancery and Lady Yarmouth's sister.[24] The legacies which George II devised in his will to his Hanoverian ministers and their assistants also come into this category.[25] It is unhistorical to dub the Hanoverians tainted because they accepted these gifts. The gifts expressed their master's appreciation, and were legitimate by the code of the time. British displeasure over this use of mostly British resources was political, and a different matter. In any case far fewer English 'goods and chattels'—to recall the famous anecdote about Madame von Schulenburg—found their way into Hanoverian pockets in the later years of George II than in the earlier years of George I.[26] Also, it is not irrelevant to recall that after the 1730s the Hanoverian ministers were without exception ancient nobility, settled in their style of life, and of high corporate self-esteem.[27] In addition, their official income was very good by German standards—4,000 thaler p.a. plus considerable emoluments.[28] In all, then, Ernst von Meier's dictum, given in 1898, still seems true in a comprehensive sense: 'Venality is the last thing with which these ministers could be charged.'[29] The adventurer-individualist out to make a fortune in the wake of his master is no feature of Hanoverian relations with Britain in the mid-eighteenth century.

* * *

To conclude. The government of Hanover was by 1740 strictly aristocratic, but hardly an oligarchy. The members of the Privy Council, the *Geheime Räte*, were the effective rulers who were invariably *altadlig*, of ancient lineage, though not always of Hanoverian lineage. They took their eminence for granted; they expected respect and obedience, and they received it. They were strictly the elector's servants and were appointed at his discretion. He might have dismissed them at his discretion, too, but he never did so: this also was part of the style of governance—the *hannoversche Milde*. They had to obey his orders, yet 'orders which pass the sea lose their force';[30]—a statement that is legally nonsense, but which can serve as a working principle when desired. Since the ministers were rarely hard workers—Münchhausen was a notable exception—they had to rely on secretaries. The 'secretariocracy' was a class in itself: expert, industrious, highly educated, utterly trustworthy, self-assured, often of 'official' families, sometimes ennobled. The same division of functions existed in the lesser *Collegia* and in the rudimentary provincial administration. It worked. Professional as well as human relations between the senior *altadlige* dignitaries and their helpmates, *bürgerlich* or '*nobilitiert*', were usually excellent. Socially the two orders stayed apart, and promotion from the lower to the higher class is unheard of in the latter two-thirds of the eighteenth century; nor was it, apparently, demanded.

As for the governance of the people, there was little of it—not merely by modern, but even by contemporary Continental standards. The observer at the close of the twentieth century may feel that eighteenth-century Hanover proves Plato's dictum, 'the State in which the rulers are most reluctant to govern is the best and most quietly governed'. However, the two great reformers of Prussia early in the nineteenth century, Friedrich Karl vom Stein and Karl August von Hardenberg, who both knew Hanover well, thought otherwise and considered her quiescence with dislike and contempt. (It is generally accepted that in the last third of the eighteenth century public standards declined in Hanover.)

One point is uncontested. Hanover in the reign of George II was a state under the rule of law—as much as any in Europe, and more than most.

And to conclude this introduction on a less ponderous note. A stone slab has survived from the entrance to the wonderful baroque gardens of Herrenhausen of about 1720 with the following inscription:

Everyone is permitted to relax ('sich ... eine Veränderung zu machen') in the Royal park. However, common people are forbidden on corporal punishment to —

I. damage statues and other exposed objects
II. throw things at swans or otherwise disturb them in their nests
III. introduce dogs
IV. catch or worry nightingales
V. occupy the benches about the great fountain when these are demanded by persons of quality or distinguished strangers
VI. defy the guards wearing the letter K on their breast.

No translation can do justice to the flavour of the original: High German with an unmistakable admixture of *platt*. Also, no formal 'document' can similarly revive the peculiar socio-political climate of Hanover under the first Georges.

Notes

1. The official, though still abbreviated, name of the state was 'Herzogtum Braunschweig-Lüneburg und dazu gehörige Länder'. In terms of the Imperial constitution certain territories ruled by the elector (including Bremen and Verden until 1733) were not 'electoral'. For this reason George II insisted that in treaties of guarantee Hanover be called his 'German lands and possessions', rather than 'the Electorate'. The reigning dukes of Brunswick-Wolfenbüttel, or 'Brunswick' for short, were also styled 'of Brunswick-Lüneburg', though obviously they were not *des Heiligen Römischen Reiches Erzschatzmeister und Kurfürst*, 'Arch-Treasurer and Elector of the Holy Roman Empire'.
2. From 1697 to 1763 the electors of Saxony were also kings of Poland—though in this case by election, not inheritance.
3. According to G. Schnath (ed.), *Geschichtlicher Atlas Niedersachsens*. Berlin, 1939, 28.
4. Henceforth Münchhausen, as distinct from his younger brother, Philip Adolph von Münchhausen, who will always be mentioned with his Christian name or initials.
5. L. von Sichart, *Geschichte der Königlich-Hannoverschen Armee*, vols. II and III/1 (Hanover, 1870), is still a standard text for the period, despite its great weaknesses from the modern viewpoint. J. Niemeyer and G. Ortenburg, *Die Churbraunschweig-Lüneburgische Armee im Siebenjährigen Kriege*, Beckum, 1976, is useful as an introduction, in addition to its delightful illustrations based on the 'Gmundener Prachtwerk'.
6. Contemporary estimates vary between 3 million and 6 million thaler; 4 million thaler seems a realistic guess.
7. The 'duchy (one-time archbishopric) of Bremen', Hanoverian since 1719, must not be confused with the Hanseatic town of Bremen, which was an Imperial free city, though the elector had certain rights in the cathedral precinct.
8. 'Prälatur', 'Ritterschaft' (and 'Rittergüter'), 'Städte'.
9. An exception is Kenneth L. Ellis, 'The Administrative Connections between Britain and Hanover', *J. Soc. of Archivists*, III, 10 (October 1969), 546-566. The quotation in my text is from Basil Williams, *The Whig Supremacy* (2nd ed., rev. C. H. Stuart), 13.
10. This is the place to mention Professor Georg Schnath's monumental *Geschichte Hannovers im Zeitalter der neunten Kur und der englischen Sukzession 1674-1714*, Hildesheim, 1938-1982, 5 vols. Ernest Augustus's *Regierungsreglement* is given in vol. 1, 688-694.
11. It was only in 1708 that the Elector of Hanover was introduced into the Electoral College at the Imperial Diet, and in 1710 that he assumed an 'arch-office'—that of arch-treasurer. By then Ernest Augustus was long dead.
12. An enumeration of the *Kuren*—still of great prestige within the Empire, though of little functional significance—may not be amiss: the historic Seven, under Charles IV's Golden

Bull of 1356, were the spiritual electorates of Mainz, Cologne, Trier; the royal crown of Bohemia (since 1620 in Habsburg possession); Brandenburg; Saxony; the Palatinate. The Thirty Years War added Bavaria.

13. By 1740 the Privy Councillors were commonly called ministers in German, as in other languages. Though it is not strictly correct, I have followed the practice for the sake of simplicity.
14. This rule was formalized only in 1720.
15. For the text, see L. T. Spittler, *Geschichte des Fürstenthums Hannover seit den Zeiten der Reformation bis zu Ende des siebenzehnten Jahrhunderts*, Göttingen, 1786; vol. II, appdx XIII, 120-132. Henceforth *Reglement II.*
16. About £9. A reflection on the country's dearth of capital, and the elector's careful habits.
17. 'Des Weyl. Herrn Premier-Ministers und Cammer-Präsidenten Herrn Gerlach Adolph von Münchhausen hinterlassener Unterricht von der Verfassung des Churfürstl. Braunschweig-Lüneburgischen Geheimten Rath und Cammer-Collegii', ed. E. von Lenthe, *Zeitschrift des Historischen Vereins für Niedersachsen*, 1855, 269-340. Henceforth *Instruction.*
18. Here the 'Instructions' of 1748 (State Papers, Regencies, 43/128, part II) have been chosen for comparison in detail. Others of the 1740s and 1750s could also serve. Where royal personages are appointed as Guardians of the Realm—George Augustus when Prince of Wales, Queen Caroline, the Duke of Cumberland in 1755—a diverging factor appears. (Frederick Prince of Wales never was appointed.)
19. Münchhausen became senior of the *Geheimes Ratskollegium* in 1753 (nominally even later, in 1764, at the death of *Geheimer Rat* von Wrisberg, who had been inactive for many years); he had been its leading member for some fifteen years.
20. See Rudolf Grieser, 'Die Deutsche Kanzlei, ihre Entstehung und Anfänge', *Blätter für deutsche Landesgeschichte*, LXXXIX, 1952, 153-168.
21. Hann. 92, I, Nr. 1.
22. For the text of the oath, see Hann. 92, I, Nr. I.
23. Sir Lewis Namier, *The Structure of Politics at the Accession of George III*, 2nd ed., London, 1960, 233/4. Namier contends that 'the [total] payments from secret service funds to Germans during Newcastle's term of office make about £21,000'. If we deduct P. von Münchhausen's pension from this sum, and a few smaller ones with no political significance also named by Namier, little remains for corrupt purposes.
24. According to an entry in F.A. 11 (*Urkunden des Gutsarchives zu Brüggen*) kept at the Niedersächsisches Hauptstaatsarchiv in Hanover.
25. For the testament of George II, see Cal. Or. 3, Abt. I, Nr. 35, K.G.
26. On this, see R. M. Hatton, *George I, Elector and King*, London, 1978, 131, 147-156.
27. It was *noblesse oblige*. In 1763 a direct tax was levied in Calenberg and Göttingen—the major part of the electorate—graded according to station and trade. The *Geheime Räte* taxed themselves at five times the second highest group. (*Hannoverische Anzeigen*, 16, 19 Sept 1763.)
28. E. von Meier, *Hannoversche Verfassungs- und Verwaltungsgeschichte 1680-1866*, 2 vols., Leipzig, 1898/99, I, 516-540.
29. *Ibid.*, I, 541.
30. Attributed to A. W. Rehberg, a senior Hanoverian official at the end of the eighteenth century, quoted in E. von Meier, *op. cit.*, I, 183.

Chapter 1
The close of the Walpole era and the French invasion threat, 1740–1741

The problem that constitutes the theme of this work is signalled by the accession of Frederick II to the throne of Prussia on 31 May 1740. However, the event which set the mould of Hanover for nearly a century—conspicuously so in foreign, perceptibly in domestic, affairs—was the accession to the throne of Great Britain of Elector George Louis as George I, twenty-six years earlier. It is therefore useful to outline the signposts of Hanoverian history from 1714 to 1740.

The personal union with a monarchy immeasurably superior in power, in resources and, last but not least, in sheer vitality had an emasculating effect on Hanover: Hanover, of considerable impact on Imperial and even European affairs during the generation before 1714, became a satellite, though often noisy at the parish-pump level. This is not say that Hanover did not occasionally benefit—in terms of eighteenth-century desiderata—by her august connection. It is merely to say that Hanover became the object of alien policies, rather than the initiator of her own. Nor is it to say that George I and George II as electors grew unconscious of their basic tie to Habsburg and their fear and envy of Hohenzollern—but their capacity to act on these convictions became much more circumscribed.

The Nordic War brought Hanover significant territorial gain through the acquisition from Sweden of the duchies of Bremen and Verden, at the Peace of Stockholm in 1719, which gave Hanover her shore on the North Sea. The acquisition and its retention were entirely due to the Hanoverian proclivities of George I, who engaged his British resources to the hilt—possibly beyond what was politically safe for him in his new kingdom. There was no repetition of such a performance. Yet smaller territorial gains (or gains hoped for, like the occupation of certain Mecklenburg counties by Hanoverian troops on an Imperial execution) can be registered right up to 1740, all due, at least indirectly, to the British presence in the background.

Hanover took part in the War of the Polish Succession (1733–1737), 6,000 of her troops fighting France on the Rhine, with little luck though with little bloodletting either. It was Viennese diplomacy that manoeuvred Hanover into this war which could bring her no gain. George II's father and grandfather were made, as dukes-electors of Hanover, of sterner stuff in pursuing their sacred egotism. (Britain kept out of the war—but then Sir Robert Walpole, though not fanatically opposed to appeasing Vienna at Hanoverian expense, cared first and last for the *entente* with Versailles.)

At the parish-pump level a running quarrel between George II and his brother-in-law, King Frederick William I of Prussia (the father and predecessor of Frederick II) was an occasion for European jitters—and amusement. Though predicated on the age-old rivalry between two dynasties, its main cause was the personal antipathy between the two monarchs—dangerous enough in the age of absolutism and sharpened by Frederick William's mania of recruiting for his army by fair means or foul, with scant respect for territorial frontiers. However, the basic unwillingness of the royal protagonists to pass the point of no return limited actual damage.

Domestically this generation foreshadows—to a lesser extent, to be sure—the quietism that settled over Hanover after the Seven Years War. The normal absence, together with the continued concern, of the elector made for a lowering of governance that was not all to the bad. Its most remarkable outcome, to the population if not to the historian, was a trend towards decreased taxation in the 1730s. It is in keeping with this environment—mental as much as political—that the men who headed the administration of Hanover from about 1720 onward were of lesser weight than the helpmates of electors Ernest Augustus and George Louis (until after the latter's translation to Britain). Münchhausen, whose star rose in the early 1730s, is the exception, but Münchhausen's genius suited the steady and intelligent pursuit of humdrum peace.

* * *

On the evening of 2 June 1740 (O.S.) the inner cabinet of the British ministry—Sir Robert Walpole, First Lord of the Treasury and since 1721 acknowledged head of the administration; Thomas Pelham-Holles, Duke of Newcastle, secretary of state for the Southern Department; Philip Yorke, Earl of Hardwicke, the Lord Chancellor; and Spencer Compton, Earl of Wilmington, Lord President of the Council—met in London to discuss Frederick II's accession to the Prussian throne, thirteen days before.[1]

It was not a happy crew, and they had viewed for some time a sombre scene. Walpole's ascendancy in government, flamboyantly maintained for long through many crises, was declining, and he himself knew it. The king, though fundamentally safe as Walpole's prop, was more difficult to manage, since death had in 1737 deprived Walpole of his best ally, Queen Caroline. The opposition in Parliament, savagely excluded from office for long, was swelling by the year in number and hopes: the Tories—country squires most of them and not very articulate in politics, but with a few able leaders—had always been irreconcilable, to Walpole's practice and style as much as to his 'Whig' principles. The 'Opposition Whigs' hated Walpole for past injuries and clamoured for power and revenge, led by the best political brains in the country—Pulteney, Lord Carteret, the Earl of Chesterfield, all Walpole's one-time allies. To these two groups were added of late the 'Patriots', young and eager members of the House of Commons who detested, or professed to detest, Walpole's debasing of national values, with William Pitt, recently deprived of his army commission for his factiousness, as their most remarkable personality. Even within his innnermost circle Walpole, ageing and ailing, had no joy. Though it is doubtful whether Newcastle was growing downright disloyal to his political chief, he was temperamentally unfit to be a support in bad weather; Hardwicke was ever cautious, and in addition something like Newcastle's mentor; Wilmington was a lightweight, and faithless to boot. As to the outer world, it was six months since the trading interest of the country, in the past Walpole's natural ally, had forced him into a war with Spain which he hated, for which he had not prepared the fighting forces, and which he could not captain. And if that was not enough, France—since 1716 Britain's treaty partner—was visibly shearing off into cooperation with Spain, the second great Bourbon power of Europe. Her ancient prime minister Cardinal Fleury was evidently no longer strong enough to stand up to more fiery spirits advocating an activist policy spearheaded against Britain, now, so it seemed, entered on to degenerate days. Though Britain could—and soon would—counter this Bourbon 'family compact' with a reactivation of William III's and the great Marlborough's 'Old System', an anti-Bourbon alliance between Britain, the Republic of the United Provinces and the house of Habsburg,[2] the danger from France loomed during those days of 1740 larger than possible succour from the traditional allies.

But at that particular meeting the news, for once, engendered brighter prospects. As Newcastle wrote the following day to his brother, secretary of state Lord Harrington, then with the king in Hanover, the conversation chiefly turned upon '… the great advantage that must necessarily arise to His Majesty and all Europe, if … that Prince be brought entirely in His Majesty's views and interests'.[3] He obviously based his optimism on a report of 4 June just received from the British chargé d'affaires (and, from August, minister) at Berlin, Captain Melchior Guy Dickens, that the 'intentions of the young king, as far as I am able to judge, are to run very cordially into his Majesty's arms'.[4] Considering the obsessive concern with freedom from external pressure which Frederick II was to demonstrate throughout his reign the notion of his intending to run very cordially into anybody's arms makes bizarre reading. Indeed, such a notion soon disappeared. However, at that moment it was shared by George II. Already, a week before this discussion in London, Gerlach von Münchhausen, the leading (though as yet not formally the senior) minister at Hanover, left for Berlin, on a mission intended to bring the young king 'entirely into His Majesty's views and interests'.[5] Such a contingency had been predicted for years—ever since Frederick William I's health deteriorated in 1734—and Münchhausen left Hanover before George II's arrival there. Officially he was charged with transmitting his master's condolences and congratulations. He was also instructed to obtain the new king's reaffirmation of the *Foedus Perpetuum* of 1693 between the then electorate of Brandenburg and the two Guelph duchies of Brunswick-Calenberg (Hanover) and Brunswick-Celle which merged under the rule of Hanover in 1705.[6] The alliance being 'perpetual', the reaffirmation was not formally necessary. But George II and, in particular, his Hanoverian ministers considered it as good a way as any of easing the young ruler at Berlin into British and, especially, Hanoverian, 'views and interests'. For once, in the summer of 1740, Britain and Hanover had a strictly identical view when gazing at Prussia: both wished to prevent Frederick from coming to an understanding with France—which London regarded as about to join Spain in her war with Britain, while Hanover looked upon France as the inveterate enemy of the *systema imperii* for which the House of Brunswick had fought with more steadfastness than the House of Hohenzollern. To Münchhausen, with his legalistic view of politics, 'selling' the 1693 treaty was a task after his own heart. Otherwise it would have been all but forgotten, and Frederick II probably spoke the truth when he said that he had not known of its existence.

Münchhausen arrived at Berlin on 6 June, leaving again for Hanover on 22 June. He was frustrated in his aims: the king did not as much as receive him in private audience to hear his entreaties at first hand. His importunities—delivered in written messages or formal audiences in the presence of Prussian ministers or courtiers, merely earned him Frederick's contemptuous appellation of 'coujon'[7] which in the context obviously means 'bore' rather than its more common usage of 'blackguard'. A tapestry from the royal manufactory and a parting communication from the minister, von Thulemeyer—then dying—that 'the will of Almighty God and of great kings is always a matter of some uncertainty'[8] were all the consolation Münchhausen received.

And yet Münchhausen's reports to George II at Herrenhausen show that his stay at Berlin nonetheless laid the foundation of his lasting assessment of Frederick II. These reports contain observations of great shrewdness by the side of the inevitable gaffes.

Münchhausen says that though the king is cautious in his relations with strangers, his intimates can approach him fairly freely. This characteristic may be expected to change, particularly in view of the king's vaulting ambitions. Indeed, he is much concerned with his own high estate. He has an exalted opinion of himself, and is unlikely to take any of his ministers into his full confidence. His mother (the sister of George II) is no exception in this respect, and she is careful not to meddle with regard to her son's politics.

Münchhausen notes the king's 'grosse Ambition' and military predilections at a time when the early, generally held, faith in his Arcadian inclinations had by no means entirely evaporated. The evidence which Münchhausen cites is varied: new regiments are raised, 'although the country much wishes for a troop reduction which is very necessary'.[9] The dispersal of Frederick William's corps of giants is meant to increase efficiency. The hated system of recruiting Prussian subjects through rural 'cantons' is to be preserved. And lastly—Münchhausen mentions it in the first place—the young king prefers the company of army officers, 'and as yet nobody else has a particular entry'.[10]

The young king's sentiments towards the powers—thus Münchhausen—cannot as yet be fathomed, except that he seems to fear rather than love Russia. Münchhausen apparently attributes a surviving resentment of the Imperial court at Vienna to the king's entourage rather than to Frederick in person: Frederick William I had much earlier acquired the Emperor Charles VI's consent to Prussia receiving one half of the duchies of Jülich and Berg upon the death of the aged and childless elector palatine, the present ruler, and there were good reasons for believing that the Emperor intended to renege on the agreement.

Münchhausen's repeated assurances to his master that the young king his nephew is well disposed towards him may have an element of the will to please. In the main, however, they probably rest on self-delusion. It was a lifelong article of faith with Münchhausen that cooperation between the Protestant powers was necessary to safeguard the peace of Europe, and in particular to protect the Empire—very much the *deutsches Vaterland* in the context—from its arch-enemy, France. It was natural for him to assume that Frederick II, free from the personal grudge against George II that had clouded his father's judgment, would arrive at the same conclusion, with its corollary, a British-cum-Hanoverian alliance. His experience in Berlin taught Münchhausen that some careful nursing might be appropriate, and perhaps some haggling over *Convenienzen*—but he was evidently optimistic as to the ultimate outcome. Regarding those conveniences—the mutual territorial concessions at the expense of third parties which take up so much of the contacts between George II and Frederick II at later stages—Münchhausen's reports show barely a hint; a word on

Jülich-Berg here, on East Friesland there, as Prussian desiderata. Münchhausen staked no Hanoverian counterclaims. His brief did not include any, and—this is a theme that will run through this work—he distrusted projects of territorial aggrandizement for Hanover.

As to Frederick, he too had to take stock, and when he had done so, he considered the British representative a better address than the Hanoverian. The theme did not crop up in his contacts with Guy Dickens until about eight weeks after Münchhausen had left Berlin.[11] Münchhausen, for his part, told the British chargé d'affaires nothing of his observations.

There is no hint of suspicion in Münchhausen's reports that the young king might soon become the greatest menace Hanover had had to face since the Thirty Years War. There is no premonition that at Berlin 'a tyrant of extraordinary military and political talents, of industry more extraordinary still, without fear, without faith, and without mercy, had ascended the throne'.[12] And yet, considering the briefness of Münchhausen's stay, his limited opportunities for appraising the king, and the previous image he must have held of the Rheinsberg Anti-Machiavel and sponger on his master's scant bounty,[13] the pen-portrait he conveys does honour to his political acumen.

In the four months between Münchhausen's return to Hanover and the death of Emperor Charles VI the pattern which Frederick envisaged for his relations with Britain and Hanover first emerges. It was to surface again and again well into the Seven Years War. Britain was—this was the basic concept—to engage her resources on the Continent on behalf of Prussia, and Prussia would enable Hanover to make territorial gains.

George II rarely failed to respond favourably. Frederick had gauged well at least two important traits of his uncle's political personality: his readiness, up to a point, to use British resources for Hanoverian interests; and his eagerness to enlarge his Hanoverian patrimony. That the pattern remained ultimately barren, a mere diplomatic *Leitmotiv*, was due to two basic factors which Frederick noticed with frustrated irritation, but which he never understood; George II as king and elector, *was* two distinct personalities; secondly, the Hanoverian government was not interested in territorial gains—not for what they were, nor for what they entailed. The second factor, in particular, must not be understood as a principle that was held unvaryingly in day-to-day transactions. The patriotic cupidity of the Hanoverian ministers too could be aroused, and they had to obey orders. But even orders could be challenged, with all deference; they could be carried out half-heartedly, or quietly neglected in the hope of a change of wind. By and large the ministers were steadfast in their views of what benefited their country.

It seems that at the root of Frederick's frustration lay his failure to grasp the limitations on his uncle's executive powers. Frederick's mind was quick rather than penetrating. As Frederick saw it, George II reigned over two realms, and undoubtedly each of these had its own traditions and laws. But he was one person, and his prerogative of deciding on foreign policy was more self-evident to his contemporaries than to modern observers with views conditioned by later developments. 'Prussia' herself was hardly as yet more than a conglomeration of territories under one ruler. One generation earlier Cleves and 'Ducal' Prussia—East Prussia to be—could have stood a constitutional comparison with Britain and Hanover that would not have seemed absurd to Continental observers unversed in British history. Even a weak ruler like Frederick I, the first king 'in Prussia' and Frederick's grandfather—the preposition is of significance—was unquestioned arbiter of foreign policy, a sphere on which the fragmentation of his territories had no bearing. That ministers in London as well as in Hanover had their own rational and deeply considered views on foreign relations which their common master was bound to take into account, never ceased to excite Frederick's contemptuous wonder. When he jeered at George II as a 'Trinity' —One and Three as convenient—or at the 'maudites perruques d'Hannovre', he misapprehended essential points, but his was an honest misapprehension.

In yet another respect these four months, from June to October 1740, set a pattern. It was to prove much easier to keep the knowledge of Continental moves—actual or designed—from British than from Hanoverian ministers. The reason was twofold: George II, in whose hands the strands of information usually—though not always—gathered, felt for Hanover. Moreover, while Continental affairs undoubtedly were a matter of importance to his British ministers, to the Hanoverian ministers they were life and death.

During the months prior to the death of the Emperor Charles VI, Frederick attempted with remarkable crudity ('Princes [are] chiefly governed by their interests')[14] to sell his alliance to either France or Britain—whosoever would bid higher. The prize that interested him, after the manner of Continental rulers in his age, was land and people. His particular object was a larger share of the Jülich-Berg inheritance, expected to fall vacant soon, than Fleury had promised his father in a secret agreement at the Hague in 1739. Frederick's preference was for an alliance with France, for reasons of personal inclination, and because the standing of France on the Continent had for some years been incomparably higher than that of Britain. But Fleury was adamant in his refusal to countenance Prussian sovereignty along further stretches of the Rhine. His calculations were not merely geared to future French incursions which the stationing of Prussian troops at Düsseldorf and opposite Cologne would severely hamper. Their mere presence would endanger that ascendancy in the spiritual electorates—above all in Cologne—which was a pillar of the French position in the Empire. Britain, though she had less to give than France in direct support, had nothing to fear from Prussian territorial expansion. Frederick therefore, in his advances to the British government, set his sights higher and staked claims to East Friesland and Mecklenburg as well. The difficulty was Hanover. Frederick must have remembered the *Discurs* his dying father addressed to him in which he stressed the rivalries between Prussia and Hanover as opposed to their absence between Prussia and Britain.[15]

The Hanoverian government would not welcome Prussian aggrandizement. Though Hanoverian jealousy of Prussia was no longer as potent as it had been earlier in the century, it was still a political factor. Both countries had legal claims to the succession in East Friesland, where the native dynasty of the Cirksenas was expected soon to die out. Also, Frederick hoped to take over Mecklenburg, on the northern and north-western approaches to Berlin—a hope he was never to abandon—and Mecklenburg was still remembered in Hanover as a sphere of expansion in the headier days of George I and Bernstorff.[16] All that remained for Frederick was to ask George II for his counterclaims, hoping that they would not clash with Prussian ambitions, and to prepare for bargaining if they did. While Frederick could not circumvent George II, he certainly tried to circumvent the Hanoverian ministers and deal with Britons—Guy Dickens at Berlin, and Harrington at Hanover. However, George kept his Hanoverian ministers posted. And it is from a Hanoverian ministerial opinion that we receive a first survey of the new situation with its evolving complexities.[17] The document, which is drawn up with great clarity, bears the unmistakable imprint of Münchhausen's authorship. 'First of all', what mattered was the opinion of 'His Majesty's English ministry'. Secondly, in so far as Hanover ('S. Kgl. M. Deutsche Sachen und Interessen') was concerned, it was of prime importance to gain the king of Prussia as an ally against France. Even if war were to ensue, this would be better than having France master of the Empire. Frederick could be expected to exact his price; the whole of the Jülich-Berg inheritance was too much and the concession, by implication, not necessary. But since it was necessary to outbid France, Frederick should receive the whole of Berg, with Düsseldorf and the Rhine line. Moreover, this would prove a gain to Hanover: Prussian acquisitions in the west were—so the Hanoverian ministers said—innocuous, and they helped to keep Prussia involved with France. Finally, the Hanoverian ministers ventured to assume that the British ministers would see no harm in those concessions to Prussia which they, the Hanoverians, had suggested in the Jülich-Berg connection.

The following points should be made in comment. First of all, the deference—verbal, may it be stated in anticipation—which the Hanoverian ministers, and Münchhausen in particular, rarely failed to show to British views, giving them precedence over those of Hanover; 'views'—though the impression conveyed is of 'interests'. Secondly, the pointed failure to note any territorial expectations for Hanover, an indicator of the Hanoverian ministers' sense of priorities and perhaps a quiet snub to the king. Lastly, the failure to take issue with Frederick's demands concerning East Friesland and Mecklenburg, territories which certainly mattered to Hanover. The rational explanation is again that the Hanoverian ministers were not interested; at least, they were not interested to the extent of endangering affairs of far greater importance to them. In this memorandum too, as in Münchhausen's reports from Berlin, there is no sense of prescience that even in the case of total failure of negotiations Frederick might become a military menace to Hanover, whether alone or in conjunction with France.

The Hanoverian ministers were correctly informed on the mainstream of feeling in the British cabinet—that Frederick's alliance was valuable in the looming war with France and that the price he put on it was negligible. Indeed, Dutch and, on different counts, Russian opposition to an increase of Prussian power on the Rhine might have been a consideration. But Holland was dependent on British good will, and British relations with Russia were flourishing, diplomatically and commercially;[18] securing Frederick with a modest concession should not have encountered insurmountable obstacles in those directions. What the Hanoverians did not appreciate were the divisions within the British cabinet. It was a blind spot they never overcame—it was so entirely outside their own experience. Newcastle set up a wail (there is no other word for it) that an alliance with Frederick would provoke France into a war with Britain for the benefit of Hanover. Nay, the more Frederick demanded, the better would the king be pleased, as he might expect greater returns for his electorate.[19] Newcastle was timid. Furthermore, as secretary of state for the Southern Department, with a war with Spain already on his hands, his apprehensions were not altogether unreasonable. However, consciously or not, his panic served to set off Walpole as being in apparent servitude to Hanover. This was an undeserved charge if there ever was one, but Walpole by then *was* failing in leadership, and the upshot of it all was that Frederick received no definite reply beyond sympathetic noises.[20] It was an approach that was never to pay with Frederick unless his diplomatic counterpart was a consummate psychologist who planned to exasperate him into extreme action. But there was no British Kaunitz about in 1740. When delaying tactics evidently failed to appease Frederick, George II paid in what he conceived to be equal coin: 'His Majesty was, by the blessing of God, with the sea and land forces he is master of, sufficiently provided for his own defence, and will be obliged, if other powers will entirely neglect the case of the public welfare, to follow their example, and confine himself to that one object of the safety of his own dominions; by which means the affairs of the Continent, and the King of Prussia's interests and pretensions in particular, would be in short time left entirely at the mercy of France.'[21] This too was a mistaken approach with one who was past master in the art of telling bluster from a genuine threat. On another level, if George II's 'one object' was to be 'the safety of his own dominions', then clearly he presented a potential enemy with a strategy—especially as his land forces were known to be vastly inferior to those of the potential enemy in question.

Thus matters hung fire, when Charles VI died unexpectedly at Vienna on 20 October 1740.

* * *

Throughout most of his reign the Emperor Charles VI had directed his statecraft towards one goal: the securing of his undivided dominions to his eldest daughter should he die without a son. It was a task complex beyond imagination, since the plausible claimants were many, prices have always been commensurate to the buyer's eagerness, and the various Habsburg estates as well as the European community had views of their own. However, when France gave her final asset to the 'Pragmatic Sanction' in 1738 the task was in the main done, if ink on parchment could do it. Bavaria was an exception, in that her non-compliance was clear, but she did not count for much on her own. The Imperial dignity—for 300 unbroken years in Habsburg hands—was a different matter, since no Pragmatic Sanction could make a woman Roman Emperor. But before Charles VI died, hopes and half-promises were current at Vienna that Francis Stephen of Lorraine, Grand Duke of Tuscany, husband of the heiress presumptive Maria Theresa, would in due course be acceptable to an 'eminent majority' of the Electors' Bench. A son of theirs might eventually reunite in his person the Imperial crown with rule over the Habsburg lands—as it indeed turned out.

Europe was thrown into a crisis unequalled since the death of another Habsburg Charles forty years earlier, King Charles II of Spain in November 1700. Then as now the survival of peace was dangerously a matter of keeping public faith; then as now it broke down. The stakes were too high.

Though the news from Vienna aroused similar reactions in Hanover and in London, for reasons not dissimilar, the emphasis as usual was different. The reaction in Hanover was not far short of alarm and, like much that follows on these pages, it is best understood from Münchhausen's *Brief Historic Relation of Events in the* [Hanoverian] *Ministry since the Death of the Emperor until the end of April 1742.*[22] His account is remarkably clear, despite some hindsight, more than some regard for George II's susceptibilities, and Münchhausen's tendency to wordiness.

According to Münchhausen, the Emperor's death presented France with another opportunity to establish her dominion over Germany by applying the principle of divide and conquer. Immediately upon receiving the news of the Emperor's death, and before George's pleasure could be known, the Hanoverian ministry therefore instructed the Hanoverian delegate to the Imperial Diet at Ratisbon to make contacts with a view to securing the *systema imperii*. At the same time confidential communications were sent to the ministries at Berlin, Dresden, Cassel, Wolfenbüttel (the 'elder' Brunswick line) 'and others' for the same purpose. These courts were all Protestant—in spite of the Saxon elector being Catholic in a Lutheran country—and normally in political rapport with Hanover, for all the animosity between George II and Frederick William I. Bavaria, naturally, was not contacted. That she was Catholic need not have mattered. But Bavaria was the one certain contester of Maria Theresa's undivided succession and, as bad or worse, practically a retainer of France. The Hanoverian ministers, on their own responsibility, suggested concerted action within the Empire on as broad a basis as possible as well as the conclusion of 'useful alliances with mighty powers'. They also called for a speedy election of a new emperor, 'suitable to the German welfare'.[23]

At the same time—allowing for the greater distance involved—London made its moves. On 31 October Harrington instructed Dickens to inform Berlin of 'His Majesty's interest in the security of the present independent system of Europe and in the preservation of the Protestant religion. And as his engagements for maintaining the indivisibility of the Austrian succession are the same as those of the King of Prussia, ... His Majesty therefore hopes the King of Prussia will immediately open himself fully to him as to the conduct he intends to hold ...'[24] In other words, the British ministry expected that the crisis would achieve what the blandishments of Münchhausen, Harrington and Dickens had so far failed to achieve: an alignment of British and Prussian policies. In the prevailing circumstances such an alignment seemed to the ministers to furnish both a rejuvenation and an extension of the Old Alliance against France.

George II, just back from Hanover, took it upon himself to see that the contemplated alignment should not leave Hanover out in the cold. In public he endorsed his British ministers' policy, which merely enjoined watchfulness, and promised cooperation with the other powers that were engaged, like Britain, in maintaining 'the Balance of Power and the Liberties of Europe'.[25] At the same time he asked his Hanoverian minister for an opinion on the advantages which might accrue to his 'German interests' from such an outcome. The phrasing quite as much as knowledge of George II's predilections suggests that he had in mind territorial gains.

In the meantime London and Berlin had already agreed to raise the status of their diplomatic representation, and Count Truchsess and Lord Hyndford were named to supersede M. Andrié and Captain Guy Dickens respectively. Was it not hence advisable, the king asked, for Hanover to have an electoral minister accredited at Berlin?[26] It is as good as certain that the British ministers did not know of the letter. The Hanoverian ministers replied that indeed they favoured a 'German' minister at Berlin. As to any tangible advantages that might accrue to Hanover, they advised against a forward policy. Thrusts in this direction might only cause chagrin at Berlin. Moreover, since the negotiations would 'doubtlessly' be held in England, Prussia might exploit concern shown for Hanover's interests in order to discredit her with 'the Nation', that is, the British public. How much better to wait until Britain signed an undertaking with Prussia and then demanded assistance from Hanover in carrying it out.[27] Though the advice bears the signature of all the ministers then at Hanover, it mirrors Münchhausen's ideas: his dislike of 'greed' as endangering an acceptable *status quo*; his sensitivity to English public opinion; his eagerness to 'oblige' Britain; his reluctance to engage Hanover in adventures on a European scale. One motive turns up for the first time—the fear of displeasing Prussia, sparked off, no doubt, by the growing suspicion that the young master at Berlin was out for mischief.

The date of the advice was 9 December 1740. For about a week previously Frederick II's resolve to invade a neighbour's land had become common knowledge. Silesia was strongly indicated: but whether Silesia, or Mecklenburg, or Bohemia—what difference did it make, politically as well as morally? Or was Hanover possibly the intended victim? On 5 December Field Marshal Schwerin of Prussia had said to Baron Ginckel, the Dutch minister in Berlin, that if Frederick were provoked by the King of England, there was little to hinder him from falling upon the electoral dominions. Ginckel had promptly reported this to Dickens, as no doubt he was expected to do. Dickens choked at 'the exorbitant height of presumption ... of thinking and talking raised here at present'.[28] But whereas London was safe enough from Prussian 'presumption', no Hanoverian minister could permit himself the luxury of indignation, so long as the spectre so suddenly arisen might yet be conjured away by prudence.

Frederick's intention of launching an invasion was realized on 16 December 1740. It is not easy to explain fully the emotional storm that shook Europe when the Prussian troops crossed into Silesia on that day. It was a storm that has echoed in the writings of historians ever since. Obviously, the Pragmatic Sanction was upset, and by implication, the balance of power. Obviously, too, a gross breach of faith had been committed. But much of the political community of Europe responded in a manner that seems to surpass the rational considerations involved. Partly it was the appeal of a young woman in distress—pretty, just orphaned, pregnant, seemingly helpless, brutally attacked. But partly at least, it was a reflex reaction to the sheer brazenness of a young ruler, just ascended to the throne, who set out to push his second-rate kingdom into the ranks of the great powers. This element of irrational reaction is particularly marked in George II and Münchhausen—each after his own manner.

George II had respectable qualities of mind and character, but he utterly lacked a capacity for insight into his own motives. From the moment Frederick invaded Silesia his uncle never ceased hating him: disappointment, fear, offended dignity, jealousy, envy, family dislike, the generation gap, genuine abhorrence—they all come into it in proportions that do not much matter. At the same time George II never failed to associate his nephew with the main chance, a capacity for *Realpolitik* which made the elder man ever ready to swallow his feelings and apprehensions when he believed a 'convenience' might ensue to Hanover. It is the incapacity to decide between these two incompatibles which is George's chief failing as a German, or indeed a European, statesman. This failing accounted for his policies more than his 'arrant political cowardice' or his *cupido habendi* which Walpole and Münchhausen, his greatest British and Hanoverian servants respectively, attributed to him, though these reproaches were not undeserved either.

The abuse which George II heaped on his nephew when the news of the Silesian invasion turned from rumour to fact is of no direct concern to this work.[29] But it was then that he first suggested by implication a carving up of Prussia. The occasion was an audience, on 16 December, to the representative of a prospective beneficiary, the

Saxon minister, von Ütterodt.[30] Ütterodt seems to have been too frightened to do more than report home; there is no evidence that he compared notes with his Austrian colleague. The king's suggestion was certainly stunning: Hanoverian armaments were at a low; Austria practically defenceless; France hovering between acceptance and evasion of her commitment to the Pragmatic Sanction; Russia—the particular patron of Saxony—immobilized by the death of the Tsaritsa Anna on 28 October 1740, and an unstable regency incapable of decision. But George II was not used to acting without taking into account the views of his Hanoverian ministers, and he stalled when the newly accredited Austrian minister, Count Ostein, invoked the military aid clauses of the 1731 Treaty of Vienna which obliged George II to protect Maria Theresa's future inheritance, both as king and as elector.[31] By then he had already written to Hanover. Characteristically for his relations with his ministers there he subordinated what was a request for advice to a superfluous order, 'to watch the Prussian court diligently'.[32] For once the Hanoverians egged their master on; evidently their anger still had the better of them.

The *Leitmotiv* of their reply was that there could be no more faith in Frederick II.[33] He was *hostis gentium*—this term is not used but it lingers between the lines. Not only should Austria oppose him to the utmost, but she must be encouraged and aided. Hessians and Danes must be taken into British pay to help cover Hanover, and the Hanoverian army must be set on a war footing. (Both Hesse-Cassel and Denmark were bound by treaty to supply Britain with auxiliaries on request—though not necessarily in order 'to cover Hanover'.) Perhaps it would be advisable to conclude agreements with Russia and with Holland—the latter in particular—also in defence of Hanover. And deception for deception: until all was ready, Frederick must be deluded into regarding George II as his friend.

The letter shows how far the ministers were bereft of their habitual circumspection. They knew that they had to deal with a master who needed—and indeed expected—restraining. This was the guideline in their relations with George II and they rarely abandoned it. The military line-up at the disposal of Maria Theresa was pitiful. Employing foreign auxiliaries in British pay for the defence of Hanover was a matter of the utmost delicacy, not to be dealt with by a casual suggestion. The same held true of agreements with Russia and Holland. And Frederick II, that most suspicious of rulers, was not likely to fall victim to dissimulation, although at that stage a miscalculation of his character was still excusable.

After a fortnight the ministers followed up this reply with a more detailed and far cooler opinion which is of interest as it responds to George II's greed for territorial acquisitions.[34] The *systema imperii* and the Balance of Europe—inseparably intertwined—ought to be preserved; this is the foremost consideration. It would be to the king's immortal glory were he to head the forces united in defence of the German fatherland. Silesia was undoubtedly covered by the king's guarantee of the Pragmatic Sanction. However—and here more deeply considered thought comes into play—with respect to Frederick it might be best not to push matters too hard. For one, an 'Imperial execution' against Frederick would weaken the Protestant interest. (It probably speaks *for* the earnestness of the ministers on this count that they added, 'though religion often comes second to secular interests'.) Then, France, which was *prima facie* an ally of Frederick in his designs against Austria and, indeed, the Empire, might after all hesitate to nurse a ruler who could in time become as redoubtable as her ancient Habsburg rival. Holland and Russia might send *dehortatoria* to the Diet at Ratisbon—a far cry from the defensive alliance which Hanover suggested earlier. And since the present outlook was dismal and dangerous, and 'certain principles' were needed for future contingencies, the ministers felt in duty bound to consider whether, apart from preserving the balance in Europe, His Majesty might not also gain power and lands in Germany—by implication, without going to war with Prussia.

Thereafter the ministers painstakingly analyse *quaestionem an*. They avoided committing themselves. It was imprudent to hold out a sure hope, they opined. Opposition was certain to be general and fierce, and hence plans for the aggrandizement of Hanover must be kept private until the chances of consummation were really bright, which was far from being the case at present. Anyhow, according to the ministers' 'alleruntertänigstem Ermessen', His Majesty's first concern should be the maintenance of the Imperial system (*Beibehaltung des Systematis Imperii*)—that is, the edifice of infinitely graded rights and duties, mutual dependences and obligations, as created in 1648 by the Peace of Westphalia, and menaced now with destruction by Frederick's ambition. However, in case all the above-mentioned difficulties were disposed of, the acquisition of the bishopric of Hildesheim was indicated. It lay at the southern doorstep of Hanover and had slipped from the grip of the Guelph dukes at the end of the Thirty Years War. Its inhabitants were largely Protestant; they had their grudges against the bishop; and the king as duke of Brunswick-Lüneburg was guarantor of their status under the Peace of Westphalia. The present incumbent was the Archbishop of Cologne, Clement Augustus, the greatest clerical pluralist in the Empire and as younger brother of the Bavarian elector a major figure on the political scene; he might be tempted to sell his rights in return for a life annuity of 100,000 thalers, 'a sum he is unlikely to receive in clear monetary revenue from the bishopric'. Certain financial concessions to the Empire might have to be made in order to purchase acquiescence from that quarter. And 'in casu extremae necessitatis', that is, if no other hope remained for the acquisition of Hildesheim, the king might have to renounce the 'alternate succession' in Osnabrück.

It is difficult to avoid the impression that the ministers hedged their recommendation of Hildesheim as an aim for expansion with provisos calculated to make George II repent of his plans. The projected annuity for Clement Augustus, which—according to the Hanoverian ministers—would turn the acquisition of Hildesheim into a losing deal financially (Clement Augustus was much younger than George II), is a nice touch. Special attention should go to the implied risk to the Osnabrück *Alternat*. The Peace of Westphalia had provided that a Catholic priest elected by the chapter should alternate with a prince of Brunswick-Lüneburg—normally a Protestant—as Bishop of Osnabrück, and as such as ruler of this not inconsiderable *Reichsstand* between Weser and Ems, to the west of Hanover. It was the only gain the Guelphs had had from that grand reshuffle of the Empire, and it spelled a major life settlement for junior members of that house; George II's grandfather had himself filled the office before he inherited Hanover (see above, p. 4). Not unnaturally, to a man as acquisitive as George II, turning this half-apanage into a straight possession was an aim as near to his heart as any; an aim of which he never lost sight until his death. To suggest that he should waive even the incomplete hold over Osnabrück which his house had held for a hundred years was an absurdity and an outrage, likely to sour a moderate prize like Hildesheim suggested as recompense.[35] (In the end Osnabrück accrued to Hanover in 1803, as her only gain from the *Reichsdeputationshauptschluss*.)

One of the phrases in the opinion of 17 January has a particular poignancy. Frederick is *dieser Herr ... ohne Treu und Religion*, 'this Lord without faith and religion'; the translation fails to do justice to the force of the German expression. These men who *were* the government of this second-rate German princedom lived in a world that differed from the London, Paris or Berlin of their time, and their language often carries implications of its own. Not that they would not dissimulate or equivocate when it suited their politics. But for a prince to be *ohne Treu und Religion* put him beyond the pale, and expressed real abhorrence.

The Hanoverian ministers should have known that George II would take their advice in the obvious sense rather than try to read between the lines.They should also have known that Baron Ernst von Steinberg, their London colleague, the 'German minister attached to the King's person' and chief of the German Chancery, would not fulfil this function on their behalf either. Steinberg was honest and reliable, loyal and industrious. But he was diffident and dull, and he had no political mind of his own.[36]

George II rarely rejected his Hanoverian ministers' advice even if it counselled unpalatable restraint. But their original opinion of 30 December 1740 had so much accorded with his mood of rage that he acted like one unleashed. During January and February 1741 the king gave Ostein a series of confidential audiences. He explicitly encouraged Ostein to apply direct to himself, especially in German affairs, which the king said he understood better than his British ministers. Steinberg was to act as go-between.

In these meetings George II evolved schemes which were intended to achieve the despoliation of the King of Prussia. He moved to a crescendo of aggressiveness. He would put his Danish and Hessian auxiliaries—British-paid!—at Maria Theresa's disposal. He outlined a three-pronged plan of operations against Frederick in the Prussian heartland, beginning with a Russian invasion of East Prussia, while he himself would lead a diversion from Hanover against Magdeburg, and the Austrians would press on through Silesia. On no account, the king felt, should Maria Theresa sign a compromise with Frederick. George II eagerly agreed with Ostein that on that occasion a few advantages might be turned over to Hanover. Would Ostein put the offer in writing? It was all utterly wild.[37]

Ostein and Maria Theresa were elated, though in Vienna, at any rate, an uneasiness lingered that the king's British ministers might prove a stumbling block. In her separate appeals to George II as king and as elector requesting him to maintain the Pragmatic Sanction by arms,[38] Maria Theresa had evoked the sanctity of treaties and the danger which Frederick posed to every *Reichsstand,* and to Hanover in particular. She had not then appealed to George II's territorial greed.[39] But now Vienna responded with a will. On 13 March 1741 the Austrian government sent Ostein a draft treaty, with authority to sign.[40] The draft provides for an offensive alliance (though nominally defensive, since Frederick had already proved himself the aggressor) between Maria Theresa, and between George II as king *and* elector (*tam qua rege quam qua sacri Romani imperii electore*), the king of Poland as elector of Saxony, and Holland, all three as guarantors of the Pragmatic Sanction, and Russia. Since George II, the States General and the 'Autocrat of All Russians' (the infant Ivan VI, referred to in the draft as 'the Third')—but not Saxony—had already agreed to declare war on Frederick and invade his lands, certain operational details were suggested; the most significant of these was the stipulation that the war should on no account start later than the end of April. The Queen of Hungary demanded for herself full restitution, or adequate compensation, but no more than that: she expressly bound herself not to claim additional Prussian territories even should they be taken by her army; the distribution of these would be subject to special agreement between the allies.

By the time the Austrian draft treaty reached London, however, George II's mood was changing. Possibly he responded to Ostein's draft treaty with an 'Approximate Project' (*Ungefährliches* [*ungefähres*] *Project*), based on the same assumptions but softened in significant points:[41] the king is consistently engaged as 'Elector of Brunswick-Lüneburg' only; the danger accruing to Hanover through involvement in the war against Frederick is stressed, the consequent obligations of *mutual* succour spelled out, and the expected gains depicted as restitution conquests *jure belli*; most important, the end-of-April deadline is replaced by a less risky promise 'to arm in his German lands as soon as this treaty is signed ... and to break camp within six weeks.' But even this somewhat deflated version no longer represented what the king by then thought feasible.

It seems that Harrington alone among the British ministers was informed throughout on how far George II was prepared to go in his Continental concerns—but until 1742 Harrington was the most obsequious secretary of state George II ever had. All the same, the British ministers were not at first hostile to the idea of a 'concert' against Frederick. They were of course committed to the Pragmatic Sanction. Its acceptance by Britain in the 'second Treaty of Vienna' in 1731 had not entailed a sacrifice of principle, and hardly one of expediency: Robert Walpole and his collaborators in foreign policy (excluding, prominently and explicitly, Walpole's brother Horatio) always remained believers in the Old System, with Habsburg as a 'natural' ally. They also had no sympathy for young rulers recklessly endangering the balance of power, already affected by the advance of France in the previous decade. Then again, Frederick's invasion put at risk the large loan which British (and Dutch) capitalists had made to Vienna in the latter days of Charles VI on the security of the Silesian revenues. At home, the turn of 1740/1741 saw a new low in Walpole's parliamentary standing, and he needed the king's good humour more than ever.

Still, hoping for the humiliation of the King of Prussia over a specific issue was one thing; ganging up on him in a war of despoliation in concert with half of Europe, another. In consequence, the British ministers, while not actually restraining the king, tried to prevent him from resorting to extreme action. At Dresden, the hub of activity in the first three months of 1741, the Austrian representatives, by way of encouragement, read to the British minister, Villiers, the outpourings of George II to Ostein. However, Villiers had express instructions from the secretary of state not to agree on a treaty, much less on a plan of operations.[42] Dickens at Berlin had no inkling of what was afoot—at least not from his superiors. Only when the king's enthusiasm reached its peak, in the first days of March, did Harrington send to Robinson, the British minister at Vienna, an attenuated picture of what was going on between the two courts.[43] Moreover, the unexpectedly heavy defeat of the opposition in the House of Commons on 13 February 1741[44] meant another boost to Walpole *vis-à-vis* the king. Public opinion, though sentimental towards Maria Theresa, was certainly not ready for a war to crush the foremost Protestant power in Germany—a power with which Britain had hitherto had no major quarrel.

It was not in the character of George II to force a showdown with his British ministers, particularly on a matter of supreme importance like war with Prussia. And the king of his own accord scuttled out of his bellicosity at some time in March 1741.

The reasons are again connected with Hanover.

* * *

As early as 20 January 1741 and again on 10 February George II had communicated to the *Geheime Räte* his plan of a secret treaty and subsequent offensive action against Prussia, with an exuberance he never showed his British ministers (Harrington possibly excepted).[45] The Hanoverian ministers in their reply of 10 February to the earlier of the king's despatches observed their own pattern of opposition to royal directives. They started with a deferential acknowledgment of 'this important object'. They followed up with a reasoned exposition of the political measures which they conceived as necessary before the king's project could be carried out; both the nature of these measures and the phrasing leave no doubt that they took the plan for what it was—a dangerous reverie.[46]

However, in the present case external factors more persuasive even than the Hanoverian ministers decided the issue. Frederick could not remain ignorant of his uncle's busy hostility. The secret had too many sharers, and Ammon, the Prussian resident at Dresden, was a keen observer. What Frederick knew was not very accurate, but it was enough to put him in a rage. As early as 30 January he told Dickens at Berlin that 'he was readier than they [his ill-wishers] to give the first box on the ear … he would join France which had made him great offers … He would kick and bite on all sides and lay everything waste before him.' On the other hand he would be pleased to have the good offices of George II, provided he acted with 'the utmost impartiality'.[47] A few days earlier Dickens first reported on Frederick's intention to form a military camp near Magdeburg, threatening Hanover and Saxony equally.[48] The rumour became certainty during March. By 4 April twenty-eight battalions of infantry and forty squadrons of cavalry would be assembled, under the command of Prince Leopold of Anhalt—the 'Alte Dessauer', drillmaster of the Prussian army.[49] This host was larger by half than the entire Hanoverian army, and immeasurably superior in training and equipment.[50]

Then, early in March, Marshal Belleisle set out on his perambulations to prepare the ground for a partition of the Habsburg dominions, and the hopes that France might after all respect the Pragmatic Sanction were shattered.[51]

In the meantime Frederick offered the carrot as well as the stick. In the last week of February 1741 he sent to Hanover—by now the more promising location from this point of view—a special envoy, Baron Erich Christoph von Plotho, one of his best diplomatists. On 1 March Plotho had a private conference with Münchhausen, 'the only person to whom he is instructed to show his confidence'.[52] Plotho developed the lines of a close cooperation between their two sovereigns. Its gist was that in return for George's good offices in obtaining Lower Silesia with Breslau for Frederick, he would use *his* good offices so that George II might keep the eight Mecklenburg bailiwicks which had been under Hanoverian sequestration since 1737. Further *Convenienzen* were not excluded. Plotho stressed that Frederick was content that his uncle should adopt towards him a benevolent neutrality; he did not expect George II to go so far as to make war on Austria.

The Hanoverian ministers' advice to their master, of 3 March 1741, is based on a preliminary opinion of Münchhausen's written two days before—immediately after his conference with Plotho. Münchhausen marshals his arguments 'for' and 'against'.

In favour, he cites the point that the enmity of Prussia was more dangerous to Hanover than that of Austria. If an aggrandizement of Prussia is inevitable, Münchhausen writes, better let her expand towards Silesia; both the European balance 'which is fairly Your Majesty's foremost concern' and the Germanic system can be preserved, even if Prussia lays hands on part of the province. (The change in preference from west to east as the thrust of Prussian expansion clearly follows the change in the image of Prussia: since Prussia has become a potential aggressor against Hanover, she can no longer be permitted to strengthen her foothold to the west of Hanover in addition to her overwhelming superiority in the east.) The arguments against acceptance have the distrust of Frederick in common. Even the *Anti-Machiavel* is cited as evidence against its author. Though Münchhausen makes no recommendation, his considered inclination is towards reaching an agreement, though not without regrets. And the Privy Council in a corporate conclusion advised the king to enter into the 'connection' *(Verbindung)* with Prussia as the least of evils. Neutrality merely means falling between two stools. Finally, they argue that, in any event, the strengthening of the army is a necessity: their ultimate aim remains to prevent French domination while avoiding any forward action against Prussia.[53]

The British angle, absent at first sight, appears obliquely: Münchhausen knew very well that 'the Balance of Europe' and, to a lesser degree, 'the Germanic system' were important points for George II to make with his British ministers. And by way of further gratifying British susceptibility the Hanoverian ministers prefaced their concluding arguments by admitting that 'they lacked complete knowledge of great world affairs'.

From that time on measures were considered for 'strengthening the army'.[54] But in all they served only to emphasize the defencelessness of Hanover against opponents such as France and Prussia. Thus it is the army's glaring inadequacy that serves to explain the actions of George II and his Hanoverian ministers in the following eighteen months.

On 17 March (N.S.) Truchsess wrote to Frederick from London that Steinberg had informed him of George II's acceptance of Plotho's offer to conclude an alliance between Prussia and 'the King of England'.[55] On 5 March (O.S.), probably the day of Truchsess's conversation with Steinberg and the day preceding his despatch to Frederick, Harrington told Robinson in Vienna that according to entirely trustworthy information France was about 'to throw off the mask' and mount an attack on Austria. France was to act together with Bavaria and Spain but would prefer an alliance with Prussia. 'In this dangerous and desperate crisis' it was absolutely necessary that Austria should bring Prussia over to its side by the cession of Lower Silesia with Breslau. George II would gladly offer his good offices as he had repeatedly been invited to do by the King of Prussia.[56]

It was a brutal reversal of the British approach to Maria Theresa. It was also the first of many instances of pressure which the British government was to apply to Austria until the Peace of Aix-la-Chapelle, to the prejudice of their relationship. In the present case, at any rate, the move was a reflex of the king's rising fear for Hanover. The Hanoverian opinion of 3 March would have reached London about 12 March at the latest, and the episode illustrates Münchhausen's standing with George II, and George II's with Harrington. That the British ministry was basically pacific, conscious of its incapacity to fight a national war which might see at any time France in addition to Spain among the enemies of Britain, and morally inclined to appeasement, all provide the necessary background to the volte-face.

Apart from the weight of the Hanoverian ministers' advice, it is impossible to be certain which factor most influenced George II to abandon his bellicosity versus Prussia. In view of two Hanoverian army camps established at that time on the Weser[57] it was probably the first rumour of a French army assembling to cross into Westphalia that caused the about-turn. At all times it was Hanover's defencelessness that was in his mind.

On 11 March 1741 the Hanoverian minister extraordinary, *Geheimer Kriegsrat* Baron August Wilhelm von Schwicheldt, had his first audience with the King of Prussia at his Silesian headquarters. Eight weeks later, on 7 May, he was joined there by the new British envoy, Lord Hyndford. Their respective missions, though they superficially harmonized, were not really compatible. Both offered Frederick benevolent neutrality combined with diplomatic pressure on Maria Theresa to make concessions in Silesia. But while Hyndford genuinely acted for the restoration of the balance in Central Europe, Schwicheldt was under strict orders to obtain Prussian support for Hanoverian territorial gains—Hildesheim and Osnabrück in the first place; then, if possible, parts of Mecklenburg, East Friesland, Paderborn—aims which, if achieved, would have radically upset that balance for which Hyndford was striving.[58] Moreover, Britain's 'benevolent neutrality' was worth a Prussian *quid pro quo*; Hanover's, as such, was not. Moreover, Schwicheldt was a bad choice, as it transpired. Active, concerned and neurotically ambitious, he lacked the feel for 'politics' that distinguished Münchhausen. Also, he was suspicious and secretive, uninspired and lacking in empathy. It seems that he and Frederick detested each other at once.[59] Henceforth Schwicheldt remained the most consistent enemy of co-operation with Prussia among the policy-makers at Hanover. Though Schwicheldt's *ad hoc* team-mate Hyndford wrote to Harrington that Schwicheldt was his 'very good friend', the context makes it clear that he disliked and distrusted him.[60] Hyndford had good reason. His own instructions ordered him, again and again, 'to cooperate with [Schwicheldt] to the utmost of his power' in the negotiations 'wherein the interests of [George II's] German dominions is concerned'.[61] Schwicheldt, on the other hand, repeatedly implored Podewils, Frederick's foreign minister, to keep the progress, and indeed the substance, of their negotiations secret from Hyndford. Frederick's disgusted incomprehension was genuine—the servants of one royal master!—but the Prussians complied. Their respective missions are well summed up by Frederick himself: 'The Hanoverian demanded that his master's neutrality should be purchased by a guarantee of the bishoprics of Hildesheim and Osnabrück, and the mortgaged bailiwicks of Mecklenburg ... The Englishman offered his master's good offices in persuading the Queen of Hungary to cede a few principalities in Lower Silesia ...' And he adds that both 'merely intended to lull the king to sleep ... with their flatteries'.[62]

The explanation for the apparent lack of coordination at the centre lies in George II's knowledge that he was employing British political assets to obtain territorial gains for Hanover in circumstances which were peculiarly ill suited for publicity. Parliamentary elections were in the offing, and Walpole's hold was visibly loosening. Moreover, before the late Parliament rose it had passed without dividing a resolution unusually favourable to Hanover. On 8 April 1741 in a speech from the throne George II again stressed his determination to stand by his engagements to Maria Theresa as necessary for the balance of power and 'the Liberties of Europe'. The House of

Commons thereupon voted £300,000 to Maria Theresa, as well as a sum for the supplies needed to activate 12,000 Danish and Hessian auxiliaries. The House also promised that it would 'effectually stand by and support Your Majesty against all insults and attacks which any prince and power, in resentment of the just measures which your Majesty has so wisely taken, shall make upon any of your Majesty's territories or dominions, though not belonging to the Crown of Great Britain ...'.[63] Not unnaturally, Frederick was confirmed in his suspicion of British and Hanoverian duplicity. Hyndford's explanation that his king was merely fulfilling his treaty obligations on terms that did not affect his good offices with either party carried little weight.[64] Evidently Hyndford, who was deeply embarrassed, did not believe in the validity of his own explanations.

The talks—Frederick with Hyndford, Frederick with Schwicheldt—failed. It is difficult to see how they could have succeeded, given Maria Theresa's 'obstinacy' along with that of her chief adviser, Johann Christoph von Bartenstein, and Frederick's enhanced prestige after the Prussian victory of Mollwitz on 10 April 1741. Obviously the immediate attractions of a French alliance were gaining ground in his eyes.

At Breslau on 4 June 1741 Podewils and the French envoy Valory initialled a defensive alliance to run for fifteen years. In secret articles Frederick waived his claims to Berg in exchange for a guarantee of Lower Silesia with Breslau; and he promised his electoral vote to the Elector of Bavaria in the forthcoming Imperial elections. France, on the other hand, engaged to supply the elector without delay with auxiliary troops to enable him to push his claims.[65]

The two partners kept their agreement secret for the time being. Frederick went on 'amusing' the British and Hanoverian representatives in his camp. 'Trompez les trompeurs!'—he was vastly amused himself. It was not until the end of June that Hanover and London felt any certainty about the Franco-Prussian treaty, although their apprehension had been growing apace.[66]

Meanwhile George II himself had arrived in Hanover at the end of June, with Harrington in attendance. Though the king was worried by the news of the Prussian–French alliance, he was not immediately frightened for Hanover. At first he believed that suitable concessions from Vienna might induce Frederick to renege on the treaty he had just concluded, 'considering his character'[67]—a remarkable judgment on Frederick's personality. It was in this spirit that Harrington signed, on 24 June 1741, an agreement with Ostein, disposing of the £300,000 the Commons had voted to Maria Theresa. The preamble said that the *casus foederis* concerning the 12,000 auxiliaries stipulated in the Austro-British treaty of 1732 had arisen. The King of Great Britain had accordingly taken Danes and Hessians into his pay in the required number and he would put them at the disposal of the Queen of Hungary without loss of time. The treaty was to be ratified within three weeks.[68] That same day George II signed another treaty (technically two treaties), this time as elector, with Ostein, in which he put at Maria Theresa's disposal as from 22 July 10,000 Hanoverian troops against payment of £200,000, to be taken out of the British subsidy. (According to a 1732 treaty the elector was bound to provide 3,000 of his own troops *in casu foederis*). The plenipotentiaries for Hanover were Münchhausen and Otto Christian von Lenthe, the junior member of the Privy Council and until lately Hanoverian representative at Vienna; for Austria, Ostein and the new Austrian envoy to Hanover, Baron Jaxheim.[69] Though the British ministers were put in the picture, they seem to have taken care not to have their master's financial measures made public. The news percolated, of course. In the House of Commons on 10 December 1742 Pitt was probably thinking of the Ostein treaty when he assumed that the king in the disposal of electoral troops was swayed by 'temptations of greater profit'.[70] (See also below, p. 56).

The 'British' treaty was ratified at Herrenhausen on 28 June. The first use Maria Theresa made of the subsidy was to redeem a promise to George II and reimburse him for 'expenses' on her behalf in Germany to the tune of £50,000—probably the first quarterly instalment which George II may have advanced out of his Hanoverian treasury.[71] This transaction too, though not strictly a breach of contract, was not of a nature to be advertised in Britain.

It was at this crucial juncture that George II began to change his mind on matters more essential than the subventions to Maria Theresa. For one, it was never put to the test whether Frederick's political ethics were as crude as his uncle believed: Maria Theresa was not yet ready to buy Frederick off, and the treaties just signed were of course ill designed to discourage her. Frederick, on the other hand, refused to comply with a British–Dutch demand that he should evacuate Silesia, signed at The Hague after months of deliberation on 24 April and delivered by Hyndford in mid-June. Then Münchhausen in an opinion of 15 July 1741 strongly advised George not to risk war for the sake of Austria or, indeed, associate with her at present in any significant manner.[72] His plea was that conditions had materially changed over the last three weeks. On the ethical plane he pleaded the Austrian ally's unreasonable obstinacy; on the practical, that the odds had become overwhelmingly unfavourable, and that no one was bound to hazard his existence for a treaty. '... One unlucky battle—under a combined attack from Prussia and France—would entail the total loss of the royal [German] lands, since we have neither resources nor fortresses ...' Münchhausen was to voice both arguments, the ethical and the practical, over and over again during the next twenty years. Unheroic as they are, they truly fitted Hanover's peculiar situation.[73]

But all these points—and Münchhausen's opinion certainly carried weight—were mere corollaries to the actual danger rising in the west. Rumours of a French army about to assemble for an assault on Westphalia and thence on Hanover had been rampant since March 1741, as we have seen. They thickened when it became known that Belleisle had achieved a concerted plan of action between Bavaria, Spain and France to despoil Maria Theresa of her territories.[74] It does not matter in this context that Bavaria never signed a written agreement with France as she did with Spain; George II came to believe that she did.[75] His bellicosity was rapidly subsiding as his panic mounted. Harrington and Bussy have left us graphic and rather moving descriptions of the king's despair.[76] Finally, on 30 July, the news reached Hanover of the crown council at Versailles ten days earlier when a final decision was taken on the formation of Maillebois's army in northern Lorraine.[77] On that same day Ostein was informed that the execution of the treaties as relating to the auxiliaries was suspended, though not as relating to the subsidy. The mumbled excuses centred on Saxony's alleged default of *her* treaty obligations.[78]

Already on 13 July Harrington had informed Newcastle on three points 'which his Majesty would have more particularly considered: 1. whether, in the desperate situation into which affairs are at present brought, through the obstinacy and ill conduct of the Court of Vienna, it can be thought ... incumbent upon his Majesty to enter into hostile operations against the King of Prussia, and, if not, 2. whether his Majesty shall not have complied with all that can be justly and reasonably expected from him by giving the above mentioned £300,000 and offering to employ the Hessian and Danish troops in the places upon the Lower Rhine or in Flanders at the option of the Court of Vienna for the security of the Empire on that side, and that of Flanders, against the dangerous views and designs of France and, lastly, whether in case the King of Prussia would be induced to engage to confine his hostile measures against the Queen of Hungary to Silesia only, it may not be advisable to enter into a treaty of neutrality with that prince'.[79]

It is necessary to stress the pusillanimity, almost amounting to treachery, of this 'proposal'—offering Maria Theresa an option of sectors where she did *not* want to employ her army, and tying down her mortal enemy—for as such she was known to regard Frederick—to operations in that sector where he was most effective. Only then can we appreciate the state of mind to which George II was reduced. His mood is also exemplified by the polite lack of interest with which he registered, on that same day, the news from the West Indies, where a major assault by British naval and land forces on the Spanish positions at Cartagena had failed disastrously.[80] The British ministers, however, reacted to the king's feeler with a decisiveness which they rarely showed when they opposed their master in foreign affairs. On 14 July (O.S.) Newcastle wrote to Harrington for the entire inner cabinet—himself, Walpole, Hardwicke and Wilmington:[81] the auxiliaries were Maria Theresa's, to be employed wherever she thought proper. A treaty of neutrality with Frederick would be 'impracticable on account of the engagements which, it now appears, [he] has contracted with France'; in other words, Parliament had passed its resolutions in April in order to strengthen the front against France and her possible allies, and not to weaken it. Of positive advice to the king in his despair there was none. And yet the reply did contain an escape clause, tucked away in a sentence of many parts: their constitutional advice went to His Majesty 'as King of Great Britain'. Probably this was not a hint, but a precautionary shedding of responsibility. Be that as it may, George II was quick to take the point. On 2 August Harrington transmitted the king's request to be told what assistance for Hanover he could depend on from England. The question has a rhetorical ring, since Harrington goes on: 'But in case it should be thought inadvisable in the present situation of affairs to send hither any assistance at all, or any such as may be sufficient and arrive in time, His Majesty will be obliged ... without any further loss of time ... to enter as Elector into a neutrality with the enemies of the House of Austria. The King would not, however, take this step without first apprizing his servants in England of the necessity ... '[82] 'The enemies', be it noted; by now it was the French army which was the immediate threat.

This time the reply from London was not entirely negative: 12,000 British troops could be furnished. If this was not enough, or too late, 'we cannot presume to interfere in any other measures that His Majesty as Elector may think proper to take for the security of his Electoral dominions'.[83] The ministers pointedly ignored the possibility of financial assistance. Among themselves they rejected it as entirely unreasonable; the more so, since the king had already pre-empted the Danish and Hessian auxiliaries for the protection of Hanover.[84] Predictably, the king did consider the offer as insufficient and too late. Later Münchhausen summarized, somewhat unfairly, 'The English ministry itself admitted that this [British] crown could not assume the greater part of the Imperial burden; much less was it capable of assisting His Majesty in his

German affairs in a real and sufficient manner ... hence nothing remained but giving way before the torrent and averting ruin from these [Hanoverian] lands by accepting neutrality and conceding the Imperial election to the Elector of Bavaria.'[85]

* * *

On 29 August 1741 Maillebois set out with about 40,000 men. On 23 September he crossed the Rhine far to the north of Cologne.[86] One month earlier, on 23 August, George II 'as elector' had signed instructions for Friedrich Karl von Hardenberg, his director of buildings, to proceed on a special mission to Paris.[87]

Hardenberg was charged with proceeding without delay to the French court 'in order to find out whether the same could be dissuaded from far-reaching undertakings which cause Us trouble'; to assure Cardinal Fleury and Secretary of State Amelot of George II's good will towards France; to enquire whether the military armaments of France, and the army rumoured to debouch into Westphalia in particular, had any bearing on the forthcoming Imperial elections; to explain that, though the king had considered giving his vote to the Duke of Lorraine (Maria Theresa's husband), his mind was by no means made up; to beg the cardinal to open his mind to him on this question, for the sake of peace in Germany; to hint that the king was prepared to vote for the King of Poland (and Elector of Saxony) if such was French policy and to concert measures with the Saxon special envoy in Paris, Ferdinand von Saul, for this purpose; to insinuate that the king of Prussia, the recent ally of France, might in time be more troublesome to her than Austria; to keep the mission secret and to invent plausible pretexts for Hardenberg's presence in Paris. Article VI of the instructions reads: 'If the Cardinal mentions the war between Us and Spain, the reply should be: indeed this matter applies to Our English affairs and concerns Our English ministry. However, the Cardinal and all the world will have noticed Our dislike of, and Our tardiness in, going into this war [*wie ungern und langsam Wir an solchen Krieg gegangen wären*]. Hence it should be easy to deduce that We incline towards making a reasonable peace.'

The instructions need few comments. Taking into account that the 'family compact' of 1733 between France and Spain had gained additional significance for Britain in December 1740, when Fleury ordered the Toulon fleet into the Caribbean, it is natural that George II should have expected inconvenient questions on the luckless war with Spain—no concern of Hanover when a French army was approaching her western frontiers. It may surprise that George II offered King Augustus as candidate for the Imperial crown, when he knew of the cooperation between France and Bavaria. But Saxony was a Protestant *Reichsstand* despite her Catholic prince; also, she was an old friend and a possible ally against Frederick.[88] The king's anxiety speaks almost painfully from every line.

While Maillebois's army deployed in Westphalia, where the bishopric of Münster was held by France's ally the Archbishop of Cologne, Hardenberg made good progress with Fleury, who made it clear from the outset that George II interested him principally as King of Great Britain. Seen from this angle the security of Hanover was a minor affair which could easily be adjusted. As to the French incursion into Germany, France wished to attack no state, Fleury asserted; but when she was menaced by hostile alliances she had to protect herself and her allies.[89] On 19 September 1741 Fleury made his crucial communication, in reply to another cry of anguish that had meanwhile arrived from Hanover.[90] Apart from asking for secrecy Fleury stated the 'sincere intents' of his king under eight heads:

1. Louis XV was prepared to withdraw his troops from the vicinity of those of George II, and of his territories, provided George II engaged not to employ his troops in Germany against the allies of France. No written undertaking was needed; a 'Royal word of honour' sufficed. 2. France believed that the Elector of Bavaria was sure to receive a plurality in the Electoral College. However, the king would feel greatly obliged if George II were to add his own vote. 3. French activities in Dunkirk were purely defensive (and hence no menace to British shipping). 4. France had no designs on the Austrian Netherlands; Louis was prepared to sign a treaty of neutrality with the Queen of Hungary covering those territories, including Luxembourg, under a guarantee of George II and the States General. 5. France had no dealings with the Stuart Pretender, directly or indirectly. 6. France would gladly offer her good offices to restore peace with Spain. 'However, in this case it seems that Your Majesty might suspend the despatch of convoys and troops to America, so that time may be gained to start negotiations and conclude them with success'. 7. The accusations that France had incited Spain to war were false. 8. The cardinal repeated his complaints concerning the damage British vessels had done to French shipping and expressed his hope of 'legitimate satisfaction'.

George II referred to the last crucial question even before he received Fleury's letter, having instructed Hardenberg on 22 September to tell the cardinal that the cardinal's grievances against Britain were separate from German affairs, which, 'according to the cardinal's own elucidation', should not be mixed. However, the cardinal should feel assured that immediately on his return to England the king would 'minutely examine those grievances and do them all justice'.[91] The king made no mention of the two points which the cardinal had singled out to reassure British national interests: the seaward fortifications of Dunkirk demolished under the terms of the Treaty of Utrecht 1713, and ever since a bugbear especially with English traders, as Dunkirk was the most convenient base for privateers in the Channel and the Narrows; and the Stuart aspirant to the crowns of England and Scotland, James 'the Third', the 'Old Pretender', about whom Walpole was supposed to be particularly anxious. Again, it was not Dunkirk or the Pretender who had made George II send Hardenberg to Paris.

Fleury complained, not without reason, that George II was less precise in his communication than he himself had been. However, both sides remained eager to reach agreement: Fleury wanted to gain British credit, at least temporarily, through the negotiations with Hanover, while George II and Münchhausen watched with dismay the French–Bavarian onslaught on Austria then under way and, worse, Maillebois's progress in Westphalia. On 5 October Fleury sent a crucial analysis: 'The matter in hand must be determined less by negotiation than by full and absolute confidence. The king [Louis XV] expresses himself plainly and gives his royal word that he will not undertake any action against Hanover [*les états d'Hannovre*]. Your Majesty gives a similar undertaking that you will not take hostile action against our allies, or hinder [*troubler*] them in pursuit of the rights which they claim to have on any part of the inheritance of the late Emperor Charles VI. Here is the ground and foundation of our treaty; or rather, of our convention, as sacred and strong as a treaty. The rest is merely detail [*n'est qu'un accessoire*].' As to the grievances against Britain, Fleury 'put his faith in the sense of equity' of the king on his return to England.[92]

Thereupon François de Bussy, the French envoy to Hanover, also in Newcastle's pay as information agent '101', finalized the matter with Münchhausen and Steinberg on 12 October, at the castle of Linsburg near Neustadt-am-Rübenberg, well away from prying eyes. Being 'on the word of two kings', no formal agreement was envisaged. But the sides did sign a protocol at Münchhausen's Hanover residence on 28 October.[93]

Firstly, in the protocol the Hanoverian ministers bore witness that George II accepted the declaration contained in Fleury's letter of 5 October. Therewith 'the principal matter' was satisfactorily settled. However, 'to avoid any inconveniences', a few 'accessory points' had to be finalized. These were that Maillebois's army was to winter in Westphalia no nearer than three German miles (about thirteen English miles) from the frontier of the electorate. No quarters were to be assigned to French troops on either side of the route which George was to take from Hanover to England. Finally, the troops on both sides were to go into winter quarters within twelve days.

Neither Fleury's letter of 5 October, nor the 'Neustadt protocol', as it came to be called, goes into the vital question of whether George II was acting as elector only. He appears as 'His Britannic Majesty and Electoral Highness'; his Hanoverian ministers, without embellishment, as 'the ministers of state'.

In addition, George II begged on the strength of the 'friendship and good intentions of His Most Christian Majesty' that the bishopric of Osnabrück be exempted from winter quarters and receive certain additional preferences—though it was not, of course, part of George's 'German dominions' or ruled at that time by a Guelph prince (see p. 26 above); but George II at no time ceased to feel a special obligation to this particular objective of his dynastic ambition. Also it is noteworthy that the Hanoverian ministers refer to France as 'guarantor of the Peace of Westphalia'. In fact, Münchhausen and his colleagues regarded France, in this capacity, as the humiliator of Germany; as the root cause of the danger she posed to them. That they should have used this phrase to flatter French vanity is an additional indicator of how earnest they were in their present cause. (This particular appeal was in vain. French troops did winter in Osnabrück and neighbouring Paderborn, where their diminishing discipline led to breaches of the peace.)[94]

As winter approached the French–Bavarian army first threatened Vienna and then took Prague. Prince Leopold of Dessau's camp had been dispersed early in October, but Frederick continued to loom as a frightening enigma: 'as experience has taught that this master's [*dieses Herrn*] true sentiments [*Gesinnung*] are impenetrable, and probably none too good towards His Majesty [George II] ...'.[95]

So George II and his Hanoverian ministers sought an agreement more binding than the Neustadt protocol. Their gropings culminated in the draft of a treaty between France and George II as elector. A 'secret and separate' article absolved him from responsibility for any action he might take as King of Great Britain. But it also stipulated that he would not permit 'quarters in his electorate to any troops in the pay of the crown of England'.[96] We do not know for certain how George II believed this obligation would square with his employment of Danish and Hessian auxiliaries; apparently he believed the suspension of the Ostein treaties (see above, p. 33) applied. In any case, Louis XV did stand by his word 'as a king', and the French invasion scare gradually subsided.

During most of this time Schwicheldt continued to stay in Silesia. By the beginning of August 1741 his orders had turned him from a negotiator for territorial gains into a frantic suppliant for his host's intercession with the French. But Frederick dawdled; he probably enjoyed the Hanoverians' fright. At first he was unwilling to get involved. Then he demanded a fee; a stiff cash payment, and the cession of the Hanoverian mortgages in Mecklenburg. At last, on the pressing advice of Podewils, he approached the French court. He had missed his chance. The principles of the neutrality were already agreed upon. On 15 October Schwicheldt left for Hanover.[97]

Hanover's gain by the Neustadt protocol is clear. The French policy-makers, on the other hand, have been condemned ever since for having made the mistake of their generation. Among those who hold this view was Frederick himself.[98] But Fleury wanted a lever against Britain and believed, however mistakenly, that he had engineered it. He disliked the war, and believed that Maillebois would have overpowered Hanover only after heavy fighting. He may have been right here, though no certainty is possible.

To what extent were the British ministry informed of the neutrality negotiations? When it was all over, Münchhausen claimed that they had 'all' been in the picture, and had approved.[99] While this is no untruth, it is an oversimplification.

The overriding consideration of George II and his Hanoverian ministers was obviously the immediate safety of Hanover. Still, they had no wish to create avoidable hostility in Britain, where any agreement with France for the benefit of Hanover was bound to arouse suspicion or worse, compelling the British ministers to interfere in Hanover's affairs. Indeed, the Hanoverians knew the force of public opinion in Britain, even if they could never comprehend its nature.[100] In their view, it might be solicitous of the position of the ministers, as well as wise, not to let Whitehall know too much too soon. Harrington, who was at Hanover, was inevitably in the picture, but his official correspondence with Newcastle has only the slightest reference to Hardenberg's mission. And Hardenberg is not mentioned by name until after the Neustadt *entente* of 12 October. At the same time he made much of George's determination to fight to the end against a French onslaught on Hanover, as indeed the king had warned Bussy.[101] In a denial of the negotiations to Robert Trevor, British minister at the Hague, Harrington was positively misleading.[102] Harrington was more outspoken in his private letters to Newcastle, though even there he did not tell all that was going on at Hanover. The ministers in London, on their part, deliberately avoided taking issue with Harrington's hints—they wanted no share of the responsibility.[103] Walpole indeed was informed by George II himself in a private letter as early as late July and showed 'reluctant acquiescence'.[104]

The situation had its farcical side, though Harrington's official reticence enabled the ministers during September and the first half of October to deny all knowledge of the negotiations, when pressed by a diplomatic community agog with rumours.[105] In the meantime Newcastle poured out his fears to Hardwicke that the Queen of Hungary was ruined for the sake of Hanover, and this would bring in its wake the wrath of the newly elected Parliament upon the ministers. As usual, Hardwicke calmed him: Maria Theresa's fate was decided by 'the circumstances and disposition of other powers', not by 'what Great Britain has done *of late*', while the opposition in Parliament would oppose whatever the ministers did. Less usual for him, Hardwicke had a complaint of his own: '... as to a neutrality between Hanover and France, our opinions were never so much as asked ...'. It is a half-truth, since he had ignored the chance to give his opinion. Hardwicke added: '... the conduct of Great

Britain ought to be the same, as if it had never happened—if that be possible'.[106]

The Neustadt undertaking of 12 October 1741 put an end to the confusion. At George's command, Harrington on 15 October sent a notification to Newcastle and to 'all British ministers abroad' that gave a reasonably clear account of 'this *purely electoral* affair'. The order was given at Newcastle's urgent request, to avert public anger from him and his colleagues.[107] The note placed the onus of the change of fronts on Holland, on Saxony and, above all, on Austria. It stated that the undertaking with France 'does not in the least tie up His Majesty's hands as king, or engage him to anything relating to his further conduct, as such, or to the affairs of England ...' Finally, after George's return to London, after some hesitation, he authorized Harrington on 26 October to show the Cabinet Council the correspondence on the negotiations, with instructions not to copy them and to return the original to the German Chancery.[108] Newcastle acquiesced. He drew up 'Considerations upon the present state of affairs' in which he accepted the neutrality and merely hoped—in terms unusually obscure—that the king was engaged in the agreement 'as elector only'.[109] Two years later he was to refer to the neutrality, in private correspondence, as the 'capitulation of the electorate'.[110]

On 24 January 1742 George II fulfilled another part of his bargain with France when Münchhausen as his 'Premier elections ambassador' at Frankfurt voted for Charles Albert of Bavaria, who became the Emperor Charles VII. Also while at Frankfurt Münchhausen negotiated a draft treaty of friendship between George II 'as elector' and Bavaria as the favoured ally of France in Germany. We may believe his later assertions that the task was distasteful to him, but he did it smoothly enough. Though the draft did not demand of George II armed or financial assistance against Maria Theresa, in the prevailing situation the treaty would have been another nail in her coffin. Yet at the same time Münchhausen believed that France would not permit the new emperor—her client—to carry out the treaty, as it was designed to increase the security of Hanover. Be that as it may, both sides agreed on the essentials of the draft.[111] So far as we know, Britain did not enter into Münchhausen's cogitations. And rightly not; if her ministers had swallowed the French neutrality, they would swallow the Bavarian treaty. However, the wheel of fortune turned dramatically just then: Maria Theresa's military situation improved sensationally, Maillebois retreated from Westphalia southwards, the new emperor was put to the chase throughout southern Germany. The treaty became an embarrassment for Hanover and was dropped.

The treaty between Hanover and France formally to embody the Neustadt protocol was not signed. 'At that time the *facies rerum* changed in England and Holland ...'[112] In our context we may discount the changes in Holland, but those in Britain are vital to the issue.

The causes of Walpole's fall lie beyond Hanover. We may believe that public opinion in London was in patriotic uproar over the 'Neutrality'.[113] Carteret and others did attack the Neustadt undertaking in Parliament in the two months preceding his fall as bringing Britain into disrepute, as a betrayal of the Queen of Hungary, and as unnecessary for Hanover's security.[114] But this subject did not figure prominently with the opposition in either house. Harrington replied in the House of Lords that 'the dominions of Great Britain and Hanover are distinct and independent'. This was the line which George II was always to take whenever a British course of action threatened Hanover. The speech from the throne on 4 December 1741 referred to that of 8 April, as though Maillebois had not neared the Weser in the meantime, or a meeting at Neustadt had never taken place.[115] Walpole's time had run out, and the 'Neutrality' issue was no more than a last irritant. He resigned on 8 February 1742, and became Earl of Orford.

On 12 February 1742 Carteret took over from Harrington as secretary of state for the Northern Department.[116] In accepting office on his personal terms, with little regard for less gifted and less forceful 'opposition Whigs', who were every bit as eager for office as he himself, he added to the handicap he would have to carry as an arrogant nobleman proverbially disdainful of the common run of politicians.

Notes

1. Public Record Office, State Papers, Regencies, 43/89. Henceforth 'Public Record Office' is omitted when quoting sources of this provenance.
2. Henceforth Holland and Austria respectively, for brevity.
3. S.P., Regencies, 43/89.
4. S.P., Foreign, 90/47.
5. The following is in the main based on F. Frensdorff (ed.), 'G. A. von Münchhausen's Berichte über seine Mission nach Berlin im Juni 1740', *Abhandlungen der königlichen Gesellschaft der Wissenschaften zu Göttingen*, Philologisch-historische Klasse, N.F. VIII, Nr. 2, Berlin, 1904, 3-87. The underlying documents were destroyed in World War II, but Frensdorff cites them virtually in their entirety.
6. The *Foedus Perpetuum* is published in Theodor von Moerner, *Kurbrandenburgs Staatsverträge von 1601 bis 1700*, Berlin, 1867, 579-580. An original copy is kept in the Niedersächsisches Hauptstaatsarchiv, Hanover, Hann. 92, LVIII, Nr. 1[a].
7. 'L'aigle noir [the highest Prussian decoration] n'est pas un ordre pour des coujons comme Münchhausen'—*Pol. Corr.*, 1, 9. The *Politische Correspondenz* merely gives dots for *coujons*, but Frensdorff and Portzek supply the clear text. (Münchhausen eventually got his 'Aigle Noir'.)
8. Frensdorff, *op. cit.*, 45.
9. Frensdorff, *op. cit.*, 37.
10. *Ibid.*
11. Dickens to Harrington, 17 Aug 1740, State Papers, Foreign, 90/48. Also, Lodge, *Great Britain and Prussia in the Eighteenth Century*, Oxford, 1923, 30.
12. T. B. Macaulay, 'Frederick the Great', in *Critical and Historical Essays*, London, 1878, 797.
13. During the years before the death of Frederick William I, George II had supported his nephew with several secret loans, amounting, it seems, in all to £12,250; Frederick repaid at his accession. The crown prince's letters to his uncle thanking him for his help in this 'delicate and dangerous [*sic*] affair' are of human interest. (Hann. 92, LVIII, Nr. 5[a]).
14. Frederick to Guy Dickens; Guy Dickens to Harrington, 17 Aug 1740 (S.P., Foreign, 90/48).
15. Cf. Ranke, *Zwölf Bücher preussischer Geschichte*, Leipzig, 1874, Book VII, 299-300.
16. For Mecklenburg in these contexts, see Mediger, *Mecklenburg, Russland und England-Hannover 1706-1721*, Hildesheim, 1967, 2 vols.
17. 22 Aug 1740. Hann. 91, LVIII, Nr. 8; also Mediger, *Moskaus Weg nach Europa*, Brunswick, 1952, 356-357 (henceforth Mediger).
18. On Anglo-Russian relations at this time, see R. Lodge, 'The first Anglo-Russian treaty', *EHR*, XLIII (1928), 354-375. The article also contains references to Hanoverian assistance to British diplomacy at the technical level.
19. Newcastle to Hardwicke, 27 July 1740; P. C. Yorke (ed.), *The Life and Correspondence of Philip Yorke, Earl of Hardwicke*, 3 vols., Cambridge, 1913, I, 243.

20. *Ibid*., p. 245; S. P., Regencies, 43/89.
21. Harrington to Count Truchsess, Frederick's emissary at Hanover; Harrington to Dickens, 10 Oct 1740, S.P., Foreign, 90/48.
22. 'Kurtze Historische Erzehlung desjenigen, so seit dem Absterben des Kaysers, bis *ad finem Aprilis* 1742, im Ministerio vorgegangen', Hanover, 4 May 1742 (Hann. 92, LXXI, 17[a], vol. I); henceforth 'Kurtze Historische Erzehlung'. Theo König in 1937 published the 'Historic Relation' from a copy which was evidently kept at Hanover for reference (*Niedersächsisches Jahrbuch für Landesgeschichte*, XIV, 1937, 200-232). The reference above is to the copy in the German Chancery files, sent to the king in London with amendments in Münchhausen's hand. The differences between the two copies are very slight. König has a valuable introduction and running comments. The quotations here refer to page numbers in König's edition.
23. Münchhausen, *Kurtze historische Erzehlung*, 205.
24. S.P., Foreign, 90/48.
25. Speech from the throne, 18 Nov 1740, *Journal of the House of Commons*, XXIII, 532.
26. 2 Nov 1740. The letter is missing from the file; I have inferred its contents from the ministers' reply (note below). See also Mediger, 360.
27. *Geheime Räte* to George II, 9 Dec 1740, Hann. LVIII, Nr. 8. By then rumours were rampant in the German chancelleries concerning Hanoverian aspirations, as well as those of Prussia and Hesse-Cassel. Hanover was credited with claims to Hildesheim. (Count Ostein at Cologne to Court Chancellor Sinzendorff at Vienna, 21 Nov 1740, Haus-, Hof- und Staatsarchiv, henceforth *HHStA*, England, 77.)
28. Dickens to Harrington, 6 Dec 1740, S.P., Foreign, 90/48.
29. E.g. C. Grünhagen, *Geschichte des ersten schlesischen Krieges*, Gotha, 1881, I, 275. The Prussian historians of Frederick II, Droysen, Naudé, Dove, Koser, Grünhagen himself, remain important for their industrious knowledgeability; their main significance today is as primary sources of German intellectual history, 1849-1918. Ranke is *sui generis*.
30. *Loc. cit.*
31. Ostein to Sinzendorff, 23 Dec 1740 (N.S.), *HHStA*, England, K. 77; also Mediger, 362-363.
32. 9, 12 Dec 1740, Hann. 92, LVIII, 8.
33. 30 Dec 1740, *ibid.*
34. 17 Jan 1741, Hann. 92, LXXI, Nr. 17b, vol. I.
35. Professor Mediger, whose treatment of these exchanges is more detailed than mine, believes that the ministers tendered their advice with no idea of insinuating their own doubts. Perhaps his view and mine are not incompatible. The Hanoverian ministers certainly regarded themselves as bound in obedience to their master in a way their British colleagues at the time no longer did, and they were loyal. On the other hand their aversion for territorial aggrandizement is documented over and again. In the present case their response may have mirrored their doubts at the subconscious level.
36. A later Austrian minister at London, Baron von Wasner, a shrewd observer, speaks of Steinberg's 'natürlicher Furchtsamkeit' (Report to Maria Theresa, 1 Feb 1746, *HHStA*, England, K. 90).
37. Ostein's reports to Maria Theresa, 16, 27 Jan, 13, 17 Feb 1741 (all N.S.), *HHStA*, England, K. 78.
38. Britain and Hanover, being separate states, had separately guaranteed the Pragmatic Sanction, the former on 16 Mar 1731, the latter on 10 April 1731; the British guarantee is part of the 'second Treaty of Vienna' (see also below). Both agreements are given by A. F. Pribram (ed.), *Österreichische Staatsverträge, England,* Innsbruck, Vienna, 1907-1913, I, 499-514, 487.
39. Maria Theresa to Ostein, 30 Dec 1740; Bartenstein (?) to O. Ch. von Lenthe, Hanoverian envoy at Vienna, 29 Dec 1740, *HHStA*, England, K. 75.
40. Maria Theresa to Ostein, 5, 18 Feb, 11, 13 Mar 1741, *HHStA*, England, K. 79. The text

of the draft treaty, in Latin, appears in Pribram, *op. cit.*, I, 561-566. For a German and English translation, Jph. Chr. Adelung, *Pragmatische Staatsgeschichte Europens von dem Ableben Kaiser Carls VI. an ...*, Gotha, III (1763), *Beilagen*, 10-18; article XII is omitted.

41. Hann. 92, LXXII, Nr. 17b, vol. I. The *Projekt* is undated, with a brief note appended in Secretary J. F. Mejer's hand of 10 Mar 1741 (O.S.), when the message from Vienna might just have arrived. Still, by then George II had already been exposed to influences strongly warning him off anti-Prussian adventures (see below), and the possibility cannot be ruled out that the *Project* was penned as early as late February when he was at his most exuberant. That the king took the *Project* very seriously is proved by the marginalia in his own hand.
42. Wratislaw and Khevenhüller to Maria Theresa, 1 Mar 1741, copy in *HHStA*, England, K. 79; Harrington to Villiers, 23 Jan 1741, S.P., 88/56.
43. On 27 Feb 1871 (O.S.), S.P., Foreign, 80/144.
44. *Cobbett's Parliamentary History*, London, 1806-1820 (henceforth *P.H.*), XI, 1388.
45. Hann. 91, LXXI, 17[b], vol. I.
46. *Ibid.*
47. Dickens to Harrington, 4 Feb 1741, S.P., Foreign, 90/49; Also J. D. E. Preuss (ed.), *Oeuvres de Fréderic le Grand*, Berlin, 1846-1857, II, 73-74 (henceforth *Oeuvres*).
48. Dickens to Harrington, 31 Jan 1741, S.P., Foreign 90/49.
49. Dickens to Harrington, 14 Mar 1741, *Ibid.*
50. For the Hanoverian army of that period, see vol. II of F. von Sichart's standard work, *Geschichte der Königlich Hannoverschen Armee,* Hanover, 1866-71, 4 vols.
51. Belleisle's tour with its French and Prusso-Germanic contexts is admirably described in Maurice Sautai, *Les préliminaires de la guerre de la succession d'Aütriche*, Paris, 1907, chs. V, VI.
52. *Geheime Räte* to George II, Hann. 92, LVIII, Nr. 8.
53. From Minutes of Privy Council session, Hanover, 1 Mar 1741, Hann. 92, LVIII, Nr. 8; *Pol. Corr.* I, 188, 219-221. Mediger (376-381) treats Plotho's mission to Hanover in detail. Frederick ordered Plotho to 'cajoler extrêmement le de Münchhausen' by giving hope of the Black Eagle and other inducements (see also above, p. 40).
54. For details, see Hann. 91, du Pontpietin I. The first of the documents in question, undated and unsigned, but apparently addressed by the Privy Council to Quartermaster General Pauli early in March 1741, bears traces of an offensive strategy aimed at Frederick. Such traces disappear immediately thereafter.
55. *Pol. Corr.*, I, 219.
56. S.P., Foreign, 80/144.
57. Sichart, *op. cit.*, II, 377.
58. For Hyndford's instruction, see Harrington to Hyndford, 10 May 1741, S.P., Foreign, Prussia, 90/49; for Schwicheldt's see Grünhagen, I, 369 ff.
59. For Schwicheldt's character portrait of Frederick, see H. Portzek, *Friedrich der Grosse und Hannover in ihrem gegenseitigen Urteil*, Hildesheim, 1958, 35-38.
60. 4 June 1741 (S.P., Foreign, 90/50).
61. The quotation is from Harrington's 'Private' letter to Hyndford, Hanover, 2 June 1741, *ibid.* It is interesting to compare this injunction to a previous occasion when British and Hanoverian interests might have come in each other's way, during the negotiations for the second Treaty of Vienna, ten years previously. Then the Hanoverian envoy, the later minister von Diede, was peremptorily ordered to stand back until the British interest was secured. (Wendy Cudmore, *Sir Robert Walpole and the Treaty of Vienna, 16 March 1731*, unpubl. M.A. thesis, London, 1978, 38-39.) But in 1731 Harrington's factual superior was Walpole, still in his prime, and not George II.
62. *Pol. Corr.*, I, 235-236, 254-255; *Oeuvres*, II, 89, 90. For Schwicheldt's efforts to obtain from Frederick 'conveniences' for Hanover, from March to July 1741, see Grünhagen, I, 368-380. The author is prejudiced against Frederick's adversaries, but his recital of events inspires confidence.

63. *J.H.C.*, XXIII, 702-706.
64. Hyndford to Harrington, 13 May 1741, S.P., Foreign, 90/50.
65. For an analysis of the secret articles, see Ranke, *Zwölf Bücher preussischer Geschichte*, Book VIII, 428-430.
66. Harrington (at Hanover) to Newcastle, 25 June 1741 (S.P., Regencies, 43/100). He had received 'undoubted intelligence' on 24 June.
67. Harrington to Newcastle (Private), 25 June 1741, S.P., Regencies, 43/28.
68. *Ibid.*; Zöhrern to Maria Theresa, London, 14 July 1741 (N.S.), *HHStA*, England, K. 78.
69. Pribram, *op. cit.*, 572-577.
70. *P.H.*, XII, 1035.
71. Copy of George II's authorization to Baron Schütz, Master of the Wardrobe at Hanover, countersigned by Steinberg, Herrenhausen, 16 Aug 1741, *HHStA*, England, K. 78. The authorization does not spell out the nature of the advance.
72. Mediger, 386-388; the file was destroyed in World War II. See also *Kurtze historische Erzehlung*, 225n.
73. Münchhausen, *Kurtze historische Erzehlung*, 211-212, for a pungent formulation. The quotation is supplied by the editor from an opinion of Münchhausen of 15 July 1741.
74. Sautai, *Preliminaires*, ch. VI; Droysen, 'Der Nymphenburger Tractat von 1741', *Zeitschrift für preussische Geschichte*, X (1873), 515-536.
75. For the text of the treaty supposedly signed between Bavaria and France as put before George II, see S.P., Foreign, 90/50, ff. 209-213.
76. Harrington to Newcastle, 2 Aug 1741, S.P., Regencies, 42/29; Sautai, *Les débuts de la guerre de la succession d'Autriche*, Paris, 1909, I, 289.
77. Sautai, *Preliminaires*, 519.
78. S.P., Regencies, 43/28. The role of Saxony is lucidly described, from the Hanoverian viewpoint, in *Kurtze historische Erzehlung*, 217-223.
79. S.P., Regencies, 43/28.
80. Harrington to Newcastle, 13 July 1741 (S.P., Regencies, 43/100).
81. S.P., Regencies, 43/50.
82. S.P., Regencies, 43/29.
83. Newcastle to Harrington, 31 July 1741, Private, S.P., Regencies, 43/30.
84. Add. MSS 3267, f. 438, 35407, ff. 75, 76; Harrington to Newcastle, 25 June 1741, Private (S.P., Regencies, 42/28).
85. *Kurtze historische Erzehlung*, 212, 214.
86. For the march of Maillebois's army, see Sautai, *Débuts*, I, 284.
87. Hann. 92, LXXXI 17^{dl}, vol. IV.
88. See also Münchhausen, *Kurtze historische Erzehlung*, 318-319.
89. Fleury to George II, 11 Sept 1741 (Hann. 92, LXXI, 17^{dl}, vol. III).
90. Hann. 92, LXXI 17^{dl}, vol. IV.
91. *Ibid.*
92. *Ibid.*
93. *Ibid.*, also König, 25.
94. One observer's comment should be preserved: 'Les filles de bonne volonté y trouvent leur compte, car elles trouvent des gens de bon appetit'; Paderborn, 23 April 1742 (Hann. 92, LXXI, 17^{l}, vol. I).
95. Münchhausen from Frankfurt (where he had been sent as Hanoverian 'election ambassador' for the imperial elections) to the ministers at Hanover, 24 February 1742 (Hann. 92, LXXI, 17^{el}).
96. George II penned his last corrections to the draft on 9 January (O.S.) 1742 (Hann. 92, LXXI, 17^{l}, vol. I).
97. For this, the second chapter of the Schwicheldt mission, see Grünhagen, I, 448-463.
98. *Oeuvres*, II, 100, III.
99. Münchhausen, *Kurtze historische Erzehlung*, 214.

100. See 'Conclusions'.
101. S.P., Regencies, 43/29; Sautai, *Débuts*, 291.
102. S.P., *ibid.*
103. Harrington to Newcastle (Private), 2, 30 Aug 1741; Hardwicke to Newcastle, 20 Aug 1741; Newcastle to Harrington, 31 July 1741; Add. MSS 32697, ff. 340-341, 378-379, 434-435.
104. Newcastle to Hardwicke, 19 July 1741, quoted in W. Coxe (ed.), *Memoirs of the Administration of the Rt. Hon. Henry Pelham*, London, 1829, I, 19.
105. S.P., Intercepted Correspondence, 107/49, *passim*. Zöhrern to Sinzendorff, London, 26 Sept 1741 (*HHStA*, England, K. 78) is characteristic in its incredulous consternation. The reports at the same time by the envoy of Hesse-Cassel at The Hague give a fascinating insight into the workings of the international news exchange there (Mann to Prince William, 3, 6 Oct 1741, *Hessisches Staatsarchiv Marburg*, 4 f, Niederlande, Nr. 675).
106. Newcastle to Hardwicke, 9, 18 Sept; Hardwicke to Newcastle, 11, 15 Sept 1741, Add. MSS 32698, ff. 15-21, 32-34, 42-44, 50-53.
107. S.P., Regencies, 43/29; Newcastle to Hardwicke, 18 Sept 1741, Add. MSS 32698, ff. 50-53, Newcastle to Harrington, 25 Sept 1741, *ibid.*, ff. 61-63.
108. Hann. 92, LXXXI, 17[d], vol. IV.
109. 1 Nov 1741, Add. MSS 35407, ff. 131-132.
110. Newcastle to Hardwicke, 24 Oct 1743, Add. MSS 32701, f. 204.
111. For an inside survey of the Bavarian treaty negotiations, see Münchhausen's 'Election diaries' of 1741/42, Hann. 92, XLV, 8; also König, *Hannover und das Reich 1740-1745*, Düsseldorf, 1938, 3-33.
112. Münchhausen, *Kurtze historische Erzehlung*, 226.
113. Zamboni, the agent of Hesse-Darmstadt in London, to the Bavarian minister Count Haslang, 24 Nov, 1 Dec 1741, 'Copies' in Cholmondeley (Houghton) MSS, Correspondence Nos. 3107, 3109, Cambridge University Library.
114. *P.H.*, XII, 254-261, 284-285, and elsewhere.
115. *J.H.C.*, XXIV, II.
116. For a full treatment of Walpole's fall and the reorganization of the administration, John B. Owen, *The Rise of the Pelhams*, London, 1957, 87-100.

Chapter 2
The Carteret years, 1742–1744

The significance of the thirty-three months that follow lies in the fact that this was one of the rare periods between 1714 and 1793 when Continental affairs took priority in British policy. It was Carteret's personality which made it so, more than his tenets, which did not differ essentially from those of the Pelhams. But he knew much better what these tenets implied, and he put the whole of his imperious personality into their implementation. His policy was not 'Hanoverian'. It was more consistently 'British' in concept and execution than that of Newcastle and Harrington until 1742. It is true that he held more of the king's liking and respect than they did, and Hanover did occupy a place in his schemes. Carteret's assertion that he 'stakes his whole on keeping the El[ector] an Englishman'[1] gives the gist of his attitude well—at least during most of his secretaryship. In his last year of office Carteret may, as some writers have suggested, have lost some of his independence of mind—though nothing of his buoyancy—for reasons that can only be surmised. It was only then that George II and his Hanoverian ministers, true to pattern, at once stepped in to fill the gap. But this is anticipating.

The Hanoverian ministers had watched Walpole's decline and fall in helpless apprehension.[2] Perhaps they were frightened that they might be brought to task for the independence they had shown of late. But when Walpole fell they adjusted with alacrity. On 22 February, Carteret asked Steinberg to a conference. According to Steinberg's notation later that night Carteret said that 'at present'—that is, with his own elevation—'minds had calmed down' in Britain, and the king could now approach his subjects, expecting their fullest cooperation. Thus this conjunction of events should be exploited to sustain 'the great world system', in danger of falling apart if French ambitions were realized. (In view of what the next generation was to bring, it must be stressed here that to Carteret 'the great world system' meant emphatically Europe—more even than to Newcastle). Cooperation with Holland must be revitalized. The King of Prussia must be requested to come in, 'with all trust but also with suitable firmness'. 'In particular, it is his [Carteret's] view that the distinction between His Majesty the King as king and as elector must cease'—which could only mean that where the interests of Britain and Hanover diverged, those of Britain came first. However, as if to make up for this implied brutality, 'the entire nation' would do all that was necessary to preserve Hanover, just as if Hanover were part of the British dominions. If Britain wanted troops, on the other hand, 'of course' the king's German troops would be the first to be called upon—a reminder to the Hanoverians that the chaffering with auxiliaries was as much a buyers' as a sellers' market. And in order to update himself on the negotiations between Hanover and France, Lord Carteret said that he intended calling at the Germany Chancery that same evening to go through the files.[3] No report of equal brevity could have given Carteret's ideas with greater precision, or mirrored his sublime self-confidence so well.

Four days later Carteret laid down his postulates before Steinberg with further elaboration:[4] Frederick should be weaned from France by a British–Dutch guarantee of the whole of Silesia, together with the Queen of Hungary's cession. An additional reason why Frederick ought to prefer their guarantee was that it would be 'national', whereas that of France depended on the good will of a few persons. (Until then sporadic British proposals had been limited to Lower Silesia. Carteret's idealization of institutional government comes unexpectedly from an aristocratic individualist, though it probably meant no more than stressing the superiority of things English. He certainly showed ignorance of Frederick.) Sixteen thousand British and 30,000-40,000 Dutch troops should be sent to the Austrian Netherlands 'so that the French should lose the fancy for starting anything there'. George ought to abide by the Neustadt protocol, but 'on his life' (*bei Leibe und bei Halse*) ought not to tie his hands with extending this commitment. Least of all, according to Carteret, should Hanover forgo British assistance, 'for without it, all treaties would not protect [Hanover], were they written on double parchment'. The Emperor, 'in French fetters', was of little account. Saxony could gain nothing from Maria Theresa. As to Russia, 'there is more to hope than to fear'. Carteret's opinion on Russia, coming as it did with such aplomb from such authority, is interesting in view of the threads subsequently taken up by the Hanoverian ministry in the later 1740s.

Carteret's ideas were not novel. Most of them, and others compatible with them, Newcastle had put into his 'Considerations upon the present state of affairs', almost four months before (see above). But while Newcastle put them to paper, Carteret carried them to the king, and imposed them on the Hanoverian ministers.

Again Steinberg was evidently a passive listener. Mention must go to the skill of *Geheimsekretär* Johann Friederich Mejer, who was present and who wrote the report: it is as if we hear Carteret speaking.

If Steinberg forwent comment, his master took action. Carteret seems to have expounded his views to George II in an earlier audience. His impact on the king was such that we have it from no less a witness than Newcastle that it was Carteret who 'put an absolute stop to the negotiations' with France; the commendation is all the more remarkable as Newcastle had been patently incapable of imposing the stop himself.[5]

On 18 February 1742 a courier carried a ciphered order from George II to Hardenberg at Paris, 'on his oath and duty' to spin out the negotiations, 'but in a good manner ... so that the French court shall have no suspicion that this is done by design'.[6] The courier arrived just in time to prevent Hardenberg from putting the last touches to a treaty on which both sides were till then in essential agreement (see p. 37 above).

In the following months Hardenberg was occupied with 'spinning out' the negotiations. The tactics were managed by Münchhausen. He did it with all his heart: he hated France; he knew the danger in acting against a major interest of Britain; he feared putting Hanover's signature to an instrument involving great-power politics. The story of Hardenberg's remaining months in Paris is dreary. Its most interesting aspect is that diplomatists of world renown like Fleury and Amelot were taken in so easily. Perhaps Hardenberg's flaunted lack of sophistication together with his rather basic French proved an asset. On 30 April 1742 (O.S.) George II informed the Hanoverian ministers that he wanted to recall Hardenberg, but he postponed the recall on their advice:[7] Maillebois was still in Westphalia. In the first half of May there were even rumours that French reinforcements were on their way. The Hanoverian army went into another flurry, together with its Hessian quasi-allies, the auxiliaries for whom Britain had paid to be at the disposal of Maria Theresa. (The Danish auxiliaries had stayed throughout the crisis in the 'principality' of Verden, where George II and the *Geheime Räte* eyed them with suspicion: Verden and the 'duchy' of Bremen had been briefly occupied by Denmark during the Nordic War, before Hanover purchased both from Sweden in 1719. Also, Denmark was traditionally friendly to France. The auxiliaries finally returned to Denmark in the summer of 1742.) However, much was happening elsewhere (see below), and on 12 July the French evacuated Osnabrück. Some further weeks of anxiety passed at Kensington Palace and in Hanover as Maillebois tarried on his retreat before turning south-east for the relief of Belleisle at Prague.

Finally Hardenberg was instructed to hand in his letter of recall. In his first draft (May 1742) George II wrote to Louis XV that his electoral envoy's presence was no longer necessary; 'the affair [*negotiation*] ... was settled [*situé*] to my satisfaction'. The final version of 29 July (O.S.) offers no explanation at all except to say that Hardenberg's departure should take place 'without delay'. On 2 September 1742 Hardenberg made his farewell visit to the cardinal and the secretary of state. Hardenberg reported on 25 September after his return to Hanover that Fleury had been most cordial. 'Bussy in London [see below] has been told,' Fleury said to Hardenberg, 'that there is no longer neutrality between us because we [the French] have broken it by a foraging party into the king's territories.' The other reason given to Bussy was that a 'convention' is not a 'treaty'. Fleury added that he had never imagined such possibilities, 'but in this world one must be prepared for everything'. Amelot was less 'measured' and trembled with emotion. Louis XV, when Hardenberg paid his parting respects, was curt—to the breach of protocol, it seems.[8] Hardenberg was fully satisfied with his performance. The cardinal's sarcasm, in particular, was lost on him.

Eighteen months later, in March 1744, the French declaration of war on Britain and Hanover was to cite British bad faith in the neutrality affair as a milestone in the deterioration of relations.[9] (There was no Hanoverian declaration of war on France, though France had expressly declared war on George II as elector of Hanover as well.)

The last word may go to Bussy. As French chargé d'affaires in London he had transmitted to his government the declaration which Fleury mentioned to Hardenberg. He spoke his mind to Steinberg, apparently in the coach on his way to a royal audience on 2 August 1742. He 'only wished' he could send Steinberg the letter that George II had written to Fleury when the French army of the Meuse was approaching Hanover. However, deference to crowned heads prevented Bussy from saying more; in particular, respect for a 'prince who had so far prided himself on his inviolable correctitude in keeping his word'.[10] The last jibe may furnish a clue as to why so clumsy a ruse on George's part succeeded at the French court until it was abandoned as having served its purpose. George II was indeed known for his straightforwardness; the deception may have come off because it was out of character. That the complaint should have come to us from Bussy, a bought traitor, adds piquancy.

The Hanoverian–French neutrality of 1741/1742 had no particular consequences for Hanover herself or for her relations with Britain. The French declaration of war, when it came, had nothing to do with Hanover, though the neutrality affair was certainly considered an additional grievance at Versailles. Fleury was dead, and his successors wanted war with Britain. Nor did the behaviour of the Hanoverian ministers play an appreciable role in the 'hate Hanover' campaign of 1743/1744 in England, as we shall see. The British political public knew little of what actually went on at Hanover, and cared less. For them it was home politics that mattered, and a campaign against Hanover was primarily intended to oust Carteret. For that purpose the 'Neutrality' did not suffice, as Carteret's stand in this instance emerged favourably in contrast to that of his rivals and enemies in the cabinet who had badly dithered.

And yet the case remains for treating the 'Neutrality' in detail, because the episode shows with peculiar clarity the primacy of Hanover in the eyes of George II, as well as the lead Hanoverian ministers could give to British policy on the Continent when the British ministers had no clear concept of their own, or were incapable of seeing it through. Conversely, it indicates Hanoverian submission to Britain immediately upon the emergence of such a minister.

George II and Münchhausen are considered men of honour and reasonable honesty. Yet in the neutrality affair their unabashed double-dealing with France still takes us by surprise. The ways of diplomacy answer for much, but not for all of it. Fleury's contempt tells us something about that too. However, it must be observed that the Hanoverians' duplicity was defensive. They saw their country in mortal danger which they could not stave off except by reneging on their political principles—and by cheating. When they were convinced that the danger was past, they instantly returned to acting by their principles however motivated by political need and by emotion. There the matter may rest.

* * *

In the half-year that had passed between Carteret's accession and the final denouement over the 'Neutrality' much had happened in the Empire.

As the danger from Prussia gradually diminished early in 1742, it was not the retreat of Maillebois as such from Westphalia that would have satisfied Hanover: had he retreated west, for instance, he might have frightened the Dutch into subsiding into their own version of a neutrality. Any event such as this, the Hanoverians feared, might undermine their line of communications with Britain, and turn British attention away from the German scene.[11] But the preliminary Peace of Breslau between Prussia and Austria in June 1742 definitely removed Frederick as an enemy of the enemies of France, and the subsequent deployment of Maillebois in Franconia cleared Hanover's western flank without merely substituting another, though less immediate, risk. And both events were, of course, the outcome at several removes of the military 'miracle of the House of Austria' which in the first days of the year had rescued Maria Theresa from a seemingly hopeless position.[12] Fulfilling Hanover's treaty obligations to Austria of June 1741 (see above) was no longer irresponsible lightheadedness.

Thus we find that one of the pillars of Hanoverian statecraft, namely German cooperation against France, became practicable once more. Another Hanoverian principle which was always to seek a concurrence of her interests with British interests (in Münchhausen's words at this time: 'celari potest, deleri non potest')[13] could again be brought into the open. But a third principle of Hanover, i.e. to back only an Emperor who had his own resources to stand up against the Empire's external foes, had to be suspended: Hanover herself had enthroned the ineffectual Charles VII of Wittelsbach.

In the event Carteret did not associate the Hanoverian ministers with the negotiations that led to the preliminaries of Breslau and the final Treaty of Berlin one month later. Although they evidently disliked being left out, and in the dark,[14] Carteret was not a man whom they cared to annoy by carping.

Carteret's hint to Steinberg in February 1742 that a large body of Hanoverian troops would be taken into British pay was not acted on for some time. When peace was concluded at Breslau he did offer Frederick twenty battalions of infantry and ten squadrons of cavalry, all Hanoverians, to protect Westphalian territories from French vengeance.[15] This was to be effected in the framework of a British–Prussian defensive alliance, and though Frederick politely declined the troops, he did accept the idea of an alliance, which was signed on 18 November 1742. At this point, the British ministers returned to Carteret's hint of transferring this Hanoverian force, some 16,000 men, to the Low Countries, to join an equal number of British troops there in readiness to fight the French. The measure itself was sound enough, in view of British treaty obligations to help in the protection of the 'Barrier', the chain of fortresses in the Austrian Netherlands from the sea to the Meuse garrisoned by Dutch troops, in view of the sensitivity of 'the Republic' in this matter, and hence of the value which Carteret and his colleagues put in the basic goodwill of Britain's ally.[16] Yet in this particular case the king may have precipitated the timing of the offer by his complaint that economy compelled him to demobilize his Hanoverian troops.[17] As late as mid-July the Hanoverian ministers intimated to the king that a dispersal of the armed camp at Nienburg, where most of the Hanoverian army was entrenched, was premature.[18]

But with Osnabrück, the main city of Westphalia, freed on 12 July and, as important, Maillebois seemingly on his way to Flanders, further opposition to the British offer became pointless, or even damaging to the security of Hanover. In this case too the king's instincts matched those of Hanoverian servants. The speech from the throne of 15 July 1742 says nothing of a decision to take the Hanoverian army into British pay, unless one takes much liberty in reading between the lines.[19] On about 22 July George II finally acceded to the cabinet's request—not merely Carteret's—to order his electoral troops into the Low Countries. The Hessians were to accompany them. There was no formal subsidies 'treaty', since the king did not sign a treaty with himself as elector. (Constitutionally he might have done so, but George II at any rate never did.[20]) However, the king as elector agreed to the conditions of the contract that his British ministers put before him, on 30 July.[21]

Carteret's motives were political rather than military in taking the Hanoverian troops. It was clear by then that Maillebois was marching south-east out of harm's way, so far as Hanover was concerned. On the other hand, carrying a large-scale offensive from the Low Countries into France was out of the question, for all the grandiose fantasies of Lord Stair, the British commander. Carteret himself showed by his remark to Steinberg quoted above that the main motive for the bargain was political indeed: to render George II more amenable to Cartertet's self-appointed 'business to make kings and emperors, and to maintain the balance of Europe'.[22]

From the Hanoverian angle, Hanoverian–British relations in the following two years revolve around the Hanoverian corps in British pay, with George II as watchdog over Hanoverian interests.[23] In Britain, not surprisingly, we hear a sustained outcry over the scandal of the 'Hanoverian Yoke', inextricably linked with the king's known preference for the country of his birth.[24]

George II had his first opportunity of promoting Hanoverian interests when he settled the terms on which his electoral troops were to serve. Apart from the number of troops and their branch of service—eleven regiments of horse, thirteen battalions of foot, three companies of artillery and 200 Lifeguards, in all slightly above 16,000 men—the terms mention only Hanoverian rights and British obligations. The pay was about one-half higher a man than that which George II's father had been able to extract in the 1702 subsidies treaty, at the opening of the War of the Spanish Succession—but then George I had been Elector George Louis only, and not yet King of Great Britain.[25] 'Recruiting expenses' (for an army already in being!) were also paid by Britain. All emoluments—enumerated in detail so as to leave no doubt—were to be geared to those applicable to British troops. (So far the less advantageous 'Dutch scale' had been applied to foreign auxiliaries.) The contract set no time limit for the Hanoverians' service.

Since the House of Commons could not grant supplies until it reconvened towards the end of 1742, stop-gap provision had to be made. At first the king ordered the Hanoverian ministers to advance the necessary funds from various electoral accounts, including his Privy Purse, the *Schatulle*. A few days later he remitted money from England, apparently from the Civil List. Then, with the troops in marching order, the Hanoverian ministry again lent money.[26] It was all done in secrecy. The constitutional aspect aside, George II did not wish himself or his Hanoverian treasury to appear flush with money before his British subjects. '"His Majesty would not for the world lend himself a farthing" [Bubb Dodington] once said of the arrangements by which George II was able to insist that the British taxpayer should foot the bill for Hanoverian troops employed against the French.'[27] As we shall see, the famous wit among British opposition politicians was not literally correct, but George II plainly had a reputation to maintain.

George II signed the marching orders for his German troops on 13 August 1742, to be carried out 'forthwith'.[28] However, the Hanoverian corps under its seventy-four-year-old commander, General Dupontpietin, did not set out until mid-September, settling into winter quarters in the Low Countries four to six weeks later. From the first, relations between Dupontpietin and the commander-in-chief, Lord Stair, were bad, though personal civility was observed. The blame for the hostility between the two men must go chiefly to George II, whose concern for the well-being of the Hanoverians, however laudable in itself, became obsessive. The suspicion haunted him that British staffs and commissaries cheated his *Landeskinder* of their due: food, drink, fodder, shelter, pay, safety.[29] He constantly pestered Carteret and Stair. Worse, he encouraged Dupontpietin, his deputies and his chief commissary to complain direct to himself. Naturally, they did.

It is hard to determine to what extent the grievances were imaginary, were caused by British bad faith, or were due to general inefficiency. No doubt all these factors played a part in the complaints. The king grew furious. Steinberg, though ever busy on royal errands, was of no account as a mediator. Carteret tried to calm matters. 'Not being acquainted with military affairs', he did so with less than his usual panache. Henry Pelham, as paymaster of the forces, did his commonsensical best to find working solutions to the problems posed by the peculiar situation. Key personage that he was—Newcastle's brother and confidant, sole commoner in the inner cabinet, leader of the ministerial cohorts in the House of Commons—his standing proved insufficient to carry weight with Stair, let alone with the Hanoverian generals backed by the king. On the operative level too George II committed a serious mistake by throwing the chain of command into confusion. Stair's commission as General of the Forces in the Low Countries gave him the entire command over British auxiliaries as well.[30] On the other hand, Dupontpietin's instructions of 13 August 1742 merely mention his duty to report on his progress to Stair and enquire about the rendezvous.[31] Dupontpietin continued to act on the assumption that in all important matters he could move only on orders from the king. In such conditions prospects of military success were bound to go overboard. Critics of George II have overlooked that his assumption of command of the 'Pragmatic Army' in the early summer of 1743 had become—though largely by his own fault—a prerequisite to anything useful being achieved at all.

It may be anticipated here that the situation essentially repeated itself three years later in the Flanders campaign of 1746. The British commander-in-chief, Sir John Ligonier, was first given, and then denied, command over the Hanoverian corps under General Sommerfeldt. Sommerfeldt merely received George II's 'express orders to consult and act in concert with [Ligonier] in everything'. The quibbling explanation which Harrington gave Ligonier for the counter-order was that the Hanoverians were not 'in the sole pay of Great Britain' but were 'serving, as the Austrians do, in consideration of a subsidy only' (see also below, p. 61).[32] One genuine reason seems to have been that Sommerfeldt was senior to Ligonier as lieutenant-general—George II was sensitive to considerations of military etiquette. For that reason, we may assume, the king strengthened his case by promoting Sommerfeldt to the rank of full general soon after.[33] However that may be, the king's underlying reluctance to have Hanoverians under the operational command of a British commander-in-chief comes out again.

The Hanoverian ministers stood aside from these squabbles, though Steinberg kept them informed of what went on in London, and on the news received from the Low Countries. The army—its command and administration—was the domain of the elector. That the ministers also had good sense, and habitually kept away from feuds, served to reinforce their caution.

On the diplomatic, as opposed to the military, level cooperation between Carteret and the Hanoverian minister went far; it was here, after all, that both sides felt competent to act. On 12 October 1742 Carteret ordered Thomas Villiers, the British minister at Dresden, to visit 'all the considerable states of the Empire', after consultations at Vienna with Maria Theresa and her advisers, and his colleague at the Viennese court, Sir Thomas Robinson. His mission was to gain allies against France, concert a plan of action and, if possible, sign treaties with the states he visited. Bavaria and Prussia were excluded from the itinerary, as allies of France. Before setting out, Villiers was to 'repair to Hanover to receive there such lights as will be given you by the King's electoral ministers'. The 'lights', drawn up at Hanover on 15 December 1742, are detailed and well reasoned. In diction and political philosophy they bear the stamp of Münchhausen's authorship. Villiers's formal instructions from London of 23 December 1742 closely follow the Hanoverian notes, with additional remarks on his relations with Robinson—a subject that was outside the Hanoverians' competence.[34] At the same time as Villiers set forth on his travels the Hanoverian ministers enjoined their representative at the Diet to avoid giving an impression that Hanover 'in order to please the English nation wished to continue the war in Germany, out of rancour against France'.[35] There was of course some truth in this charge, and it became increasingly difficult to deny it as the 'Pragmatic Army', newly so styled, began moving from the Low Countries eastward.

Villiers succeeded in his mission to the extent of drawing Saxony into the anti-French camp, though the negotiations between Dresden and Vienna were not concluded until December 1743. Considering Saxony's notorious fickleness this was a doubtful gain, while her military weakness was not yet as well recognized then as it was to be three years later. Indeed, Villiers's four-month peregrination—Dresden, after all, was his base—remained barren of results. But it is a good example of a genuine division of labour between Britain and Hanover, in an enterprise of interest to both.

While all this was afoot, the British–Prussian alliance—the first 'Treaty of Westminster' between the two states—was signed on 19 November 1742 (O.S.). The negotiations were not as smooth as Carteret had hoped for in the heady days after the Peace of Breslau. Frederick's guarantee of Hanover was covered by the term '[George II's] possessions and subjects situated in Europe'. (Britain's 'Spanish' and 'Mediterranean' possessions, i.e. Gibraltar and Minorca, were exempted from the Prussian guarantee in a secret article).[36] Frederick also offered to exchange the recognition of his claims of succession to Mecklenburg and East Friesland for his assent to annul the Osnabrück 'alternate' in favour of full Hanoverian rule. His offer was declined—almost certainly on the advice of the Hanoverian ministers, who are on record to this effect three months later. According to their argument, East Friesland in Prussian hands would harm British and Dutch trading interests.[37] They were probably sincere in their protestations, though no particular harm occurred to those interests when East Friesland did become Prussian in 1744. But their underlying motive—if we judge them by their steadily expressed preferences over the preceding two years—was their suspicion of Prussian aggrandizement in the west, and their lack of interest in territorial acquisitions for Hanover.

Late in 1742 the British cabinet yielded to Austrian demands to move British forces from the Low Countries, where they were not doing anything effective, to central Germany, where there was much for them to do. Frederick saw this decision in the worst possible light. He took, or affected to take, Carteret's fire-eating propensities at their face value: the Pragmatic Army, Frederick's attitude implied, was out to aggrandize Hanover; dethrone Charles VII; install Francis Stephan, Maria Theresa's husband; and interfere in the due process of the Jülich-Berg inheritance. (In 1741 Frederick had waived his own claims in return for a French guarantee of Silesia (see above); but he had done so in favour of the innocuous Sulzbach-Wittelsbach, and not a rival power like Saxony which he feared had the support of George II.) On 20 December 1742 Frederick said to Hyndford what constitutes the epitome of his political attitude to George II: 'I would have him remember that Hanover is at a very little distance from me, and that I can enter there when I please!'[38] Not untypically for Frederick, this was five days after he had ratified the treaty of 'perpetual, firm and unalterable friendship' with his uncle. Carteret and Hyndford went into frenzies of explanation—frenzied in intensity, that is, but meek in content. Hyndford's later claims of his own audacity in countering the challenge is mere bragging. At last, towards the end of January 1743, Frederick ungraciously withdrew his threat of armed intervention; he was not, after all, wholly averse to having the French in trouble in central Germany.[39] His suspicions of the Pragmatic Army, however, reappear in his manifestoes at the start of the Second Silesian War (see below).

Even so the Hanoverian ministers remained committed to the utmost caution. They urged George II to delay the march of the Pragmatic Army, chiefly by dilating on the difficulties and dangers inherent in a forward course. Their entire voluminous correspondence during those weeks bears out their fear that Hanover might have to pay for a military activism which was no longer her direct concern.[40] The king did his best. It consisted mainly in sabotaging Stair's marching orders by withholding from Dupontpietin the direct order Dupontpietin was expecting from the king himself. Stair alternated between rage and despair. Again Carteret was of little help. Newcastle later alleged that Carteret too, in addition to his subservience to George II, dreaded what Frederick might inflict on Hanover if provoked, and that George II's irresolution was mirrored by Carteret's own hesitation.[41] This is a partial explanation at best. Irresolution was no trait of Carteret's character. It is more likely that Carteret, honestly diffident about interfering in military operations, did not want to strain his relations with the king over a matter like a march in mid-winter from the Low Countries. It is at this stage that Carteret claimed to have warned the king, ever since he assumed the secretaryship, against separating his Hanoverian from his British interests. Carteret added that, in the contrary case, if the king were ever to subordinate regard for his British crown to that of his German lands, or let himself be intimidated because of them, he or his successors would risk losing both. The king, said Carteret, was much impressed. Carteret, so he said, had good reason for complacency; he was 'well content' (*vergnügt*). But since the occasion of Carteret's assertion was a propitiatory talk with Baron Wasner, the Austrian minister, who was anxious to see the Pragmatic Army move into Germany, Carteret's optimism is suspect. Maria Theresa and her ministers, at any rate, were sceptical, though they fervently hoped that Carteret was right in his assessment of the situation.[42]

In May 1743 the Pragmatic Army finally appeared on the Main. At the end of that month George II took over from Stair as commander-in-chief.

The campaign of 1743 took its course, and the battle of Dettingen was won over the French on 27 June. The story need not be retold here. Under the eye of their common sovereign the British and Hanoverian troops, from the generals to the rank and file, kept in decent harmony—whatever the subsequent tittle-tattle concerning the fighting, and the real squabbles later.[43] There was no scope for those acts of insubordination and non-cooperation which in 1759 robbed Prince Ferdinand at Minden, and Loudon and Saltikov at Kunersdorf, of the full fruits of their victories over the French and the Prussians, respectively. That much credit should go to George II as commander-in-chief. The king can also be cleared of another charge, the most trivial and the most famous of all: though he did wear the yellow sash of Hanover on the field of Dettingen, he did not wear it to flaunt his attachment to his Hanoverian rather than to his British troops. The yellow sash, together with the worn tunic and the 'Ramillies' tricorn, were of no more significance to the king than a sentimental memory. The garments were his accoutrement at the battle of Oudenaarde thirty-five years before, when he had charged against the French as electoral prince.[44]

After Dettingen the Pragmatic Army took part in no further operation of importance, and the electoral and the British troops went into winter quarters in the Low Countries in November. The king stayed with the army until November and went home to an adoring Hanover. His sojourn in the field had also meant that he was near at hand while Carteret was conducting the Hanau negotiations, and on 14 July

1743, less than three weeks after Dettingen, the so-called Treaty of Hanau was signed with Prince William of Hesse.

Prince William was an outstanding personage on the mid-century scene: regent of Hesse-Cassel in the permanent absence of his elder brother, the landgrave, who was also King of Sweden; on reasonable terms with Frederick of Prussia, with the Wittelsbach Emperor, *and* with the court of Vienna; a keen politician and gifted diplomat; like his father, an inveterate trader in his native subjects for foreign army service (his son and his grandson were to follow in his footsteps). As disposer of 'the Hessians' his good will was of particular consequence to George II. In the present case Prince William acted on behalf of Emperor Charles VII, constitutionally elected but evicted from his Bavarian patrimony. The design of the treaty was to cut the Emperor's dependence on France and get the French out of Germany. Its gist was that Maria Theresa should recognize Charles as Emperor and her army was to evacuate Bavaria. In return the Emperor should waive all claims on the territorial inheritance of Charles VI. Also, financial provision would be made for the Emperor to maintain his dignity.[45] The understanding was sensible. The hitch was that Maria Theresa, ignorant of the talks, held Bavaria, which she hoped to keep in compensation for Silesia. Only Britain could conceivably press her into acceptance, by withholding—or threatening to withhold—subsidies. Before this could be attempted, the British ministry had to make available an interim subsidy for Charles VII until a permanent solution was found to his financial needs. Carteret wrote to his colleagues, although he had powers to bind the British government on the spot. But he apparently believed that since the Cabinet Council would have to consent to the arrangement in any case, it would be wise to have their consent in advance.

As often, Carteret proved a bad psychologist. Newcastle promptly scotched the initiative of 'his lively Brother [Secretary] abroad'. Perhaps he really believed that the proposal served merely 'German'—that is, Hanoverian—'politics, German measures, and (what perhaps is near as bad as either) German manners').[46] Perhaps he was only jealous of Carteret's pre-eminence. It is likely that both motives came into play. The chance was lost. No doubt this experience played a role in Carteret's growing reticence towards his colleagues.

An alternative explanation of Carteret's behaviour in writing to his colleagues can also be proferred: George II realized at the last that Maria Theresa could not be persuaded to accept the Hanau terms—or what would be left of them—for less than the cession of Bavaria. Such a concentration of Habsburg power in the south of Germany was intolerable to Hanover and, indeed, to the entire 'Evangelical interest'. Carteret, coerced by the king, decided to back out of the agreement. He sent his message to London in bad faith, knowing that it would be rejected.[47] But in the absence of positive evidence this conspiratorial theory seems over-contrived.

In retrospect Carteret's decline dates from the Hanau fiasco. It is of interest whether the Hanoverian ministers played a part in the negotiations. The king, with Carteret on the spot, is unlikely to have left them in the dark. The concept was certainly to their liking: security for the Emperor, who had, after all, received George II's vote; general recognition of Maria Theresa's undivided heritage—unavoidably without Silesia; peace for the Empire; and above all, the removal of the French. Moreover, the recent Villiers mission had shown that Carteret could and did cooperate with Münchhausen in major undertakings. Unfortunately, there seem to be no clear-cut indications either way of Hanoverian intervention.[48] There is one intriguing hint: during the gestation period of the 'treaty' Münchhausen went out of his way to assure the Austrian envoy at Hanover, Baron Jaxheim, that George's British and German ministers would come to no arrangements without the Queen of Hungary's full knowledge and consent. In any case Jaxheim, so Münchhausen assured him, could safely take the waters at Pyrmont—nothing was likely to happen for some time. When shortly afterwards news began to percolate of the Hanau events, Jaxheim hinted to his superior at Vienna that Münchhausen's protestations had been a feint.[49] He was probably right.

Newcastle's aversion to allowing the French army to leave Germany unmolested, which he expressed in his letter to the Earl of Orford, was shared by Münchhausen.[50] Newcastle's reasoning was the more rational: a French army mauled in Germany would be that much less dangerous in the Low Countries. On the other hand Münchhausen, who was not much interested in the Low Countries, might have considered the wisdom of building bridges to a retreating enemy. But Münchhausen's hatred of the French was only overcome at moments of intense fear, and Dettingen had induced in Hanover a euphoria greater than that which the modest success justified. The point of punitive action against the French was not put to the test; it is of psychological interest only.

* * *

The British scene must now be surveyed.

Newcastle's attack on Carteret's supposed 'German' proclivities echoes—as his tactical twists often do—the noisier trend of public opinion at home.

Even since the Hanoverian dynasty mounted the British throne, by grace of Parliament and in pursuit of a certain political system, aversion to the electorate had been a political factor in Britain. The aversion was strongest in Tory circles—naturally so, since the new dynasty indelibly suggested 'Whig'. But the feeling was widely diffused.[51] Only after 1760 did dislike of Hanover fade away as a factor in home politics, as George III could no longer be regarded as 'Hanoverian' in a politically significant sense. During the two generations in between, the sentiment occasionally materialized into bursts of action. The fiercest of these bouts raged from December 1742 to November 1744. It is outside the scope of this work to describe the phenomena in detail or analyse them in depth. However, the salient points must be made.

The causes of the outbreak of anti-Hanoverian feeling in 1742-44 were twofold. The first was jealousy of Carteret, 'the sole minister', and this factor would have predominated under any circumstances. His former associates who were left in the cold when he made his peace with the king in February 1742 fuelled this jealousy with their resentment.[52] The other cause, so entwined with the former that it is difficult to treat them apart, is the hire of the Hanoverian troops. Pitt fused the two sources of antagonism as he, above all, knew how, when he called Carteret the 'Hanover troop minister'.[53] Here an explanation is needed. Since the king and his ministers habitually hired foreign troops in time of war, why should it have been reprehensible to take the king's German subjects, who were so much more reliable, militarily and politically?[54] The answer was made—and honestly made—that the king, being a Hanoverian first and foremost, would always use his own troops for Hanoverian and not for British ends. The events of the summer of 1741, though not strictly a parallel, were a good illustration of what to expect from the king when he was under a strain. All the same, whatever might have been the objective validity of the case and the personal sincerity of the contenders, the Hanoverian issue must be seen as secondary. When Carteret fell and Pitt made his peace with the administration, the campaign petered out. 'Anti-Hanoverianism' reverted to its normal level of irritation.

Still, the campaign was more than mere 'faction' politics. It mobilized most of the political nation from top to bottom. It was sustained in Parliament, with Chesterfield and Pitt as its protagonists in the Lords and Commons, respectively. It spawned a flood of treatises and pamphlets—some of high intellectual content, others scurrilous; many managed to combine something of both. The debate was carried on among private gentlemen and in the press. It gave a boost to caricature, witty or obscene.[55] It excited the man in the street, who may not have spared the king's person as Parliament was constrained to do.[56] It generated threats of rebellion and murder, directed at Carteret and the Speaker of the House, Onslow, a pillar of the Whig establishment.[57]

Many of the arguments, from the restrained and rational to the abusive or trivial, are to be found in the parliamentary debates. At their most convincing they appear in the 'Protest' registered in the House of Lords on 9 December 1743, to which were appended the signatures of Chesterfield, Marlborough (lately at Dettingen) and twenty-three other peers, 'that such jealousies and animosities have arisen ... between the troops of Great Britain and those of Hanover, that they can no longer act together'.[58] The most famous is Pitt's fanfare, delivered on 10 December 1742, 'this great, this powerful, this formidable kingdom is considered only as a province of a despicable electorate'.[59] Earlier in his oration Pitt had accused the ministers of diverting the Hanoverian troops from their proper objective—'for it is not to be imagined that His Majesty ... would not have sent his proportion of troops to the Austrian army, had not the temptations of greater profit been industriously laid before him'—a sneer at the sovereign that seeks its equal in the history of Parliament. Among the treatises, the most sophisticated are probably Chesterfield's *The Case of the Hanoverian Troops in the Pay of Great Britain* ... and *Natural Reflections on the Present Conduct of His Prussian Majesty*. The latter was published in August 1744, immediately after Frederick had broken the Peace of Breslau and invaded Bohemia, a series of events to which we shall return. Among the less sustained attacks, one thrust, with reference to Dettingen, is memorable: 'The [British] fools escaped, because they had to deal with [French] madmen ... But fools seldom improve, while the mad have their intervals ...'.[60] *An Attempt towards a Natural History of the Hanover Rat*[61] constitutes the low mark in scurrility.

There was no lack of replies, inside and outside Parliament: many were lively, too, and some put forward an excellent case for the Hanoverian connection.[62] It might be maintained with sense and conviction, after all, that Hanover served as a strategic diversion for any French war effort against Britain. But this reasoning always remained confined to the few—the self-conscious defence of an unpopular cause.

All the same, the administration carried all the votes on the Hanoverian troops with a comfortable majority. Towards the end of 1743 the Pelhams and Hardwicke, ever more angered by Carteret, considered withholding their support for a renewal of the financial appropriation after its expiry. On the advice of Lord Orford, as Walpole, their late chief now was, not to offend the king, they refrained from doing so. The contract only terminated after the resignation of the Earl of Granville (Carteret's style since October 1744) in November 1744.[63]

What was the effect of the campaign on the king as elector, and on his Hanoverian ministers? In one respect, essential to this work, the campaign is of importance, for it induced George II to ask his Hanoverian ministers for an opinion as to what effect a possible separation of the crowns would have upon Hanover. He formulated his request somewhat differently, but this is how the ministers understood their brief. (As their opinion denotes their fundamental outlook and is little affected by the situation of the moment, it is treated separately.)

In the sphere of practical politics it is difficult to discern any effect that the anti-Hanover campaign had on the Hanoverian policy-makers. It was not in the nature of George II to be deflected from a course of action by mere impudence, however hotly he might resent it. He carried his British ministers, who in turn carried a majority in Parliament, and it was this that mattered. Münchhausen and his colleagues, for their part, were indeed conscious of what 'the Nation' across the sea thought and said, but they had no real understanding of the way the British polity worked, and they spoke a common language only with George II. They knew Milord Carteret, the king's first minister—a term less obnoxious to Hanover than to Whitehall, Westminster, or Grub Street. They found him masterful but friendly. For them it was a time of menace and challenges. The money came in for troops which they knew would defend Hanover in an emergency. Occasionally they re-stated the need of giving priority to British interests while pursuing those of Hanover.[64] Though this was not their absolutely truthful view of the matter, it was not mere cant either. It was a guideline that served well while Carteret was in office.

* * *

In article II of the Treaty of Worms, signed on 13 September 1743, the allies guaranteed to each other the territories 'which they possessed at present or ought to possess [… *ou doivent posséder*]' by virtue of certain named treaties among which that of Breslau/Berlin was absent. Article XIII provided for a situation in which Maria Theresa might draw on her troops in Italy 'to make use of a greater number … in Germany'. The evidence suggests that the phrasing and the omission had no hidden meaning. This interpretation receives strength from a secret 'Separate Act of Declaration', attached to the treaty, which obligated Britain to do her best to obtain 'compensation' for Maria Theresa for Silesia, 'in view of the great sacrifice which the Queen must make … for the good of all Europe'.[65]

It speaks ill for Carteret's diplomatic management that he packed the open treaty with contents that might have disquieted a ruler less suspicious than Frederick, while the provision which testified to Carteret's good faith was kept from Frederick's knowledge. And Frederick, as Carteret knew well, always looked for breaches of faith. When the main body of the treaty was presented to Frederick early in February 1744—he never knew of the Separate Declaration while it mattered—articles II and XIII raised him to a fever of suspicion which his ministers tried in vain to assuage.[66] This was the point of departure for his 'Second Silesian War'. His special envoy to Versailles, Count Rothenburg, left Berlin about 21 February 1744, in deepest secrecy, without the knowledge even of Podewils.[67] Frederick's resolve can only have been strengthened by the Treaty of Amity and Mutual Defence between Austria and Saxony signed at Vienna on 20 December 1743, which was the outcome of the Villiers mission. An open article of the latter treaty invites the Tsaritsa Elizabeth, and George

II 'as king and as elector', to become co-signatories. A secret article promised Saxony 'a facilitation of communications between Poland and Electoral Saxony', 'provided She [i.e. Maria Theresa] suffers no injury'.[68] This meant, of course, that the postulated land bridge between Saxony and Poland was to be carved from Brandenburg and not from Silesia, in the event that Saxony increased her military aid to the allies.

At Hanau Carteret had rebuffed Frederick's attempt to involve Prussia in the negotiations. Frederick retaliated for the slight to his envoy, Finckenstein, whom Hyndford refers to as 'this little spy', by coming near to insulting Hyndford.[69] The matter is significant because it bears on Hyndford's later relations with the Hanoverian ministers. Carteret, however, was slow to take offence. He put a good face on Frederick's refusal to honour his obligation under the 1742 Treaty of Westminster to provide auxiliaries, after France had declared war on Britain and Hanover on 15 March 1744. Frederick added insult to injury by explaining that the treaty was defensive, and Britain might have provoked France by her aggression at sea.[70]

Frederick gave another earnest of his hostility to George II by setting up the 'Union of Frankfurt', signed on 22 May 1744, with the Emperor, Prince William of Hesse (nominally with his brother, the King of Sweden) and the Elector Palatine—the former two, like Frederick, offended parties in the Hanau episode.[71] Prince William's adherence was especially painful to George II, as it added the Hessians, hitherto his paid allies, to the potential assailants of Hanover. When rumours of the Union first proliferated, George II feared a French–Prussian plot involving the occupation of Hanover in order to force Maria Theresa into evacuating Bavaria. Münchhausen, although in a more balanced frame of mind, still saw the Union as an attempt to strangle the 'liberty of Germany', and the weaker German states in particular.[72] Frederick justified both fears in so far as he was able, by urging his ally, the king of France, to invade Hanover in concert with his own scheduled invasion of Bohemia.[73]

Three days after the Union of Frankfurt was signed, the last Cirksena prince of East Friesland died on 25 May 1744. Frederick had the Prussian eagles put up at Emden within the day—in vindication of his own, and in defiance of his uncle's, claims to the succession. The Hanoverian government contented itself for the time being with an ineffectual demonstration on the spot by a senior official.[74] On 23 June Frederick sent a final note to Hyndford refusing military aid for the protection of Hanover under the treaty of 1742, in reply to a somewhat wheedling request delivered to him over a month before. In his 'unkind and piquant answer' Frederick stated that his help was evidently not called for, since the king had hired out his electoral troops for service elsewhere (i.e. to Britain in the Low Countries). Frederick had originally intended totally to deny that Hanover was covered by the treaty, but Podewils dissuaded him from carrying matters that far.[75] Finally, in the second week of August, with Maria Theresa's main army engaged in Alsace, Frederick entered Bohemia. He had just concluded agreements with Charles VII and with France which granted him Bohemia east of the Elbe as his share of the expected spoils.

George II so far had borne Frederick's provocations with forbearance. However, his anger was merely pent up. It may have been the spectre of his nephew back on the path of military glory and territorial gain that finally precipitated his outburst of rage against Frederick. It was early 1741 all over again. It is idle, though tempting, to speculate how George II would have reacted if another French army had marched into Westphalia. However, in the summer of 1744 morale was higher in Hanover than three years before, and with some reason. The south-western flank of the electorate had gained an additional measure of security through a subsidies treaty concluded in November 1743 between George II and the ever needy Archbishop Elector of Cologne, hitherto an ally of France, for a period of three years; the financial clauses were activated through an additional agreement in April 1744.[76] The good performance of the Austrian army in Alsace, and the failure of the French army effectively to pursue the Austrians when they rushed back in August to meet Frederick in Bohemia, also served to steady nerves at Hanover. Though from that month onward rumours of French invasions and Prussian coups abounded, no immediate danger to Hanover seems to have been feared.[77]

Again George II became instrumental in a diplomatic campaign to put an end to Frederick's audacity. Prussia was to be carved up: Silesia to revert to Austria; Magdeburg, the 'Saalekreis' and a corridor towards Poland to Saxony; Pomerania to Sweden; East Friesland and Cleves to Holland; East Prussia to Poland in exchange for parts of eastern Poland to Russia; Halberstadt and certain Westphalian counties to Hanover.[78] Frederick was to come under the ban of the Empire. The remnants of his dominions were to go to his brother, Prince Augustus William, the heir presumptive, an inoffensive soul. The plan probably originated with Count Heinrich von Brühl, chief minister to the King of Poland (and Elector of Saxony). The Imperial ban to be imposed on Frederick was George II's own contribution to the scheme.[79] Maria Theresa readily fell in with the plan, but stipulated that her right to the whole of Silesia did not depend on conquests her allies might, or might not, make elsewhere. It was only on the eve of the 1745 campaign that she brought herself to buy off Saxony, on paper, with a small concession in this respect. It was of course a quarrel over the skin of a living bear.[80] It should be said that the elimination of the Hohenzollern *electorate* was not a war aim—either then or later.[81] Frederick's enemies were conservatives; the Hohenzollern electorate was a pillar of the Empire, and thus of Christendom. (The tsaritsa and Bestushev, her Grand Chancellor, were not conservatives in the sense applied here; but then Russia when viewed from the West was as yet only doubtfully part of 'Christendom'.[82]) Frederick's personal fate, and the status Prussia had acquired over the preceding century, were no part of the time-hallowed world order; they were therefore expendable. It is thus that the recurring expression, 'écraser la Prusse', must be understood.

The British ministers regarded the plan of the wholesale despoliation of Prussia with scepticism, though the return of Silesia was no more than Austria's due (see below).[83] The exception among them was Carteret, who has been blamed ever since for not restraining his king firmly enough. It is this charge that has led certain historians to assert that Carteret lost his independence of mind during the later term of his office. Wasner stressed that it was Carteret, unlike the other British ministers, who talked to him with vivacity of the plan to partition Prussia.[84] But by then Carteret was no longer a minister. That Carteret was old-fashioned in that he looked more to the king and less to Parliament than did his colleagues begs the question why he did so if, as his critics claim, his sovereign's policy was not in the national interest. And to say that his sole support at the time lay with the king is of course merely another way of damning him.

It is a more correct assessment and a better defence of Carteret to state that his and the king's anti-Prussian line of late 1744 was not, in fact, against the British national interest. Frederick had given ample proof of his ingrained hostility to Britain and he had returned to the fray as the active ally of France. If his sustained thrust of expansion southwards succeeded, it was bound to shatter the Old System of alliances, still overwhelmingly regarded in Britain as necessary for the balance of power. Moreover, by trying to concentrate diplomatic activities at The Hague, where Robert Trevor, an outspoken critic of George II, was British minister, Carteret tried in effect to bend the main effort towards France and away from Prussia.[85] All in all, to say that Carteret uncritically succumbed to the king's Hanoverian idiosyncrasies seems a misinterpretation of events and of personalities; such self-abnegation would have been out of Carteret's character. (It is certain that the king's Hanoverian ministers were victims of Carteret's besetting sin—his negligence in keeping colleagues informed. When Britain concluded, and later ratified, the subsidies treaty with the Archbishop Elector of Cologne in April–August 1744—a matter of importance to Hanover—the Hanoverians bitterly complained among themselves of not being put in the picture.[86] They do not seem to have complained to the king or to Carteret himself.)

As in the first months of 1741, the Hanoverian ministers were in an awkward position when Frederick invaded Bohemia in August 1744. They shared their master's fear and hatred of Frederick. But they utterly lacked his bellicosity, and they *always* visualized the fate of their country should Frederick, with or without French aid, mount an offensive against Hanover. Münchhausen, to the fore as in every crisis, took the line of loyally cooperating with George II on the diplomatic level, but of carefully avoiding any step that might precipitate Hanover into war.[87] To this extent he and Carteret were well matched *vis-à-vis* the king. However, ganging up against their master for their master's good was a ticklish matter. No letters between the two ministers on this subject seem to have survived—if ever there were any. Since they were both at Hanover for most of this period, no exchange of notes was really necessary for them to coordinate their views.

Carteret's last months in office saw a crisis in the relations between Britain and Holland, again brought about by George's concern for his electorate. Though Frederick's renewed entry into the war had not made George panic, practical measures for the security of Hanover were nonetheless needed. In August and September 1744 preparations were made to remove the Hanoverian treasury to Bremen, and thence to Holland. It seems that the resolve was kept secret even from Carteret.[88] What could not be kept secret was the king's order to detach the Hanoverian troops from the allied army in the Low Countries, and march them into Cologne and Westphalia to cover the electorate. As French pressure on the frontier of the Austrian Netherlands was mounting steadily, the Dutch were much put out. They went so far as to demand that the British government hire non-Hanoverian troops for service there, while the 16,000 Hanoverians stayed put at electoral expense. But since they themselves refused to declare war on France, such a far-reaching request did not carry much weight. Even so, relations between Britain and Holland were upset to a degree not known since the 'Restraining Orders' of 1712. At the same time Trevor, in irritation and contempt, and the Pelham group in the cabinet shared the Dutch view that the king was motivated by Hanoverian interests alone, though they could not openly say so.[89] When Trevor wrote to Pelham, since August 1743 the notional prime minister, that 'when any guarantee or advantage is in question, Hanover is a distinct independent state, and nowise involved in the measures, nor even fate, of England', he was stating his own view as well as that of the Dutch. Pelham's reply illuminates his personality as much as it expresses an opinion: 'I am sorry to find the people where you are so well informed ... The melancholy picture you have drawn [is] too like the original in every feature ...'[90] For all the despondent tone, the ministers' resistance to the execution of the king's order was persistent and in the main successful. In retrospect it is possible to see it as a sign of the inner cabinet's growing influence in matters of foreign policy hitherto held to fall within the purview of the royal prerogative. They themselves certainly saw the issue merely in a practical light and not as a constitutional tussle: the Netherlands theatre was vital to the war; a good understanding with Holland, 'that solid national concert',[91] was still regarded as a main prop of national policy.

The Hanoverian ministers, on the other hand, gave George II what stiffening they could. They were conscious of their disadvantage in not having an adequate counterweight to Hardwicke, who was usually the British ministers' spokesman with the king on these matters; Steinberg, their London colleague, was not his match.[92] The dispute was finally settled by a compromise: at the beginning of December 1744 it was agreed between all concerned that half the Hanoverian troops should stay in Brabant to cover Holland, while the other half would be deployed on the middle Rhine, within the framework of a composite army under the Austrian general, the Duke of Arenberg. By then the situation of Hanover had eased. Though the possibility of a French invasion was not as yet written off, Frederick was in a dangerous position in Bohemia. Moreover, Granville's last diplomatic scheme was coming to fruition in the Quadruple Alliance which promised Saxon troops for the west if need be (see below). And so in December the 8,000 Hanoverians marched off to the east. As the subsidy contract of 1742 lapsed on 25 December 1744, in any event the newly constituted ministry in London had an additional argument at its disposal to calm public opinion, opposed to the Hanover connection.

The matter was hardly at an end, however, since Hanoverian troops were needed in the war in numbers far greater than the electoral government could, let alone was willing to, underwrite. Again the British ministers found a way out. The £300,000 subsidy to Austria was to be increased, and the Hanoverians would come under Maria Theresa's nominal command whilst continuing to serve in the west. A period of intense haggling then ensued over the amount of the subsidy and the size of the Hanoverian corps. George II in his capacity of elector was, as usual, advised by Münchhausen. Lenthe, who represented the War Chancery on the Hanoverian Privy Council, acted as financial expert. Steinberg acted for the king in London. Hardwicke again took first place on the British side, with Under-secretary of State Weston in charge of current contacts with Steinberg. Baron Wasner, the Austrian minister, represented Maria Theresa. It appears that for all the conflicting interests the negotiations ran smoothly enough. Nor were there any underhand deals. Weston seems to have held a watching brief over Steinberg on Hardwicke's behalf.[93]

Finally it was settled that Hanover would receive £200,000 for 14,000 soldiers, and the Austrian subsidy was to be increased by that amount. The House of Commons agreed with tolerable grace—not least because Pitt had by then found a common language with the ministers regarding his political future. A generous repatriation allowance was also voted to the Hanoverians on the—fictitious—termination of their service in British pay. The Hanoverians were not explicitly named in debate as the German troops Maria Theresa was to hire, but evidently no one was uncertain as to their identity. The supplementary treaty with Austria was signed on 13 April 1745 (N.S.).[94] A special step was thought necessary to assuage Dutch criticism. Some time before his departure for Hanover in May, George II ordered Schwicheldt on a mission to The Hague to declare that he, as elector, would furnish at his own expense a contingent of 6,000 Hanoverian troops 'to the common cause, whose destination and employment shall be settled at ... the Hague'. In return, Hanover was to be treated in allied councils as an equal.[95] As these were the 6,000 troops who were under arms even during the period of the direct British subsidy, everybody concerned was satisfied—except, perhaps, the Hanoverian rank and file themselves.

Notes

1. Under-Secretary Edward Weston to Robert Trevor, 19 Mar 1742, *Trevor Papers*, HMC, Fourteenth Report, App. 9, 82; also quoted (not quite accurately) in Basil Williams, *Carteret and Newcastle*, Cambridge, 1943, 123.
2. Jaxheim to Sinzendorff, 4 Feb 1742, *HHStA*, Staatskanzlei Hannover, Fasz. 2.
3. Hann. 92, LXXI, 17^{d}, vol. I
4. 26 Feb 1742 (*ibid.*).
5. Newcastle to Hardwicke, 24 Oct 1743, Add. MSS 32701, f. 207.
6. Hann. 92, LXXI, 17^{dI}, vol. I.
7. *Ibid.*
8. Hann. 92, LXXI, 17^{dI}, vol. III. See also the frigid note of Louis XV to George II on this occasion (*ibid.*).
9. For the texts of the French and British declarations of war in 1744, see N. Tindal, *The Continuation of Mr. Rapin's History of England*, London, 1759, XXI (IX), 28-32.
10. Hann. 92, LXXI, 17^{I}, vol. III.
11. See the interesting memorandum of the Hanoverian ministry of 27 March 1742 which analyses this contingency. (Hann. 92, LXXI, 17^{d}, vol. I.)
12. As a narrative of these years in Germany, A. Dove, *Deutsche Geschichte 1740-1745*, Gotha, 1883, is still useful, despite the author's cloying adulation of Frederick.
13. *Kurtze historische Erzehlung*, 230.
14. See *Geheime Räte* to Minister von Hugo at Frankfurt, 13 July 1742 (Hann. 92, LXXI, 17^{d}, vol. II).
15. Carteret to Hyndford, 18 June (O.S.); Podewils to Hyndford, 16 July 1742 (S.P., Foreign, 90/54). Also Carteret to Hyndford, 10 June 1742 (Hann. 92, LXXI, 17^{d}, vol. II).
16. Throughout the eighteenth century the Barrier never lived up to the original Dutch concept of its place in the national defence; the fortresses were finally evacuated in 1782, at the request of Emperor Joseph II as sovereign of the Austrian Netherlands. For the genesis of the 'Barrier treaties', see Roderick Geikie and Isabel A. Montgomery, *The Dutch Barrier 1705-1719*, Cambridge, 1930. Alice C. Carter, *Neutrality or Commitment: The Evolution of Dutch Foreign Policy 1667- 1795*, London, 1975, surveys the overall scene with great empathy into the Dutch viewpoint.
17. See Newcastle's letter to Hardwicke of 24 Oct 1743, quoted in Coxe, *Memoirs of the Administration of the Rt. Hon. Henry Pelham*, London, 1829, I, 429.
18. Hann. 92, LXXI, 17^{d}, vol. II.
19. *J.H.C.*, XXIV, 335.
20. See Karl Bingmann, *Das rechtliche Vehältnis zwischen Grossbritannien und Hannover, 1714-1837*, Celle, 1925; I. B. Campbell, *The International Legal Relations between Great Britain and Hanover 1714-1837*, unpubl. Ph.D. thesis, Cambridge, 1965.
21. For all that concerns this theme, in its widest context, see Gert Brauer, *Die hannoversch-englischen Subsidienverträge 1702-1748*, Aalen, 1962.
22. Quoted in Mahon, *History of England ... 1713-1783*, London, 1853-1854, III, 135.

23. For a consecutive description of the king's concern, see Brauer, *op. cit.*, 129-149.
24. Erwin von Wiese, *Die englische parlamentarische Opposition ... (1740-1744),* Waldenburg, 1883, is still useful, in spite of its dated value judgments and the patchy source material.
25. *J.H.C.*, XXIV, 357-360; Brauer, *op. cit.*, 133.
26. George II to *Geheime Räte*, 3 Aug, 12 Sept 1742; *Geheime Räte* to George II, 17 Aug, 1 Sept 1742, Hann. 92, LXXI, Nr. 17^{d}, vol. III; LXXV, Nr. 3. The king ordered that the *Schatulle* be given priority of repayment.
27. Carswell, J., *The Old Cause*, London, 1954, 232-233.
28. Hann. 91, du Pontpietin I.
29. Lenthe, 34, gives a particularly revealing utterance of the king. Brauer, *op. cit.*, 138-142, is admirable on this, and the consequences. The chief primary sources are Add. MSS 35452-35459 and Hann. 92, LXXV, Nr. 2, *passim.*
30. Stair's commission of 21 Apr 1742, Add. MSS. 35452, f. 80 also Pelham to Stair, 16 Jan 1743, Add. MSS. 35455, f. 74.
31. Hann. 91, du Pontpietin I. Brauer (*op. cit.*, 140) points out that in a similar situation George I had explicitly instructed his Hanoverian generals to take their orders from 'the commanding English general'. George I was a professional soldier; his son was not.
32. Harrington to Ligonier, 11 July 1746 (O.S.), S.P., 87/20; also Campbell, *op. cit.*, 528-529.
33. For the Hanoverian corps in Flanders in 1746 and Sommerfeldt's promotion, Sichart, *op. cit.*, II, 429-448.
34. Add. MSS 22530, ff. 19, 29-41. Also B. Williams, *op. cit.*, 128, and Theo König, *Hannover und das Reich, 1740-1745*, Düsseldorf, 1938; 38-39. König makes Villiers's mission more of a Hanoverian enterprise than I would accept. For the Hanoverian guidelines of 15 Dec 1742, Cal. Br. 11, 2057.
35. König, 39.
36. For the Treaty of Westminster, including the secret article, S.P., Foreign, 108/415.
37. *Geheime Räte* to George II, 9 Feb, 4 Mar 1743, Hann. 92, LVIII, Nr. 8; also Ranke, *Zwölf Bücher preussischer Geschichte*, Leipzig, 1875, Book X, 28-29.
38. Hyndford to Carteret, 20 Dec 1742 (S.P., Foreign, 90/55). Hyndford believed the king was 'after ... much wine'; this did not affect the impact he made on his listener.
39. Hyndford to Carteret, 15, 22 Jan, 16 Feb; Hyndford to Frederick II, 29 Jan; Podewils and Borcke to Hyndford, 29 Jan 1743 (S.P., Foreign, 90/56).
40. *Geheime Räte* to George II, Mar/Apr 1743 (Hann. 92, LXXI, Nr. 17^{gl}, vol. I).
41. Newcastle to Hardwicke, 13 Oct 1743, Add. MSS 32701, ff. 215-216.
42. Wasner to Maria Theresa, 8 Jan 1743 (N.S.), *HHStA*, England, K. 83; Maria Theresa to Wasner, 23 Jan 1743, *ibid.*, K. 84.
43. The letters of Lt-Col. Charles Russell give a good picture of the Hanoverians as they appeared to a British officer who fought in the campaign. (*Frankland–Russell–Astley MSS, Hist. MSS. Comm.* 52, 1900, 247 *seq.*). Russell was prejudiced, but not altogether unfair.
44. See W. von Wersebe, *Geschichte der Hannoverschen Armee*, Hanover, 1928, 139. The explanation is plausible and I accept it. John Wootton in his painting 'George II at the battle of Dettingen' (National Army Museum, London) tactfully changed the yellow sash for the blue ribbon of the Garter.
45. An extensive summary of the Hanau 'treaty' is in Sir Richard Lodge, *Studies in Eighteeth Century Diplomacy 1740-1748*, London, 1930, 17-18. For Prince William's version, published one year later, see R. Koser (ed.), *Preussische Staatsschriften* (1740-1745), Berlin, 1877, 633-638. Also, Lodge, 'The so-called "Treaty of Hanau" of 1743', *EHR*, XXXVIII (1923), 384-407, and 'The Hanau Controversy in 1744 and the Fall of Carteret', *op. cit.*, 509-531.
46. See Newcastle's malicious analysis of Carteret's proposals in his letter to Lord Orford, Add. MSS 32700, ff. 314-317; quoted by Lodge, *Studies*, 23-24.
47. This seems to be the view of Wiese, *op. cit.*, 30-31.
48. Prince William's correspondence with his chief diplomatist, Alt, usually a mine of

information, here deserts the student: during the weeks in question, Alt was with William at Hanau (*Hessisches Staatsarchiv Marburg*, 4 f, England, 240).

49. Jaxheim to Count Ulfeld, 20, 27, 28 July, 1, 8 Aug 1743, *HHStA*, Staatskanzlei, Hannover, Fasz. 2.
50. Münchhausen to Hugo (Ratisbon), 2 Aug 1743, Br. 11, E. I, 547.
51. Squire Western remains of course the undying symbol of Tory contempt for 'Hanoverian dogs'. But it cannot be said that the Tories showed particular initiative in this respect in workaday politics. Significantly, so meticulous an observer as Professor Colley hardly mentions the Hanover nexus in the relevant chapters of her study, for the years 1742-1760. (Linda Colley, *In Defiance of Oligarchy: The Tory Party 1714-1760*, Cambridge, 1982, chs. 9, 10.)
52. For Carteret's decline and fall—not, as such, part of this study—see Owen, *op. cit.*, chs. V, VI.
53. In the House of Commons on 19 Jan 1744 (*P.H.*, XIII, 465).
54. This argument figures prominently in the defence put up for the administration.
55. See M. Dorothy George, *English Political Caricature*, Oxford, 1959, vol. I, *To 1792*, ch. IV. M. Schlenke, *England und das friderizianische Preussen 1740-1763*, Munich, 1963, gives much background material.
56. Lord Egmont relates that a Thames waterman, espying the king alone on the terrace of Richmond, cursed him for a Hanoverian dog. The king could only shake his stick at him in helpless rage (R. A. Roberts ed., *Diary of ... Lord Egmont*, H. MSS. Comm. 16th Report, 1920-1923, 3 vols., henceforth *Egmont Diaries*; II, 424). Regrettably for the present story, the year was 1737.
57. *Egmont Diaries*, III, 279; entry for 18 Dec 1743.
58. *Journal of the House of Lords*, XXVI, 277.
59. *P.H.*, XII, 1035. The *Parliamentary History* is not an immaculate source for these years. However, this particular speech is well authenticated; the internal evidence too for its genuineness is overwhelming. See also B. Williams, *The Life of William Pitt*, London, 1913, 2 vols., I, 105-106.
60. 'Nobleman', *The Mysterious Congress. ... Accounting ... particularly for the Resignation of the Earl of S[tai]r*, London, Cooper, 1743, 10.
61. Also published by Cooper, London, 1744. The sadistic obscenity of the pamphlet throws light on the legal permissiveness of England in the mid-eighteenth century.
62. The best known of these treatises, and one of the sanest, is Horatio Walpole's anonymously published *The Interest of Great Britain Steadily Pursued*, London, Roberts, 1743.
63. See Owen, *op. cit.*, 187; Brauer, *op. cit.*, 148-152.
64. E.g. *Geheime Räte* to George II, 26 March 1743, Hann. 92, LVIII, 8. The context—the 'expectancy' of East Friesland—makes it probable that in this case the ministers were influenced by their lack of enthusiasm for territorial acquisition. (See also above.)
65. For the Separate Declaration, see S.P., Foreign, 108/160. The treaty without the secret articles appears, *inter alia*, in C. Jenkinson, *A Collection of All the Treaties of Peace ...*, London, 1785, 3 vols., II, 355-370. At Worms Carteret sought to achieve for Italy what he had hoped Hanau would do for Germany: extinguish Bourbon predominance. Here as there he remained unsuccessful, though at Worms diplomatic and, in consequence, military action progressed much further.
66. *Pol. Corr.*, III, 26-29, 35-42.
67. L. von. Ranke, *Zwölf Bücher preussischer Geschichte*, Book X, 94-98.
68. For the text see F. A. W. Wenck, *Codex iuris gentium*, Leipzig, 1781-1795, 3 vols., I, 722-733.
69. For the Glogau incident of 12 Aug 1743, see Hyndford to Carteret, 15 Aug 1743, S.P., Foreign, 90/57; for the characterization of Finckenstein, Hyndford to Carteret, 20 July 1743, *ibid.*
70. Frederick to Hyndford, 21 Apr 1744, *Staatsschriften*, I, 571-572.

71. For the text of the treaty, see Wenck, *op. cit.*, II, 163-169.
72. George II, pro Memoria of 27 March; Münchhausen, unsigned note, 14 April (?) 1744; Cal. Br. 11, 2097; König, 44.
73. 12 July 1744, *Pol. Corr.*, III, 208.
74. For a monographic treatment of the conflict between Prussia and Hanover over East Friesland, see Hermann Rother, *Die Auseinandersetzung zwischen Preussen und Hannover um Ostfriesland von 1690-1744*, diss., Göttingen, 1951. Also, Onno Klopp, *Geschichte Ostfrieslands von 1470-1751*, Hanover, 1856. Later Klopp became a rabid hater of Frederick, but here his treatment is reasonably balanced.
75. Hyndford to Carteret, 27 June 1744, S.P., Foreign, 90/59; *Staatsschriften*, I, 572-573.
76. Hann. 10, Cöln, Nr. 1; *Lenthe*, 63.
77. On Frederick's tentative plans against Hanover, see König, 46 note 48. *Lenthe*, 62, mirrors the vague concern with a French invasion.
78. Ranke, *op. cit.*, 142-145; Mediger, 407. 'East Prussia' should be 'Ducal Prussia', but the anachronism stands for clarity.
79. See Villiers to Carteret (Granville), 6 Oct, 4 Dec 1744, S.P., Foreign, 88/62; Wasner to Maria Theresa, 9 Feb 1745 (N.S.), *HHStA*, England, K. 88.
80. Maria Theresa's expression, as quoted in Arneth, III, 399.
81. According to Ranke (*Zur Geschichte von Oesterreich und Preussen zwischen den Friedensschlüssen zu Aachen und Hubertusburg*, Leipzig, 1875, 336), who would not have disregarded evidence to the contrary.
82. On this fascinating subject see M. S. Anderson, *Britain's Discovery of Russia 1553-1815*, London, 1958, chs. IV, V (i). Also, of course, Mediger, *passim*.
83. See the tenor of the despatches of Villiers from Grodno and Warsaw, of Robinson from Vienna, and of Trevor from The Hague, during these months (S.P., Foreign, 88/62, 80/165 and 166, 84/406 and 407, respectively.
84. Wasner to Maria Theresa, 9 Feb 1745 (N.S.), *HHStA*, England, K. 88.
85. For this, the 'Project from The Hague', see Carteret to Trevor, 31 Aug, and Trevor to Carteret, 22 Sept 1744 (S.P., Foreign, 84/406), and subsequent exchanges until Carteret's fall (*loc. cit.*, and 407). For an example of Trevor's indiscretion—he criticized George II even to outsiders—see Carteret to Hyndford, 8 Mar 1743, S.P., Foreign, 90/56.
86. *Lenthe*, 55.
87. Johannes Ziekursch, *Sachsen und Preussen um die Mitte des 18. Jahrhunderts*, Breslau, 1904; Münchhausen's position is better documented for 1745 than for the second half of 1744.
88. König, note 48; Hann. 92, LXXI, 17^k (25 Sept 44).
89. For Trevor's reports see S.P., Foreign, 84/406, 407. Trevor's reports to Granville of 10 and 20/21/22 Nov 1744 (84/407) are particularly illuminating on the Dutch scene; for a proper evaluation of the reports, it must be taken into account that Trevor was more reserved with Carteret than with sympathetic spirits like Pelham and Harrington. See also Brauer, *op. cit.*, 160-166.
90. Quoted by Brauer, 164.
91. Newcastle to Trevor, 28 Sept 1744 (quoted by Brauer, 167, from Buckinghamshire MSS, 100). Also, Granville to Trevor, 22 Nov 1744 (S.P., Foreign, 84/407).
92. Complaints of Steinberg's ineptitude appear in Lenthe's letters to Schwicheldt (at Bonn at that time) (*Lenthe*, 55 and elsewhere).
93. Hann. 92, LXXV, Nr. 6, provides an insight into the mechanism of the deal. See also Hardwicke's notes of his audience with the king on 4 Jan 1745, in which the king complained, 'smiling', that 'ministers are kings in this country' (Add. MSS 35870, ff. 87092; 32704; f. 73). Also Harrington to Trevor at The Hague, 22 Feb 1745, S.P., Foreign, 84/408; George II to Schwicheldt, also at The Hague, 8 Feb 1745, Cal. Br. 24, (Holland) 3236. These last two letters are centrepieces of an intensive correspondence on the subject. For Pitt's position, see Owen, *op. cit.*, 248-256.
94. *P.H.*, XIII, 1173-1201 for 18 Feb (*sic*) 1745; 1201-1202 for 22 Feb 1745; *J.H.C.*, XXIV,

757; S.P., Foreign, 108/168. Brauer, 169, quotes a letter from Horace Walpole to Horace Mann of 4 March 1745 which gives particulars of the tripartite deal.

95. Nicolas Tindal, *The Continuation of Mr. Rapin's History of England*, IX (XXI), 126-127. Also Harrington to Trevor, 22 Feb 1745 (S.P., Foreign, 84/408).

Chapter 3

The last years of the War of the Austrian Succession, 1745–1748

With Granville's fall on 24 November 1744, any chance that the partition of Prussia might have served as a serious goal of British policy vanished. Harrington resumed his post as secretary of state for the Northern Department. So far as George II was concerned, he resumed the secretaryship a changed man—for reasons that are not clear. Henceforth he gave his political loyalty to the team in which he served, rather than to the king. That Harrington was so unwise as to be more outspoken than his colleagues when facing the king on the latter's favourite ideas, and that his colleagues, and his 'brother' Newcastle in particular, were of doubtful loyalty, fatally affected his subsequent career. But it also drove the king during the sixteen months that followed into a deviousness that has no parallel in the reign.

On 8 January 1745 Britain, Holland, Austria and Saxony signed a defensive treaty at Warsaw.[1] The purpose of this second 'Quadruple Alliance' was to preserve the system of Europe and the Empire as it was embodied in the Pragmatic Sanction. To redress the damage done to that system by Frederick's eruption into Bohemia, Saxony pledged to come to the aid of Maria Theresa with an army of 30,000—a very great force—paid for by Britain and Holland.[2] Once Bohemia was out of danger, Saxony would be on call to send 10,000 men to the Low Countries or to serve the Empire at the behest of her paymasters, for a smaller sum. In return she would fully share the fruits—as yet undefined—of victory. Russia was invited to join the alliance.

It was a moderate and sensible scheme from the British viewpoint; nor was it at the time unduly utopian. There was a strong case for clipping Frederick's wings. He had broken the Peace of Breslau, and it was no perfidy to argue that he had thereby forfeited the British guarantee of Silesia contained in that peace. When Silesia reverted to Austria, she might compensate Saxony with a strip in the north of the province to provide Saxony with a land bridge to Poland—ardently desired by the Saxon ministers, if less so by the Poles. Any further stripping of Frederick's domains was not in the British interest, and Granville himself had provided in the treaty for a prospective strengthening of the war effort in the west. When the alliance was signed the auguries for such an outcome seemed favourable—to a diplomatic community not as yet conscious of Frederick's fanatical tenacity in holding on to what he considered his own. The Prussian army had been driven out of Bohemia in November 1744 through the generalship of Field Marshal Traun. On 20 December *Amtmann* Meyer of Elbingerode in the Hartz on his own initiative arrested Marshal Belleisle as he was crossing Hanoverian territory on his way to Berlin. The ministers at Hanover—including Münchhausen—were badly frightened, but George II asserted himself, and Belleisle departed for England as a prisoner of war.[3] His disappearance from the scene of war was a severe blow to Prussian-French cooperation.

Then, on 20 January 1745, the unexpected death of Charles VII changed the German situation overnight. The Hanoverian ministers felt a relief which they did not trouble to disguise; now the Imperial crown could, and should, return to the House of Austria in the person of Maria Theresa's husband, the Duke of Lorraine. Thus the Bavarian interlude would remain as the awful memory of an Emperor who, through lack of resources, turned into a puppet of over-mighty protectors, such as France and Prussia. The *systema imperii* would be restored and, by implication, the Balance of Europe well served. George II agreed.[4] Events soon justified the reasoning of the ministers. The Union of Frankfurt, bereft of its ostensible chief, fell apart. The late Emperor's son and new Elector of Bavaria, young Maximilian Joseph, had no serious pretensions to the Imperial crown, and his country was at its last gasp. He could feel lucky when Maria Theresa, in the Treaty of Füssen on 22 April 1745, restored Bavaria to him against his renunciation of all claims to the inheritance of Charles VI. He also gave her the promise of his vote for her husband at the impending Imperial election.[5] Maximilian Joseph's defection from the anti-Habsburg front was another blow to Frederick, and its first diplomatic result was a settlement, early in May, between Austria and Saxony of their respective shares of Prussia, now an apparent prey.[6] However, the British ministers had by then changed their strategic outlook and abandoned any idea of harassing Prussia, and neither George II nor his Hanoverian ministers felt in a position to challenge them openly. A 'Convention' for consultation and mutual defence, which Hanover and Saxony signed on 12 April 1745 and which provided for the accession of Britain and Holland, remained unratified and unsung, and was never communicated, it seems, to the British ministry.[7] After further months of talk Hanoverian ministers signed on 8 July the draft of a 'Secret convention against Prussia' which provided for the division of spoils. Hanover's portion—modest when compared to that of Saxony—comprised in the main Halberstadt to the east and Minden to the west.[8] Five weeks after the shattering Saxon defeat of Hohenfriedberg at Frederick's hands (see below) the project remained of necessity a non-starter.

Early in 1745 Frederick, conscious of his rapidly worsening position, approached the British government through his minister in London, Andrié. He suggested that he might withdraw from the war, if necessary on the basis of the *status quo ante bellum*. Harrington and his colleagues, eager to shift the centre of the war westwards, were sympathetic. The Hanoverian ministers, informed by Steinberg and the king himself, were not. The latest developments had made the humbling of Prussia a distinct possibility, and they were at one with their master not to extend to Frederick a helping hand. George II needed no encouragement in his hostility to Frederick, but as usual he felt reassured when he knew his ministers at Hanover were with him, and his self-confidence grew when he, in turn, could reassure them of a compatability of views.[9] Because of opposition from the king, an arrangement between Britain and Prussia was held up for months. It is another instance of the pull Hanoverian attitudes had on British Continental policies in a fluid situation. The situation solidified when, early in the summer of 1745, Frederick's power for good or ill drastically improved. On 11 May the battle of Fontenoy exposed and increased the allies' weakness in the Low Countries. On 4 June Frederick's victory over the Austrians and Saxons at Hohenfriedberg restored his fortunes and shattered all hope of his military discomfiture in the circumstances then prevailing. A Prussian army, again assembled near Magdeburg ostensibly against Saxony, might after all change front westwards.[10] Russia refused to join the Quadruple Alliance. A Jacobite invasion of Britain was imminent, with French strategic, and perhaps operational, support.

Frederick proved a good learner: he remained content with his earlier terms. On 26 August 1745 Harrington and Andrié signed the 'Convention of Hanover' under which Britain engaged to mediate a peace between Prussia and Austria based on the 1742 Treaty of Breslau, to be concluded within six weeks.[11] The Hanoverian ministers later claimed that Harrington had tried to conceal the negotiations from them, and therefore they had not been able properly to evaluate their import; they did not claim to have been ignorant of the fact. How little Harrington took George II's faith for granted is shown by his extracting from him an explicit promise to support the convention.[12]

Immediately after the signature the king and Harrington left Hanover for England. There was no time to lose. Prince Charles Edward had raised his standard at Glenfinnan on 19 August, and within weeks much of Scotland professed allegiance to 'James VIII' of the House of Stuart.

To the chagrin of Frederick and the British ministers it took four months, two fresh major Prussian victories and the military subjugation of Saxony until peace was signed at last at Dresden on 25 December 1745. In the main the delay must be attributed to Maria Theresa, who was not forewarned of the Convention of Hanover, and whose obduracy matched Frederick's.

Throughout July and August 1745, until the eve of the Convention of Hanover, the Hanoverian ministers and George II himself pressed on Harrington voluminous opinions which warned against an accommodation with Frederick. It appears they worked in conjunction with the Austrian ambassador-at-large, Count Khevenhüller. The gist of their arguments was that France could not be beaten by direct assault, as the campaigns of 1744 and 1745 had again demonstrated. A successful defence was the best that could be expected. An indirect approach was needed. The power of France could be eroded by strengthening her opponents and by crippling her allies. On both counts Frederick must be reduced. He was the arch-enemy of Austria, Britain's natural ally; so long as Silesia, by general agreement the core of Prussia's claim to great-power status, remained in his hands, Austria could not, and would not, deploy her resources where Britain needed them. Also, they argued, Frederick's recent invasion of Bohemia proved that his malevolence was incurable. Moreover, the evil he caused would not die with him, since his successor was sure to be imbued with his spirit: if we substitute 'state' for 'successor', we have here a curious premonition of Prussia's later role in history, and Frederick's responsibility.[13]

With the convention signed, the Hanoverian ministers and their master tried to make it nugatory. All told, their machinations were feeble and bear a brief description.

When the courts of Dresden and Vienna were informed of the undertaking the British ministers had assumed with respect to them, they lost no time in signifying their displeasure and disagreement. Villiers and Robinson, the British ministers at the two courts, met with strict refusals to conform to the convention. Count Brühl's principal aide, Saul, had protracted talks with Bussche ('M. de Busch' of contemporary English sources), the Hanoverian minister at Dresden. Bartenstein, again Maria Theresa's chief adviser in foreign affairs, conferred with Münchhausen at Frankfurt, where the latter served as Hanover's ambassador at the Imperial election made necessary by Charles VII's death. Baron von Wasner, the Austrian minister in London, kept up pressure on George II, through Steinberg as well as in audiences with the king. He found an adviser and staunch ally in Frederick, Prince of Wales, who, whatever his differences with his father, was at one with him in his concern for Hanover.[14] Wasner gained in dignity—though hardly in effectiveness, for he was an able diplomatist and represented of course the vastly stronger power—by the presence of Count Flemming, the Saxon foreign minister, who came to London for the purpose.

The Austrian and Saxon argument was that Frederick was incorrigible and Prussian's present power overweening. Austria and Saxony were determined to put Frederick down and had just—on 29 August 1745—concluded a new treaty for this purpose.[15] If Frederick had succeeded in hoodwinking the maritime powers, the greater the pity; Austria and Saxony continued to believe that common interests tied them to Britain and Holland, and hoped for their allies' speedy disenchantment. Might not George II, as elector at least, act according to his just and reiterated beliefs? A new venue was taken when, about October 1745, Maria Theresa decided to explore a separate peace with France as the less dangerous of Austria's two major foes—the diplomatic revolution of 1756 was casting its foreshadows.

George II and the Hanoverians were entirely sympathetic, and showed it. The king went so far as to complain to Wasner—as he had done to Wasner's predecessor Ostein four years before—of his British ministers' ill intentions, with which he, the king, was powerless to cope. He enjoined the empress—as she now was since her husband's election as Emperor Francis I on 13 September 1745—not to quote him, as he merely wished to assist her in deciding upon her next steps.[16] This plea for discretion was unnecessary, since Villiers and Robinson were left in the dark in any case so far as it lay in the hands of the courts to which they were accredited. Andrié's *démarches* in London show Frederick's resentment.[17] Münchhausen at Frankfurt indicated the need for caution in dealing with Prussia[18]—a line that became reinforced by Frederick's fresh victory over the Austrians in Bohemia at Soor on 30 September. The British ministers, who sincerely wished for a peace between Prussia and Austria (a policy which even Granville, in opposition, supported),[19] may not have known in detail of the Austrian, Saxon and, indeed, Hanoverian intrigue, but were in no doubt of the king's general attitude. The Jacobite rising demanded all their attention: an English army had been dispersed at Prestonpans on 21 September; early in November Charles Edward and his host advanced south into England and by 4 December they were at Derby, 120 miles from London. Pelham was pacific by nature and easily dejected. Newcastle had not as yet found his aplomb in foreign affairs. In fact the king, who was no natural dissembler, told Harrington soon after their return from Hanover that he would have no more to do with the convention.[20] So the ministers scowled at the uneasy Wasner and wrote to Vienna and Dresden 'in the strongest manner'.[21] But there was no bite in their displeasure, and the other side knew it. Lastly, the Austrian peace move towards France, though it at first incensed the king, suited the wishes of at least Pelham and Harrington among the ministers.[22]

* * *

Thus matters hung fire until Frederick lost patience. On 23 November he pounced on Saxony to forestall, as he believed with good reason, a Saxon–Austrian attack on his heartlands. After a month it was all over—Saxony occupied, her king in flight, her army smashed at Kesselsdorf on 15 December and peace signed at Dresden on Christmas Day 1745 on the lines of the Hanover convention except that Saxony was condemned to pay damages to Prussia.[23] If ever the phrase about cutting the Gordian knot was realized in history, Frederick realized it in those five weeks. Hanover had no part in the peace. A fortnight after its conclusion her ministers were still ignorant of its provisions.[24]

Frederick also achieved something else. It is no accident that on his return from Dresden to Berlin he was first acclaimed 'the Great'. His successes, his very survival, could no longer be attributed to the luck of an impudent and treacherous adventurer. Münchhausen, for one, had sensed the impending catastrophe when rumours of the campaign first reached him. On 14 November he wrote direct to Maria Theresa and implored her to include Hanover in any peace she might make.[25] Later neither he nor his colleagues, nor George II himself, ever forgot the shock which the collapse of Saxony and, at bottom, the realization of Frederick's terrible prowess had given them. Frederick remained in their eyes the foremost threat to Hanover for another ten years. But they never again joined in plots for his destruction. Other schemes had to be devised to neutralize his menace. Also, they would never again deceive the British ministry on a matter of major policy, though admittedly the line between 'deception' and 'equivocation', as between 'major policy' and 'stratagem', is difficult to draw.

Before the Convention of Hanover of August 1745 Harrington had urged Hyndford, then British ambassador at Petersburg, to obtain Russian auxiliaries for service in the Empire—which in the circumstances meant that they would be used against Prussia—in return for British subsidies. After the convention—of which Hyndford was not informed for fully two months—Harrington countermanded these instructions.[26] The Tsaritsa Elizabeth and her chief adviser, the Grand Chancellor Bestushev, were deeply disappointed. Bestushev and Hyndford shared one fundamental emotion: they hated Frederick. Both believed, too, that only a combination of Russian manpower and British subsidies could destroy him. When the Hanover convention and the Peace of Dresden restored Frederick's security and prestige, Hyndford decided to ignore the events so far as he could. Obviously, he could not conclude a treaty without his government. When Chesterfield followed Harrington as secretary of state for the Northern Department in October 1746 he proved singularly inconsistent, wavering between his earlier support of Frederick and a present pugnaciousness. In a moment of panic Chesterfield even pressed on Russia, at the behest of George II, suggestions that amounted to preventive war against Prussia.[27] It was a mere flash in the pan.

Hyndford did his best: while engaged in a frustrating endeavour to hold his official superiors to an activist line, he also explored another avenue—behind their backs. He took up direct contact with the king through the Hanoverian ministers. His formal addressees were Heinrich Grote,[28] *Kammerpräsident* and formally senior to Münchhausen in the Privy Council at Hanover, and Steinberg. The correspondence was largely in cypher. Hyndford implored his correspondents not to reveal the exchanges to the British ministers.[29] George II himself, through Steinberg, promised Hyndford the necessary secrecy, together with high praise for Hyndford's 'zeal and personal attachment'.[30] Indeed, in February 1747 George II informed Hyndford, again through Steinberg, that in future he would receive his instructions concerning the treaty negotiations from the *British* ministry, whose proper concern they were.[31] But the letter was loosely phrased, as well as particularly gracious in tune, and the correspondence went on for some time as before.

But whatever the hopes of the conspirators, their machine ran idle. The intrigue dried up when the Hanoverian ministers discouraged Hyndford's entreaties that they should cooperate in introducing a bias against Prussia into the treaties of June and November 1747, whose object was quite different (see below). Strictly Hanoverian business, as well as occasional private confidences, crop up in the correspondence of Hyndford with Steinberg and Grote until Hyndford's departure from Petersburg in the autumn of 1749, but these items fall into the usual pattern of Hanoverian–British exchanges. In extenuation of Hyndford's peculiar behaviour it must also be remembered that at that time a British ambassador was still the king's servant in a meaningful sense. The significance of the episode possibly lies less in Hyndford's 'disloyalty' to the secretary of state than in his evident bad conscience, a feeling which he shared with the king himself.[32]

* * *

The Peace of Aix-la-Chapelle, May–October 1748, is remarkable chiefly in that it settled so few of the issues which had led to the war.[33] Peace negotiations had been conducted on and off between Britain and France since the end of 1745. The British ministry was united in its desire for a speedy peace since the beginning of 1748 when it became clear that the Dutch were destitute militarily, financially and morally.[34] The interests of Hanover came up in the negotiations, with some success. The Austrian negotiators were instructed to keep in touch with Münchhausen, whose good will towards Austria was implicitly recognized.[35] 'The territories and possessions in Germany' of the King of Great Britain as elector were guaranteed in the definitive treaty—an improvement on the preliminary drafts, which spoke only of the 'Electorate' (see 'Introduction'). The king also induced Newcastle—secretary of state for the Northern Department since Chesterfield's resignation in February 1748—to press for the recognition of a debt allegedly owed Hanover by Spain since the reign of her last Habsburg king.[36] In the preliminaries, Holland and France duly undertook to use their good offices to obtain payment. The claim is mentioned in article XVIII of the definitive peace treaty as subject to amicable settlement; this seems to have been the end of the matter. The king also informed Newcastle that East Friesland should not be included in any guarantee to Frederick,[37] and the treaties named no possessions of Prussia apart from Silesia and Glatz. Altogether it cannot be said that the tribute to Hanoverian interests was excessive, or disproportionate to the causes at stake.

The question of territorial aggrandizement for the House of Hanover in Germany, however, falls into a different category. Its originator was Frederick, who, in 1748, used it as bait (*l'amorce d'Hanovre*) to George II in order to have Prussia accepted in place of Austria as an ally of the maritime powers. The occasion of the offer was the mission of Henry Legge as special envoy to Berlin, where Britain had not been represented at all for almost a year.[38] The gist of Frederick's offer was to turn the 'alternate' of Osnabrück into a Hanoverian possession—a secundogeniture for the Duke of Cumberland, if George II so wished. George II, predictably, was enthusiastic, the Duke of Cumberland guarded. Münchhausen was deeply suspicious; his normal coolness towards real estate was enhanced in this case by a premonition of *timeo Danaos et dona ferentes*.[39] He need not have worried. Nothing came of the mission. For one, it is inconceivable that France and Austria—the former a guarantor of the Peace of Westphalia, the latter by tradition and interest a champion of the weaker against the stronger *Reichsstände*—would have given their assent. But the immediate stumbling block was Newcastle. He was convinced that no system of alliances which excluded Austria was worth having. If Prussia could be gained as a member in addition to Austria, she would be welcomed; but to be nothing but an additional partner was the opposite of what Frederick had in mind.[40]

In a different sense, too, these summer months of 1748 are of importance to the relations between Hanover and Britain. On 8 July 1748 Newcastle arrived in Hanover to join the king, having crossed the sea for the first time. His initial prejudices against the Hanoverian ministers were soon dispelled. As early as 17 July he wrote to his brother secretary, the Duke of Bedford: 'I must do justice to our brother ministers here; hitherto they seem very reasonable, and I believe will not *insist* upon anything that can any ways give any rubs, or obstruct our general affairs.'[41] The future was to show that his optimism was justified. Particularly with Münchhausen, Newcastle established a *rapport* which lasted as long as he remained in office. Münchhausen, a judge of character and not averse to laying on flattery with a trowel, took Newcastle by storm.[42] But their relationship went deeper. Of the same age, they shared their European outlook: they both believed in the Old System and were reluctant to recognize its irretrievable decay. Both 'saw France everywhere'.[43] They both marvelled at the vast potential of Russia which could be harnessed for good or for evil. Their loyalty to the House of Hanover was unshakable without being blind. Their industry was awe-inspiring, and their hands were 'extremely clean', by the standards of their time.[44] They also shared much that was not rational, or not entirely so: both loved power *and* its trappings; both were passionately 'political'. It was said of Münchhausen that he dealt with the breeches of a delinquent as he would with matters of high finance;[45] it might have been said of Newcastle. Both loved to 'oblige'—not just in expectation of a due, but because they were fundamentally kind men; both were worriers who sought relief from stress in indefatigable letter-writing. They shared the belief—somewhat naive, considering their enormous experience by that time—in the efficacy of diplomatic combinations. Also, their personal styles matched in a way that is difficult to define, but which made them harmonize without friction or jealousy.

No comparison must be overdone. Newcastle's idiosyncrasies were his own—and the soil of Hanover did not grow satirical chroniclers like Lord Hervey and Horace Walpole. Also, the political civilizations in which they moved greatly differed, except in that both civilizations were very civilized.

There is no doubt that the effusive friendliness of Newcastle's and Münchhausen's correspondence ever since their first meeting in the summer of 1748 is more than diplomatic conventionality, and it cannot be brushed off as a relationship between Hanoverian toady and English dupe. It was also to have important political consequences.

* * *

It might have been more logical for their purposes if the Hanoverian ministers had striven for a close alliance between Prussia and Hanover–Britain once they had given up the hope of assisting in Frederick's overthrow. Horatio Walpole thought so.[46] But their dislike of Frederick was too deeply rooted for such a heroic reversal and it took them almost ten years to come round to the strategy of an alliance with Prussia.

Between 1746 and 1755 Hanover's preoccupation with Frederick crystallized into one of its major variants; namely, the sustained attempt to achieve an alliance which would be as wide as possible, but would without question have Britain and Russia as central to the scheme. Hanover would remain discreetly in the background. Frederick was believed to 'fear Russia more than God',[47] and an alliance such as that envisaged might induce him to respect Hanover. The old dread of France, so potent as recently as 1741, had receded at Hanover for the time being: partly because of the indifferent performance of the French army on German soil since 1741, and partly because Münchhausen, over-sensitive to diplomatic fluctuations, was impressed by the decline of French standing in the Empire as witnessed by the defection of Bavaria and the waverings of Cologne. But in the main it was plain terror of Frederick that made the French threat diminish—his genius and his power; his ruthlessness and his unpredictability; his malevolence towards Hanover. But if the concept of a containing alliance crystallized at Hanover early in 1746, it was not until the working relationship between Münchhausen and Newcastle was established two years later that any practical steps could even be attempted.

The British–Russian alliance was visualized as truly defensive, for by the time of the Peace of Dresden the idea of an alliance bent on Frederick's destruction was seen at Hanover as chimerical. At best Frederick would take Hanover to ruin along with himself. This was sound. What was unsound was the Hanoverian attempt to manipulate forces, none of which Hanover could control. For one, Britain and Russia had national objectives to which Hanover was marginal or irrelevant. When the aim was achieved at last, with the Convention of Petersburg late in 1755, it proved counterproductive. It was impossible to tie down the tsaritsa and Bestuzhev to the concept of defensiveness, essential to Hanoverian thinking. The second Westminster convention of January 1756 between Britain and Prussia, a direct outcome of that of Petersburg, was intended as a reassurance to Frederick; it triggered the descent into Armageddon instead. But it was France, the enemy of old, and not Prussia, that ruled and misruled Hanover for six months in 1757/58, and by so doing injured her political will beyond recovery.

* * *

On 5 January 1746, when the instruments of the Dresden peace had just arrived, Maria Theresa instructed Wasner to place a double proposition before George II as elector. The one concerned an alliance between Austria and Hanover on the lines of the Austro-Saxon treaty of 13 May 1744, itself an elaboration of that of 20 December 1743.[48] Maria Theresa expressed the view that, provided the Hanoverians were not too timid to accept, there were no differences in principle between the partners. But even then, knowing that the Hanoverian ministry 'was in the habit of appropriating everything to its own use, without contributing anything useful to the general cause', the operative clauses had to be carefully defined, viz. 18,000 Hanoverian troops were to come to the aid of Austria when she was attacked. The second proposition concerned a defensive, armed, Quadruple Alliance between Austria, Hanover, Saxony and Russia. This—obviously a matter of the highest international importance—would be acceptable to British opinion if it was properly explained that the alliance would only become operative upon 'yet another' breach of peace by Prussia. As to Hanover, Wasner ought to make it clear that here was her one chance to get hold of East Friesland, in the hands of Prussia since 1744.[49]

The offer, taken as a whole, is interesting for its unflattering estimate of the Hanoverians: their selfishness, greed and cowardice. At the same time it lacks perceptiveness. With Saxony's recent fate before their eyes, the Hanoverians had good reason for 'timidity'. As to territorial acquisitiveness, Maria Theresa and her advisers should have been able to distinguish between George II and his Hanoverian ministers—who, for all their deferential bearing, were among the most independent-minded ministers in monarchical Europe. And as regards selfishness, the pot was calling the kettle black; the House of Habsburg was notorious for seeing the world as revolving about its own particular concerns. And then, of course, the East Frisian carrot suggests that the Quadruple Alliance might not have been entirely defensive in intent after all.

On 27 January (N.S.) Wasner met Steinberg. Steinberg was friendly but noncommittal. His first report on the king's reaction came two days later. The king was highly pleased, Steinberg told Wasner, and had no query at all as to the principle behind the proposed alliances. As to procedure, the king would at once order his Hanoverian ministers to have talks with those of Maria Theresa and 'set to work'. To make doubly sure that the proposals were being considered seriously Wasner begged George II to let him know what information it was advisable to give the British ministers.[50] It seems Wasner never got a reply. He had approached George just when relations between the king and his British ministers were moving towards the worst crisis of the reign. The members of the inner cabinet—Newcastle and Pelham, Hardwicke and Harrington—with the backing of most of the Cabinet Council, were fast reaching the conclusion that their chief enemies from among the earlier 'Opposition Whigs'—Granville and Bath—had engrossed for themselves the king's confidence to a degree that made it impossible for the ministers 'to do the king's business in Parliament', and hence that 'they who dictate in private should be employed in public'. They resigned on 11 February 1746—to return in triumph after three days when the king, Granville and Bath had become convinced that as yet 'the Pelhams' alone could form an administration supported by the political public.[51] When this interlude was past, George II for once was in no mood to try his British ministers with Hanoverian extravaganzas. Wasner, usually quick on the uptake, did not make the connection. His reports complain, first in irritation and then in despondency, that his repeated reminders to the king had met with evasiveness. The one concession Wasner was prepared to make in explaining the king's conduct amounted to an added insult: 'though I will not deny that he is of good will so long as there is no question of money, troops or even a minor risk'.[52] Finally Wasner despaired of his assignment to involve George II as elector. On 6 May 1746 he advised that all that could be expected was that George II should urge his *British* ministers in the right direction. Wasner did not know that he had set in motion another essay at grand policy-making at Hanover, based on Vienna's concept of an 'Armed Alliance' directed against Prussia, but with the difference that Hanover's part was to be taken by Britain.

George II, in fact, had promptly fulfilled his promise to order his Hanoverian ministers 'to set to work'—after his own fashion, having written to them on 17 January 1746, the day after Wasner's conference with Steinberg. He did not *order* them to set to work, but he did ask their opinion, leaving them in no doubt that he much liked the double project. ('I approve of the whole subject,' went the king's pencilled scrawl, and as an afterthought he stipulated that any aid to Russia should be 'any time' in troops, and 'never' in money—a characteristic touch, but not a promising line, considering the known assets and needs of Russia.)[53] The Hanoverian ministers' reply was given on 8 February 1746. As often in cases of importance, it was based on individual *vota* of the *Geheime Räte*, if not always on each councillor's *votum*.[54] Though the opinion stretches over twenty-eight folio pages it can be adequately summarized in a few sentences: Hanover, for her own safety, had to be allied to mighty powers and, though this was a necessary condition, it was not the only condition, for Prussia could easily overwhelm her before any help arrived. As it was widely known that only fear of Russia and circumspection (*Ménagement*) *vis-à-vis* the 'English nation' restrained Frederick in his lust for aggrandizement, Britain should take Hanover's place in the projected alliance. Hanover would then not only be protected but would not incur Frederick's wrath either. And if war were to break out, British subsidies would keep German, and for that matter Russian, troops in the highest state of preparedness that could be expected. And (since George II had, after all, set out on the assumption that Hanover would accede to the alliance) once the four-power alliance against Frederick—Austria, Saxony, Russia and *Britain*—was complete, His Majesty could still accede 'as elector', on conditions which it was too early to discuss.

George II reacted according to pattern. He immediately on 7 February 1746 ordered his Hanoverian ministers, with imperiousness though in gracious terms, to 'take as their directive' point by point the suggestions they had just made to him.[55] On the other hand, in the prevailing political circumstances he did not as yet 'urge his British ministers in the right direction'. Furthermore, the Hanoverian ministers failed to cooperate with the Austrian representatives, even though Steinberg told Wasner that such was the king's will.[56] They informed Bussche, the Hanoverian envoy at Vienna, of the projected Quadruple Alliance and instructed him to keep posted and report back to them—if the occasion arose—but to take no initiative.[57] It became Münchhausen's recurring argument in his talks with the Austrians that George II as elector was in any case doing more than what was due to Austria, and that Russian aid in particular fell within the *puré Anglicana*, outside the Hanoverian ministry's pale.[58] When talks between the Hanoverian ministers and the Austrian representatives finally took place at Hanover in the autumn of 1748, while Newcastle was there, no results materialized. The Hanoverians would not have Hanover directly involved.[59] Somewhat unenthusiastically Münchhausen at the time favoured a defensive alliance against France between the maritime powers, Austria, and a postulated 'Association' of south-western German states (the 'Vordere Kreise').[60] But this was a different matter.

The subsidy treaties concluded between Britain and Russia in 1747 (see above) do not fall into the grand design of forging a protective ring round Hanover. They served a momentary intention of Newcastle—that of breathing a new spirit into the war in the Low Countries. The alliances were concluded for one year only, with an option of another year's extension, not taken up in the event. The Hanoverian ministers used their good offices with Hyndford to obtain maximal information and, more guardedly, to check him when his anti-Prussian bias threatened to divert the negotiations from their limited objective. The outcome was as they could have wished it to be. Early in 1748 a Russian auxiliary corps moved ponderously westward, avoiding Prussian territory. It was sent back when the Peace of Aix-la-Chapelle was signed in October 1748. As a warning signal to Frederick this was well enough.[61] But it was a far cry from the memorandum of 8 February 1746 which first envisaged the new alignment against him.

Since August 1748 the Hanoverian interest in London had been aided by an adventitious development: Münchhausen's younger brother, Philip Adolph, had relieved Steinberg as head of the Germany Chancery. Philip Adolph von Münchhausen's relations with his brother recall those between Horatio and Robert Walpole rather than those of Henry Pelham and Newcastle. The Münchhausens loved and trusted each other. They shared their outlook and their way of thinking. Philip accepted his brother's pre-eminence. But by virtue of his daily contacts with George II he occupied a position of special importance. He was an expert, a confidential go-between, and he spoke his mind to his brother—though never without ceremonious courtesy. On the other hand, his exposure to British influences—unofficial and official—caused his colleagues at Hanover occasionally to take his opinions with a grain of salt; he had become, after all, something of an expatriate. In vigour of mind he was a great advance on Steinberg (who continued to serve on the Hanover Privy Council as the elder Münchhausen's unofficial aide in foreign affairs). Last but not least, Philip von Münchhausen was the ideal link between his brother and Newcastle.

Notes

1. For the text of the treaty, including its secret articles, see Wenck, *op. cit.*, II, 171-179.
2. For Vienna's displeasure at the limited British aims *vis-à-vis* Frederick, see Maria Theresa to Wasner, 2 Feb 1745, *HHStA*, England, K. 89.
3. The best description of Belleisle's arrest is that given by a clerk of Meier's in a letter to his brother (*Lenthe*, 113-115). For first reactions at Hanover and St James's, see Hann. 92, LXXI, 18.
4. Memorandum of the *Geheime Räte*, drafted by Münchhausen, 5 Feb 1745; *Geheime Räte* to George II, 28 Feb 1745, quoting the king's approval of 29 Jan/9 Feb 1745, Cal. Br. 11, 2132.
5. For the text of the treaty, see Wenck, *op. cit.*, II, 180-190.
6. For an abstract of the agreement, see Ranke, *op. cit.*, Book XI, 147.
7. Cal. Br. 24, Saxony, 6897.
8. G. J. Droysen, *Geschichte der preussischen Politik*, V, 2, Berlin, Leipzig, 1886, 518; Mediger, 407.
9. E.g., *Geheime Räte* to George II, 9 Mar, 4 Apr 1745 (including a Saxon 'Plan of Operations'), Hann. 9^d, 38. For George II's aggressiveness at this time, and his British ministers' acquiescence, see Stone to Newcastle, 16 Feb 1745, Add. MSS 32704, f. 72.
10. Newcastle to Harrington, 14 June 1745, S.P., Foreign, 43/113; for a concise appreciation in general terms, Newcastle to Harrington, 5 July 1745, S.P., Foreign, 43/37.
11. For the text of the Convention of Hanover, Wenck, II, 191-194.
12. Grote to Hyndford, 9 Nov 1745, Add. MSS 11380, f. 169; Newcastle to Hardwicke, 15 Sept 1745, Yorke, I, 635.
13. The memoranda are collected in Hann. 9^d, Nr. 42, and Hann. 92, LXXV, Nr. 7, vol. IV. The most telling is a dissertation of 16 July, apparently by Diede. It was sent to Harrington by order of Münchhausen; for an unknown reason Harrington never saw it. Borkowsky, 57-59, and Mediger, 401-406, analyse this document in greater detail. It is this memorandum which convinces Professor Mediger that at that time Diede and Münchhausen aspired to build Hanover up as the guardian of the Empire against France, through territorial acquisitions in the west.
14. The Prince of Wales had first come to England at the age of twenty; he was his grandfather's representative in the electorate so long as George I was in England. The

Austrian and anti-Prussian sympathies of the Prince play a considerable role in Wasner's reports at that time (*HHStA*, England, K. 88, 90 *passim*). Two letters of the Prince to Münchhausen of 30 August and—apparently—19 November 1745 stress the Prince's devotion to 'notre chère patrie' and back Münchhausen in his contacts with the Austrian and Saxon courts (Hann. 91, Münchhausen I, Nr. 16). In general, the Prince emerges from the sources as much superior to the 'Poor Fred' of popular tradition. (See also his 'Political Testament' of 1749 in which he enjoined his eldest son to 'be always kind' to Hanover—and to make provision for the separation of the crowns; Sir George Young, *Poor Fred*, London, 1937, 172-175.)

15. For its text, see Arneth, III, 422-424. Frederick had just declared war on Saxony. At Hohenfriedberg the Saxons had fought as auxiliaries of Austria—like the British at Dettingen.
16. Wasner to Maria Theresa, 12 Oct 1745 (N.S.), *HHStA*, England, K. 88.
17. For Frederick's mounting suspicion, see *Pol. Corr.*, IV, 8 Sept to 11 Dec 1745, *passim*.
18. Cal. Br. 11, E. I, 2157, Hann. 92, LXXV, Nr. 7, vol. V, for Sept–Oct 1745. This is the tenor of his reports and the way he was understood by his colleagues and the king, though I have found no explicit warning to that effect.
19. Thus Hardwicke to Philip Yorke, 19 Sept 1745 (Yorke, I, 455).
20. Newcastle to Hardwicke, 15 Sept 1745 (Yorke, I, 635).
21. Newcastle to Chesterfield, 5 Sept (?) 1745; Lodge (ed.), *The Private Correspondence of Chesterfield and Newcastle 1744-46*, London, 1930, 63. Newcastle's subsequent letters give an insight into the ministry's uncertainty. Also Wasner to Maria Theresa, 12, 26 Oct 1745 (N.S.), *HHStA*, England, K. 88.
22. Lodge, *Studies*, ch. 4.
23. For the terms of the Peace of Dresden, see Wenck, II, 194-202, 207-215.
24. Lenthe to Schwicheldt, 7 Jan 1746; *Lenthe*, 244.
25. *HHStA*, Staatskanzlei Hannover, K. 2.
26. Hyndford Papers, Add. MSS 11389; particularly important are Harrington to Hyndford, 15 Oct, 22 Nov (ff. 126, 196-197); Hyndford to Harrington, 22 Oct 1745 (ff. 140-141). In the letter of 22 October Hyndford sends his 'most earnest entreaty' for information on the Hanover convention of which he had heard rumours.
27. Chesterfield to Hyndford, 14 Aug 1747, Hyndford Papers, Add. MSS 11384, ff. 95-98.
28. The Grote (as the Hake) were *not* commoners but ancient nobility (*Uradel*). There were several noble families in Lower Saxony that did not use the predicate 'von'.
29. Hyndford to Grote, 6 May; to Steinberg, 10 June 1746 (O.S.), Cal. Br. 24, Russland, 6618; Hann. 92, LXXV, Nr. 13.
30. Steinberg to Hyndford, 3 June 1746, Add. MSS 11381, f. 234.
31. Steinberg to Hyndford, 10 Feb 1747, Hann. 92, LXXV, Nr. 13.
32. Since we have access to the clear as well as to the two sets of deciphered copies (the one for the Hanoverian ministry, Cal. Br. 24, Russland, 6618, the other for the German Chancery, Hann. 92, LXXV, Nr. 13), the correspondence may be of interest to students of cryptography. The variants between the clear and the deciphered copies, and between the two deciphered copies, are slight, but they are interesting and on occasion comical. Sir R. Lodge ('Lord Hyndford's Embassy to Russia, 1744-9', *EHR*, XLVI, 1931, 48-76, 389-422) mentions in two footnotes based on the Hyndford Papers that Hyndford was in confidential correspondence with Steinberg. He does not analyse its significance. For the Hanoverians' soft-pedalling, see the tenor of Grote's letters to Hyndford, Add. MSS 11383, 11384, and Mediger, 433-436. For the text of the three treaties, see de Martens (ed.), *Recueil des traités et conventions conclus par la Russie* … , IX, 'Angleterre', Petersburg, 1892, 134-172. The foremost monograph covering the entire episode is still Ernst Borkowsky, *Die englische Friedensvermittlung im Jahre 1745*, Berlin, 1884. The weakness of this work lies in the author's failure to consult British archives and, on a different level, his emotional commitment to Frederick. For a more detailed critique of Borkowsky, see

Mediger, 708.

33. For the text of the preliminary peace, Wenck, II, 310-334; of the definitive peace, Wenck, II, 337-428.
34. The best description, within the general context of the war, is Lodge, *Studies*, ch. VIII.
35. Maria Theresa to Wasner, 4 Sept 1748, *HHStA*, England, K. 95.
36. Newcastle to Sandwich, 8 Apr 1748, 'Private', S.P., Foreign, 84/431.
37. *Id.* to *id.*, 'Separate', *ibid.*
38. The standard monograph is Lodge, 'The Mission of Henry Legge to Berlin, 1748', *Transactions of the R. Hist. Soc.*, 1931, 1-38.
39. *Ibid.*; Add. MSS 32812, ff. 279, 281, 336, 338; 32813, f. 87.
40. I think that Sir Richard Lodge in his *Studies in Eighteenth Century European Diplomacy* is unfair to Hanover. His charge 'Never had there been a more barefaced and noxious attempt to obtrude electoral demands into negotiations in which vital English interests were concerned' (372) is not proven. The Hanoverian ministers as a group cannot be stigmatized as 'docile' (370) without important qualifications. (Only for Steinberg among the ministers concerned at the time in foreign affairs does the description hold true.) Lodge's metaphor of 'lion' and 'jackals' (372-373) is equally inept. The ministers hardly fed on the king's prey, and it is not easy to picture George II as a 'lion'. It is true that German modes of expression might mislead a historian of *English* politics, though I find no evidence that Lodge used the Hanoverian archives. In Lodge's 'The Mission of Henry Legge' the Hanoverian ministers play a more respectable part than in the *Studies*. The French and Austrian historians of the negotiations, the Duc de Broglie (*La Paix d'Aix-la-Chapelle*, Paris, 1892) and Adolf Beer ('Zur Geschichte des Friedens von Aachen im Jahre 1748', *Archiv für österreichische Geschichte*, XLVII, 1871, 3-195), pay almost no regard to the role of Hanover. However, neither of them seems to have used *British* unpublished sources.
41. Lord John Russell (ed.), *Correspondence of John, Fourth Duke of Bedford*, 3 vols., London, 1842-1846; I, 401-402.
42. Newcastle to Bedford, 18 July 1748, *op. cit.*, 463.
43. I found this phrase in its eighteenth century context used by W.F. Reddaway, *EHR*, XXXI (1916), 61.
44. Chesterfield's epitaph of Newcastle, quoted by B. Williams, *Carteret and Newcastle*, Cambridge, 1943, 224. I have examined an episode that sheds light on Münchhausen's financial mores. The short article appears in *Niedersächsisches Jahrbuch für Landesgeschichte*, 52 (1980), 311-316.
45. Quoted by W. von Hassel, *Die schlesischen Kriege und das Kurfürstenthum Hannover*, Hanover, 1879, 252.
46. See his letter to the Duke of Cumberland, 26 Aug 1747, in *Memoirs of Horatio, Lord Walpole*, Coxe (ed.), London, 1820, vol. II, 211. Horatio had been the advocate of an Anglo-Prussian alliance for long.
47. Attributed to Hyndford in Koser, *König Friedrich der Grosse*, Stuttgart, Berlin, 1893, 1903, I, 580.
48. For the Austro-Saxon treaty, see Arneth, III, 431, 559.
49. *HHStA*, England, K. 91.
50. Wasner to Maria Theresa, 1 Feb 1746 (N.S.), *ibid.*, as also Wasner's following reports.
51. For this, see Owen, *op. cit.*, 293 ff.
52. Report of 18 Mar 1746 (N.S.).
53. Hann. 92, LXXV, Nr. 7, vol. VI.
54. Cal. Br. 24, Oesterreich I, 4473. Mediger (*op. cit.*, 413 ff.) analyses the genesis of the opinion and stresses the role Geheimer Rat Diede played in its inception. The file also contains the draft of the collegiate opinion by the side of the final version that went to George II—an interesting example of eighteenth century German style editing.
55. *Ibid.*
56. Baron Jaxheim, the Austrian envoy at Hanover in 1746, has nothing to report on an

impending Quadruple Alliance, though he was frequently invited to join the Hanoverian ministers in their Geheime Ratsstube, where he was treated with a great show of confidence; *HHStA*, Staatskanzlei, Hannover, Fasz. 3.

57. *Geheime Räte* to Bussche, 27 Mar 1746, Hann. 92, LXXV, Nr. 7, vol. VI.
58. For an instance of this excuse, used with crucial timing, see Count Raab, Austrian envoy at Hanover, to Maria Theresa, 27 Aug 1747, *HHStA*, Staatskanzlei Hannover, Fasz. 3.
59. This is my conclusion in the absence of positive evidence in the relevant files, Hann. 92, LXXV, Nr. 7, vol. VIII; *HHStA*, England, K. 94. See also Pribram, II, 44.
60. E.g. his memorandum for Maria Theresa of 30 June 1748, *HHStA*, Staatskanzlei Hannover, Fasz. 3.
61. *Pol. Corr.* VI, *passim*, shows Frederick's intense preoccupation with the presence of Russian troops in Central Europe.

Chapter 4
The Münchhausen–Newcastle partnership, 1749–1756

If the forging of a protective alliance remains the *Leitmotiv* of Hanoverian thinking for a decade, short-term attention centred on different issues. It is significant that all of these hinged on British policies or difficulties.

As early as February 1749 Münchhausen had proved his worth as diplomat-friend of Newcastle when he mediated between the Austrian government and Newcastle in a quarrel over a subsidy of £100,000 that broke out within weeks of the conclusion of the definitive peace treaty of Aix-la-Chapelle. Austria claimed that this sum remained her due from Britain, and though her case was doubtful the empress and her ministers were in an ugly mood—not quite without reason. Münchhausen persuaded Newcastle in letters of genuine eloquence that whatever the contractual merits of the claim, the object of the quarrel, 'an inconsiderable [*très médiocre*] sum compared to the sacrifices of the past', was not worth endangering the Old Alliance for. Newcastle gave in, though with some trepidation: 'It remains to be seen whether I myself shall not be the sacrifice, or better, the dupe, of my blind attachment to the House of Austria and the conservation of the *bon Système*.'[1]

The King of the Romans project, which also challenged their partnership, was a proposition of a different sort.[2] The Hanoverian archives do not refute the contention that the idea was fathered late in 1749 by Sir Charles Hanbury Williams, 'poet, wit and diplomatist', a confidant of Newcastle, and the British minister at Dresden–Warsaw in 1749.[3] The scheme was that Britain, with the participation of Holland and Austria, should bribe the electors to elect Maria Theresa's eldest son, the archduke Joseph, as 'King of the Romans'—the traditional title of the designated heir to the Emperor. At one stroke George II would have the credit for having secured the new Lorraine dynasty on the Imperial throne, Maria Theresa would be grateful, and the Old System would be vindicated. More specifically, a dispute over a future imperial election with its dangers to the general peace would become less likely.

This is not the place to examine the strength and weakness of the proposition. Suffice it to say that no one who mattered was enthusiastic about it except Newcastle and, for a brief time, George II.[4] Among the Hanoverian ministers an exception was the younger Münchhausen, who seems to have fallen under Newcastle's sway at this point. Münchhausen himself was uneasy. He felt that Newcastle, for all his experience, did not realize that the *Kurfürsten* might be bribed, but that it was risky to try to buy them so openly; that Maria Theresa would give little thanks for the patronizing interference of a foreign government in what she considered her family freehold anyway; that the very idea was an insult to the Empire, for which, with all its terrible shortcomings, Münchhausen cared deeply. And these reservations held good in addition to the political difficulties: Frederick, as Elector of Brandenburg, would at best sell his acquiescence dear, and not for cash; Louis XV and his ministers, with France a guarantor of the Imperial constitution, would be presented with added chances to make trouble. Moreover, Münchhausen knew well that Newcastle's power in the British cabinet was limited to fair weather, and money demands meant squalls.

But Münchhausen had no choice. A prime principle of his policy was to prove that the Hanoverian–British relationship was useful to Britain as well. For practical purposes Newcastle had become the maker of foreign policy. By the end of 1749 the King of the Romans project was, as Newcastle termed it, 'a child of my own'.[5] Mere gossip, whispered to Newcastle, that the Hanoverian ministers were in doubt about the project sent them into protestations of loyalty to Newcastle which bordered on the hysterical. Newcastle accepted the protestations gracefully, but clearly he had been perturbed.[6] Münchhausen did not wish to try their friendship further. Moreover, Newcastle's objective of perpetuating the House of Austria in the Imperial dignity was of course unobjectionable to the Hanover minister. And so Münchhausen became Newcastle's chief agent in the negotiations with the empress, the electors and the diplomatists—all shifty and suspicious, most of them greedy, none with his heart in the matter.

Münchhausen did his best; his colleagues were loyal. But his best was confined to diplomatic dexterity and informed advice.[7] This was not enough when the question was one of money, and here Newcastle's pull was severely limited. Granting that Britain, Holland and Austria were all, for different reasons, insufficiently generous, another source remained to be tapped. After forty years of careful management, and ten years of profitable troop transactions, in a country as yet unscathed by war or occupation, the king's Hanoverian *Schatulle*—his privy purse—had become a European by-word for a treasure of almost mythical proportions.[8] If the glory and interest of George II were so intimately involved, and the English difficult to approach, might not the electorate supply the presumably moderate sums needed to satisfy the uncommitted members of the Electoral College?

In the heyday of his short-lived enthusiasm for the project the unlikely happened: George II dug into his own pocket to further the political initiative of a British minister. On 20 February 1750 the Hanoverian minister at Bonn (the Archbishop of Cologne's residence), Borch, signed a treaty at Schloss Neuhaus near Paderborn which promised the archbishop-elector a four years' annual subsidy of 400,000 Dutch florins (approximately £40,000), to be paid in equal parts by Holland (vitally interested in buttressing her Rhenish flank) and George II. Also, the king undertook to stand security for the Dutch portion. In return, the archbishop *inter alia* promised 'without hesitation' (*ne balance pas*) to follow the king's vote in the assemblies of the Empire, including the Electoral College. George II is referred to as 'Elector of Brunswick-Luneburg', with the 'King of Great Britain' omitted.[9] Newcastle, in a letter of 7 February 1751 to Burrish, the British minister at Bonn (and other German courts), stressed that the treaty was 'made in His Majesty's electoral capacity … and neither is, nor will be, laid before Parliament'.[10]

This financial offering remained unique. As the success of the project seemed within reach, Pelham ungraciously relented to make modest British allocations available for the purchase of Bavaria first, and of Saxony somewhat later. In between Newcastle discovered to his dismay that the appetite thrives on feeding. The Elector of Cologne threatened to renege unless he was bought over again, and ultimately did so; the Elector Palatine began by making impossible demands. George II's brief mood of financial recklessness evaporated. But until the final demise of the project Münchhausen, in talks with the Austrian minister, J. W. von Vorster—whose government was eager that others should shoulder the burden—would raise the feasibility of Hanoverian payments, and in the same breath deplore 'that all misfortune came from the king's exaggerated regard for money, and his refusal to disburse' (*dass alles Unglück daher rühre, dass der König das Geld gar zu hoch achte, und von einigen Abgaben nichts wissen wolle*).[11] The modern observer can only marvel at Münchhausen's apparent disloyalty to his absent monarch, his equally apparent confidence that an Austrian indiscretion would do him no harm, and his show of pusillanimity. The Austrians saw a concerted drive to shift pressures from Hanover to London, and back if need be, while Münchhausen probably intended nothing more Machiavellian than to comment on his disillusion with a project that he had to foster nevertheless. In this spirit he commiserated with Newcastle, 'the principal author and prime mover' of the project, who was risking his standing with his colleagues and with the public.[12]

It is worth noting that the King of the Romans project served Münchhausen not merely as an opportunity to demonstrate to Newcastle his good will and ability to be of use. He also asked for a political *quid pro quo*. Münchhausen, and to a lesser extent his colleagues, had one serious grievance against Austria: the persecution of Protestants throughout the Habsburg domains, unbloody, mostly petty, but certainly persistent. Unlike his contemporaries among British ministers, Münchhausen was not only Protestant, but a Protestant deeply committed to helping his brethren. And with the traditional defenders of Protestantism among the electors in eclipse—the Elector of Saxony a Catholic convert, the Elector of Brandenburg an agnostic—the stand of Hanover became a matter of importance. At the instance of Münchhausen Hanoverian remonstrances were a recurrent feature of Diet proceedings at Ratisbon, to the annoyance of the Austrians, who appreciated Münchhausen's general benevolence but deplored his 'quite incomprehensible fanaticism' in matters of religion.[13] Though this charge is unfounded, it is revealing that it was made at the behest of Maria Theresa, who was indeed a religious bigot.

However, Münchhausen was enough in earnest to harness Newcastle to the Protestant cause in the summer of 1750, when the project was still hopeful, and his own assistance crucial. The occasions were humdrum—the vested liberty to elect a Protestant Burggrave of Friedberg; the Catholic proselytizing zeal of the princes of Hohenhohe-Waldburg. Münchhausen's wrapping was formidable: a '*Note* touchant les griefs du Corps evangélique dans l'Empire'. Newcastle was unenthusiastic, but Münchhausen must be 'obliged'. And thus Newcastle remonstrated with the Austrian authorities through the minister in Vienna, Robert Keith and, more important, since Keith was pleasant rather than commanding, with Count Willem Bentinck, the Dutch *stadtholder*'s right hand then on 'project' business in Vienna (and a correspondent of Newcastle). Such oppression, warned Newcastle, might unite the Protestant powers in the Empire. Frederick had already offered to cooperate with George II! The Austrian authorities remained unflustered and, apart from uttering soothing noises, did nothing.[14] It appears that Münchhausen never repeated this gambit.

* * *

When the King of the Romans project faded out in 1753, Hanoverian–British relations came under more substantial strain, again because of Prussia, for by 1752 there were two major issues pending which made Hanover acutely fear Prussian ill will.

The former concerned East Friesland. George II had not immediately reacted to Prussia's seizure of the principality in May 1744 (see above, p. 58), because he was in no position to resist the take-over by force. But he had an arguable case for succeeding to the last native prince and he saw himself worsted by his nephew out of territory he considered his own. He was not the man to swallow such an insult philosophically, and since force was out of the question he tried the organs of the Empire—the Diet of Ratisbon first, the Aulic Council at Vienna later. In the end Frederick's claim was upheld—not merely because he was in possession, but also because his title to East Friesland was based on a decree of Emperor Leopold I which Maria Theresa as Leopold's granddaughter would not easily set at naught.[15] Though George II was ultimately to waive his claim to East Friesland in the Westminster treaty of 1756, at the end of 1752 George II's campaign was in full swing, while Frederick's annoyance was acute. It was not Münchhausen's campaign, and Frederick could cite him as being on record against its pursuit.[16]

Indirectly connected with this issue was another, positive, grievance that Frederick held against Britain. East Friesland gave him the port of Emden, long decayed since the days when it had been a rival to Hamburg and Bremen but capable—so Frederick believed—of regaining its former importance and of turning into a gold mine for the hungry Prussian treasury. His attempts to develop Emden have received varying treatment from historians. He himself believed that his indifferent success was largely due to the depredations of British privateers in the last years of the war, and the backing they received from the British courts of Admiralty. For years Frederick exercised restraint, either because he believed that ultimately British justice would prevail or because the time was not ripe for a showdown. Finally, in October 1752, Frederick allocated the remainder of the Silesian debt which Prussia had assumed under the Treaty of Breslau in 1742, and which was due to British and Dutch creditors, as compensation to his subjects whose claims against Britain had in the meanwhile been acknowledged by a *Prussian* commission. The sums involved were not very considerable: Prussian claims, including interest, were about £33,000, deducted from the outstanding debt of £45,000.[17] But Frederick's high-handedness roused a storm in Britain, with calls for reprisals. Frederick was surprised and angered. He had not meant to provoke a quarrel and he had in the past been convinced of his righteousness even when his case was weaker than at present.

When the storm broke—with the East Frisian quarrel between George and Frederick also at its height—the Hanoverian ministers instantly feared their country might be made to pay for the battle of the giants. They could not reason with Frederick, but they could approach their own king and his British ministers, and they did so with a will. As it turned out, their fears soon gained substance. During the second half of September 1752 reports from Colonel Joseph Yorke, Hardwicke's son, and minister at The Hague, reached Hanover which 'contained a very extraordinary intelligence that the King of Prussia had actually sent two engineers to form a march-route from Halberstadt to Wesel'.[18] Granting that 'a march-route from Halberstadt to Wesel' would run along the southern frontier of the electorate, Newcastle displayed a nervousness which was probably imparted to him by the Hanoverian ministers, and which they certainly shared. Shortly afterwards information started to come in from the east on impending call-ups and troop concentrations between Magdeburg and

Halberstadt; the reports reached panic intensity early in 1753.[19] The picture tallied with intelligence which George II and the younger Münchhausen forwarded to Hanover at the same time that Frederick definitely intended to invade Hanover. Would the Privy Council, George II requested of the Hanoverian ministers, immediately submit plans drawn up in conjunction with General Sommerfeldt, the commander-in chief, 'for concentrating our troops so that they may not be seized, and keep at the same time their rear free, together with their sustenance'. Also, the Hartz (because of its metal ores the prime cash-producing region of the electorate) must be covered. Also, 'the salvage of the valuables, moneys and important papers' at Hanover must be attended to.[20]

The ministers forwarded their plan, coordinated with Sommerfeldt and Quartermaster General Pauli, to the king on 6 February 1753. Its outline was as follows. A field battle against the Prussian army was not feasible. The Hanoverian army would be best off to retreat north-east, under the guns of Stade. Thus a passage would be kept open to the sea, to England, and Denmark (where George II's daughter Louisa had been queen consort 1746–51). The Hartz just could not be protected.[21] The king accepted the plan by return of courier, taking exception only to a few expensive details such as the provision of tents, which he hoped were not yet necessary. He did not grudge, however, a wide call-up of Hanover's youth in case of invasion: 'We have every reason to believe that these young men will prefer to join Our, their native sovereign's, war service for some short time rather than fall into the hands and war service of Prussia, which entails lifelong slavery'—a true if somewhat startling observation. He ended with the fervent prayer: 'And the Highest in His mercy may avert from our German lands danger and misfortune ...'[22]

Frederick of course knew what went on in Hanover. Taking into account the atmosphere of alarm, he probably learned more rumour than hard fact. He vehemently vowed that his intentions towards Hanover were entirely peaceful. The evidence points to his sincerity. He did indeed order Prince Henry at the time to draw up a plan of operations against Hanover, but it is probable that this was a mere contingency plan occasioned by the crisis, and not vice versa. Perhaps he also wanted to exercise his gifted young brother.[23] His uncle, at any rate in private, scornfully rejected these protests of peaceful intent. In fact, Frederick suspected that it was George II who wanted to provoke a war over East Friesland, for which the Silesian loan would serve as a pretext.[24]

The scare subsided as it gradually became clear to Hanover that the 'two engineers', the call-ups and the troop movements across the border had no sinister objective. But the episode has lessons for the student of history, just as it had at the time. First of all, it was a posthumous tribute to the statecraft of George I. A crisis had occurred, and the *Regierungsreglement* of 1714 (see Introduction, pp. 6–7) had again been vindicated. The *Geheimes Ratskollegium* of a quasi-absolutist state had coped with a dangerous situation under a minimum of guidance in the absence of the prince, and had achieved an outcome to his satisfaction. The all-important cooperation with the military had functioned as prescribed: the generals had acted as professional advisers to the civilian government, and not as policy-makers or manipulators. Secondly, the plan of operations outlined in 1753 was to hold good in 1757, both before the battle of Hastenbeck and after. This need not have been so, for with Frederick transformed from prospective enemy to actual ally an essential element had changed. But as the plan of 1753 was held valid during lesser alarms that recurred in 1754 and 1755, we may assume that sheer inertia was one factor in the different strategic situation of 1757. (See below, p. 112.)

A third point is the most important for the shaping of events. The shock of a looming Prussian invasion in 1752/53 galvanized the Hanoverian ministers into a new effort to envelop Hanover with protective alliances.

Wasner's virtual rebuff early in 1746 had not deterred Austria from working for a 'defensive armed Quadruple Alliance' against Frederick. Largely on Wasner's advice (see above, p. 74) the idea of including Hanover was temporarily shelved, but not given up. An important advance towards the goal, though easy to achieve in the prevailing circumstances, was the 'Alliance of the two Empresses' between Austria and Russia of 2 June 1746. Concluded for twenty-five years, it committed the parties to mutual assistance if either of them, or Poland, were attacked. The fourth article of a 'secret and separate' amendment stipulated that if Austria were to come to the aid of Russia in consequence of a Prussian attack on Russia or Poland—that is, not on Austria herself—the Treaty of Dresden would be considered void. Austria would then be free to recover Silesia and Glatz with Russia's help. In the main body of the treaty an invitation to the King of Great Britain to join *as elector* was particularly solicited.[25]

It was not love of England that kept Austria wooing Britain until the latter finally acceded to the 1746 alliance in 1750. A survey of Austrian desiderata sent to the Austrian chargé d'affaires at Hanover early in 1749 expresses the bitterness felt towards Britain by Vienna—far more strongly felt by now than the age-old enmity for France. But the conflict with Prussia overshadowed every other consideration, and for the effective pursuit of the conflict the 'armed alliance' with Hanover *and* Britain was still considered to be of overriding importance.[26] Only eight weeks later, in March 1749, Kaunitz submitted to Maria Theresa his historic memorandum on foreign policy. Among his foremost conclusions was the assertion that, in spite of their basic community of interests with Austria, no active assistance could be expected from the maritime powers in the inevitable settling of accounts with Prussia. Holland was in decay. As for Britain, though George II and the Prince of Wales indeed hated Frederick with good reason, as did the Hanoverian ministers, this constituted a political disadvantage, paradoxically enough: 'the Nation'—Parliament, 'the Great'—feared that the influence of the royal family in foreign affairs might endanger the constitution. Newcastle may have been excepted from this generalization; Kaunitz's colleague at the State Conference, Count J. J. Khevenhüller, wrote in his own memorandum that, of all the people who mattered in Britain, Newcastle was 'still the one with the most honest opinions' (*noch am redlichsten denkende*) plainly in the sense of 'being of the honest party'. Also Khevenhüller believed that Newcastle 'can frequently be guided by sensible representations made in a pleasing manner' (*dass sich Newcastle durch verständige und mit guter Art vorgebrachte Erinnerungen öfters leiten lasse*). Kaunitz's implication was that it was not merely useless to try and accommodate Britain, but that it might even be prejudicial to Austria's cause, since such attempts would put France off, a much more promising candidate for an alliance against Prussia.[27] But six more years were to pass before this doctrine was to become Austrian high policy.

When George II joined the alliance on 30 October 1750, after years of haggling, he did so as King of Great Britain only; to this extent he had his way, with the consistent backing of the Hanoverian ministers. He also carried his refusal to accede to Separate Article No. 4 (see above). On the other hand George II did not receive the unequivocal guarantee for Hanover he had demanded. What he did get was declarations from Austria and Russia that they would come to Hanover's defence if she were attacked 'solely in resentment [*uniquement en haine*] against His [George II's] accession to the treaty'.[28] As the 1752/1753 crisis was to show, this did not cover all the contingencies which might befall Hanover, and was not the sort of defensive treaty Hanover had wished for.

* * *

The opportunity to raise afresh the issue of an alliance that would promise Hanover maximum security at minimum risk was handed to the Hanoverian ministers when their apprehension of a Prussian swoop was at its height. It happened thus: on 13 February 1753 George II sent Münchhausen and Steinberg a request on behalf of Newcastle to let him know what could be done for the security of Hanover in face of the Prussian menace. In particular, British naval action against Emden or a Baltic port seemed to Newcastle a promising line if the Prussian threat were to materialize. (In view of the origin of the present quarrel this was a logical line to follow.) Would Münchhausen and Steinberg provide, therefore, topographical and military information bearing on the suggestion? The king also asked, at Newcastle's behest, that the reply be clothed as a response to a royal (i.e. 'electoral') order—a significant touch.[29] The reply was given on 23 February. It came from the Privy Council in its collegiate capacity, after the usual votes had been taken severally. The Hanoverians went beyond what Newcastle could have expected. They dismissed an isolated British action against Prussian ports as being of little avail to Hanover. Only a prior alliance with Russia and Austria might hold Frederick back from attempting to invade. But it was unlikely that Austria would stir without Russia, or Russia without subsidies, and, as the alliance was intended to safeguard Hanover rather than avenge her fall, the subsidies ought to be paid as retainers in time of peace.[30]

Within days of the arrival of the opinion of 23 February 1753, on 9 March, Newcastle instructed Guy Dickens, now minister at Petersburg, to demand Russian military aid in case Frederick attacked Hanover, 'under the Defensive Alliances of 1741 and 1742, and by the King's accession to the treaty of 1746'.[31] In fact, the *casus foederis* was not at all clear: the British accession of 1750 to the Austrian–Russian alliance of 1746 specified in its appendant declarations that Russia (and Austria) had to come to the rescue of Hanover, if she was attacked because of the personal union with Britain, and 'in resentment of' the British accession. Moreover, no attack had as yet materialized. Perhaps because of these flaws, and certainly under the impact of the Hanoverian memorandum, Newcastle made a leap forward. If the tsaritsa complied with the request to mobilize Russian troops along her western frontier in order to relieve Prussian pressure on Hanover, not only would Britain reimburse her for her expenses; also, 'if the troubles should be soon and happily ended, then, and in that case, some part of that subsidy may be continued ...'. But Bestuzhev was not disposed to haggle over interpretation. He wanted to entangle Britain against Frederick; he also wanted subsidies. Britain—in contrast to France—had never willingly provided subsidies in time of peace. Pelham, with a vivid memory of the King of the Romans delusion, was more unwilling than most to tread this path. In any case, by the time Bestuzhev's reply reached London, the Hanoverian invasion scare was over.

There is evidence that in September 1753 Newcastle asked the German Chancery in London to submit a case that Frederick constituted a threat to Britain, and hence that it was a British interest to check his aggressive intent. The resulting memorandum—if indeed it resulted from this request—is in French, dated 24 September 1753, without address or signature, but written in the unmistakable hand of *Geheimer Kabinettsekretär* Johann Friedrich Mejer, assistant to the younger Münchhausen. It repeats the essential arguments of the opinion of 23 February, though with much greater attention paid to British susceptibilities. It repeated that Frederick's basic motivation was 'the desire of conquests at the expense of public tranquillity' but went on to state that he was the ally of France, the country bent on commercial expansion to the detriment of Britain. Furthermore, in order to embarrass Britain, Frederick welcomed Jacobites to his dominions—the Earl Marischal Keith and, apparently, Prince Charles Edward himself. Frederick had broken the solemn agreements respecting the Silesian loan, and had undermined the King of the Romans project. Though the sentiments of France might be peacefully inclined, Frederick would not rest until he had enticed her into a war which could not fail to become general, 'if his back is free and he has nothing to fear for himself'. Therefore it ought to be clear that for the sake of her own interests, and not those of Hanover, Britain ought to take measures, however costly, to make Frederick's aggressive policy too risky for him to pursue. As to Hanover, there were no territorial disputes between her and Prussia, with the exception of East Friesland, which was to come for adjudication before the Aulic Council. For all his ill will Frederick would not be able to stir France to bellicose action over the issue of East Friesland and hence, if Frederick did molest Hanover, he would do so only because of Britain.[32]

The memo is marked by its circumspection. It points to an armed defensive alliance against Frederick without ever spelling out the idea in so many words. (The operative key clause is obviously 'if his back is free'.) The implication that Hanover should not suffer for a quarrel not of her own making is clear, however. But the argument that she has nothing to fear from Frederick on her own account is strained and unconvincing.

If the content of the memorandum seems tailor-made for Pelham, its style and editing are awkward and repetitious—remarkably like Newcastle's missives. We have seen that Newcastle took an interest in the safety of Hanover which he was at pains to keep from the knowledge, it appears, even of his brother. It is conceivable that Newcastle not merely asked the younger Münchhausen for the memorandum and suggested its general sense, but that he dictated it in detail. Philip Adolph—intelligent, loyal, predisposed to humour Newcastle in a tactical matter—may have taken the dictation and let his secretary write it out.

Newcastle's authorship of the memorandum is no more than an intriguing possibility. However, there is no reasonable doubt that he used its arguments in the Cabinet Council, as he had used those of the Hanoverian ministers' opinion of 23 February. Again the sequence of events is striking. On 2 October Newcastle formally conceded to Bestuzhev the principle of peacetime subsidies as part of a new treaty, though the offer was far smaller than Bestuzhev had demanded.[33]

It is difficult to pontificate on the Hanoverian share in these British 'quantum leaps'. Undoubtedly, by 1753, with the final breakdown of the King of the Romans project, Newcastle was ready for a new departure. *Post hoc* is not always *propter hoc*. Still, a case can easily be made out that here it is so; that it was the Hanoverian ministers' persuasion, from Hanover and in London, which pushed the British ministers twice over major hurdles on the road that led to the Convention of Petersburg and thus—however circuitously—to the Seven Years War. What comes out clearly is the intimate cooperation between Newcastle and the chief Hanoverian ministers, the faith Newcastle had in Münchhausen's integrity and political wisdom and, last not least, Newcastle's genuine belief that Hanover should not suffer from British quarrels with Prussia, among others. To this extent 'Hanoverian influence' is proven. Undoubtedly Newcastle also yielded to the fears and wishes of the king more readily than did Walpole and Pitt. Undoubtedly, too, he did so less than has popularly been assumed. Yet this imponderable does not invalidate his political reasoning in this matter; nor, one may add, does it besmirch his political honour.

Two more years were to pass before the British ministry adopted formulae that satisfied the tsaritsa and her advisers. There are many reasons for the delay. Business with Elisabeth Petrovna was always time-consuming and nerve-racking. Dickens, no forceful personality at the best of times, was by now elderly and an invalid. The Treasury had not become generous even after the First Lord had agreed in principle to give taxpayers' money for a Russian subsidy in peace time. The political danger of assuming burdens for the sake of Hanover was there, and indeed it materialized when agreement with Russia was reached.

In the course of 1754 two developments made progress easier. In March Pelham died. Not merely did Newcastle become his successor as 'Prime Minister', but he secured two secretaries of state who accepted his direction without questioning—the Earl of Holdernesse (North) and Sir Thomas Robinson (South). And the rapidly deteriorating situation in North America had by the end of that year made another war with France a near certainty. A conclusion with Russia grew more urgent, and its costs less of a domestic risk. Obviously, Hanover might have been left to the mercy of France and her ally, Prussia, possibly to be indemnified after the war. Pitt thought so;[34] Newcastle was not the man to act thus.

Münchhausen did his best during these two years to keep Newcastle on his toes.[35] When the negotiations recommenced in the summer of 1755, some of the credit ought to go to him, even if in the circumstances of the time his part was no longer a major factor in the finalizing of the treaty.

In June 1755 Sir Charles Hanbury Williams, Newcastle's confidant and by now a senior diplomat with experience at Dresden–Warsaw, Berlin and Vienna, arrived at Petersburg to supersede Dickens. His instructions from Holdernesse gave him new latitude for financial concessions.[36] On 9 August 1755 Williams signed with Bestuzhev and Vice-chancellor Count Vorontsov the treaty which has since been known as the Convention of Petersburg; an amended version was signed on 30 September. There were hitches before the tsaritsa ratified the convention on 21 February 1756. But by the end of 1755 the convention seemed secure—in time to assist in developments unforeseen by its Western promoters.

The convention was in form a renewal for four years of the 'Treaty of Defensive Alliance' of 1742. The operative clauses of the 1755 version stipulated that a Russian army of 55,000 men should henceforth be assembled in Livonia in readiness to march as soon as Britain or her allies, or the king's German dominions, were attacked. 'Forty or fifty galleys' were to stand by to transport this force 'in order to make a descent'. In return Britain agreed to pay Russia £100,000 p.a., until the actual 'requisition' of the troops into British service and pay under the *casus foederis*.[37]

At the time when Williams set out with his amended instructions, Newcastle and

Münchhausen misread the future on two major counts. Firstly, they assumed that the Russian policy-makers were entirely motivated by cupidity. But the tsaritsa's enmity towards Frederick, at any rate, played a part in her motivations that was no weaker than her desire for British subsidies. She did not intend Frederick to remain overawed for the sake of his own safety. Secondly, by the time the convention was signed in Petersburg it had dawned on both Newcastle and Münchhausen that a fundamental realignment with Prussia was possible, and by the time the convention was ratified, that realignment was a fact.

* * *

Before we consider Hanover's part in the 'Reversal of Alliances', it is necessary to turn our attention elsewhere.

The British–Russian treaty negotiations had not taken place in a diplomatic vacuum. Indeed, the Hanoverian undercurrent in British policy formulation was much strengthened in 1755 by George II's prolonged stay in the electorate from May to September that year. The king, naturally enough, had insisted on the journey in the face of anguished expostulations from Newcastle. If, in those dangerous times, electoral concerns were regarded as an irritating irrelevance by the British ministers, they were of a desperate interest to the king, who had nightmares of French armies on the Weser rather than on the Ohio. It probably eased Newcastle's discomfiture that Holdernesse as secretary for the Northern Department went with the king. Holdernesse was as safe a man as he could have hoped for.

A first step to protect Hanover from the mounting storm was a British subsidy treaty with Hesse-Cassel, where the regent, Prince William, had become landgrave on the death of his childless brother, the King of Sweden, in 1751. Hanover was not officially a party to the treaty. The treaty was negotiated on the king's behalf by Holdernesse, who signed alone. However, among the Hanoverian ministers at least the brothers Münchhausen were in the picture and apparently assisted in smoothing out difficulties. After the signing a Hanoverian army official worked with Holdernesse over the details of implementation.[38] Hanoverian liaison is the less remarkable since—beyond the common interest and a tradition of cooperation—personal ties at the top were particularly close; one of the Hessian signatories, Dietrich Diede zum Füstenstein, was a relation of *Geheimer Rat* Diede. The gist of the treaty was that the landgrave should hold 8,000 of his troops in readiness for service under the King of Great Britain over four years, the number to be increased to 12,000 on request. The landgrave's monetary reward was finely graded, but the basic retainer was about £36,000 p.a., as from signature. The troops were not to be employed 'on board the fleet or beyond the sea ... excepting always for the defence of Great Britain and Ireland'. It was a significant limitation, considering British needs at the time, and the use made of Hessian troops one generation later. The terms were stiff: the Hessians had succeeded in making their partners believe that they were contending against a pre-emptive bid from Frederick.[39] The importance of the treaty to George II and Newcastle is shown by Newcastle's decision to sanction the advance of the first instalment of 99,000 thaler ('crowns') out of the Civil List. It was a step of debatable constitutional propriety, and politically risky. Henry Legge, the Chancellor of the Exchequer, strenuously opposed it. But Parliament was not in session, and time was precious.[40]

Gratifying as the treaty was to the king and his Hanoverian ministers, it precipitated another anti-Hanoverian campaign in England. Though lively, it was less sweeping and virulent than that of the early 1740s. It is difficult to explain phenomena like these entirely in rational terms, but new life was breathed into the old grievance that the king's foreign dominions were saddling England with expenditure in blood, money and political disadvantages. On the other hand, war with France loomed larger in 1755 than in 1742, and the obligation to do something for Hanover had more meaning to more of the public. Factional passions ran not quite so high: for better or worse Newcastle was no Walpole or Carteret. And last but not least, Pitt, though still removed from the centre of power and disdainful of the men who feebly pretended to guide the nation, did not show that terrible verve which his earlier banishment had given him. Still, the malaise affected circles not normally hostile to traditional Whig politics. In the prevailing situation the City came to view concern for Hanover as damaging to British interests on the seas and overseas.[41] The crop of anti-Hanoverian pamphlets was considerable. Among the more serious, pride of place goes to *Deliberate Thoughts on ... Our Late Treaties ... in Regard to Hanover*, published in 1756 but written in late summer 1755.[42] The author was Samuel Martin, Legge's secretary at the Treasury. The pamphlet entirely lacks cant. It is deferential to Newcastle, and it respects the king's love for the land of his birth. It also recognizes that Hanover is in mortal danger from France 'and her confederates', through British quarrels and no fault of her own. It admits her claim on British protection. Nonetheless, coming to Hanover's aid would not merely harm Britain—it would bankrupt her. Hanover, therefore, ought to be left to her fate.

At the extreme end of invective stand the six letters Dr John Shebbeare addressed 'to the People of England' between 1755 and 1757.[43] For audacious wit they seek their equal in that audacious and witty century. The motto alone of the *Sixth Letter*, a near-blasphemous quotation from the Book of Revelation, is a stroke of genius; if it does not merit, it at least explains, the pillory and prison to which Shebbeare was subsequently sentenced: 'And I looked, and behold a pale horse: and the name that sat on him was Death, and Hell followed with him.' The pale horse, as everybody knew, was the emblem of Hanover, and the sovereign was presumably cast as Death, or Hell.

Parliament too was outspoken when the session opened, but not quite as harassing as it had been twelve and thirteen years before. Newcastle, unlike Carteret then, had calculated the voting chances with his usual acumen. Henry Fox, just appointed secretary of state for the Southern Department in place of the ineffectual Robinson, skilfully steered the Hessian and Russian treaties through the Commons when they came up for debate on 10 December 1755. Pitt's anti-Hanoverian rhetoric on this occasion reads far beneath his inflammatory best, though we may be influenced by our knowledge of the measures he himself was to take in the near future. The financial clauses, amounting to a reimbursement of the Civil List for the advances made to Hesse-Cassel, were approved on 15 December with a resounding majority of 259 against 72. In the House of Lords the opposition to the treaties was led by Lord Temple, Pitt's brother-in-law. Apart from Newcastle the chief supporter was Granville, since 1751 Lord President of the Council, and essentially in agreement with Newcastle's policies. Chesterfield managed to unite his approbation of the Russian treaty—for which he himself had worked when secretary of state—with his penchant for Frederick by claiming that the treaty was to the latter's advantage. As to the Hessian treaty, Chesterfield approved of the principle but believed with reason that the landgrave had got too much. The Lords too confirmed the treaties by rejecting an adverse motion by a large majority.[44]

Kaunitz, since May 1753 in charge of Austrian foreign affairs, had actively encouraged Newcastle in the treaty-making process with Russia and Hesse-Cassel. His interest in a military link-up between Britain as paymaster and Russia, Austria's chief partner against Frederick, was obvious. Hessian auxiliaries, in British service, he felt, might also take some of the weight off British demands on Austria.

Despite these sanguine views, the first half of 1755 was to see the doom of the Old System, moribund as it had been for years. The reasons run deep. British treatment of Austria had been maladroit since 1741—at once hectoring, patronizing and uneven. With the improving atmosphere between Vienna and Versailles, the understanding Austria had reached with the tsaritsa and Bestuzhev, and Haugwitz's economic reforms, Maria Theresa and Kaunitz were able to believe that the British alliance was expendable. The occasion for the open break came with British demands for both a more effective Austrian presence in the Low Countries, *and* defensive arrangements for Hanover in time of need. Austria, obviously, was as little ready to tie her resources to the one objective as to the other. In particular her policy-makers resented that George II made demands on behalf of Hanover while he was not prepared to reciprocate as elector. It is one of Kaunitz's greatest successes as a master of diplomatic management that he left the onus for the failure on the shoulders of Britain. Keith in Vienna remained optimistic, plainly a victim of Kaunitz's persuasiveness. At Whitehall and Herrenhausen, where wider perspectives prevailed, it was clear by July 1755 that Britain could not count on Austria against France.[45]

Münchhausen was deeply disturbed. He had done his best to prevent the breach.[46] Though Holdernesse kept him informed of events he decided—just before the British broke off negotiations with Austria—on a final attempt. It was a plan for mutual defence against France and Prussia on a grand scale, embracing Hanover, Saxony and Austria, and it involved three armies. 'Some' British financial aid to Hanover was a prerequisite. Münchhausen wrote to Newcastle—an unusual step at that time, since Newcastle was no longer secretary of state. Evidently Münchhausen saw himself as virtually one prime minister addressing another. Also, the need was supreme: His Majesty's *electoral* lands could not 'be abandoned to the enemies of *England*'—a clear hint of British responsibility. In his letter Münchhausen indicated that the plan had originated with Holdernesse, who also wrote to Newcastle in greater detail by the same messengers; the internal evidence as well as Holdernesse's cautious phrasing leave no doubt that the idea was Münchhausen's. The king gave his approval. It was a forlorn hope. Austria was no longer interested in 'defence' against Frederick, if she had ever been so since 1746. But the matter never advanced that far. Newcastle refused. The vast expenses for defence which Britain already shouldered did not permit her 'to sustain the burden of a Continental war' as well—which was a fair interpretation of Münchhausen's suggestion. Newcastle accepted that 'justice, duty and gratitude' compelled Britain to act for the safety of Hanover; indeed, he wrote in this sense to Holdernesse too. In discharge of this obligation, he offered British money to raise the Hanoverian army to 30,000—adding to its strength by half—and to take more German troops into the elector's pay. It was one of the rare cases when Newcastle gave Münchhausen a substantive 'No', and he felt the need to quote Hardwicke in support of his stand. Of course, Pitt waiting in the wings must have loomed large in his mind too. From a different level of observation, it is yet again a case where Münchhausen came up against the limits of his influence: he and his colleagues might conceive ideas and initiate processes. Ultimately they could not dictate to forces immeasurably stronger than Hanover.[47]

But by the time Newcastle's letter reached Münchhausen, Münchhausen had opened another vista, of truly historic impact.

* * *

In the last five years of George II's life, Hanover was an ally of Prussia. Put more precisely, her defensive system was based on cooperation—soon to turn into a treaty—between Britain and Prussia.

Despite Chesterfield's belief in the matter, Frederick did not see the Petersburg convention as a boon to himself. His basic attitude towards Hanover remained unfriendly but not actively aggressive. As to Britain, the quarrel over compensation to Prussian merchants and repayment of the Silesian loan was still unresolved. Moreover, Frederick highly valued his alliance with France. As war between France and Britain became probable he showed in his own inimitable way where his sympathies lay. Early in April 1755 he gave the French minister in Berlin, La Touche, the unsolicited advice that once war was declared a French army should invade Hanover: 'this is the surest way to teach that ... a lesson'. La Touche thought proper to omit in his report the epithet which the King of Prussia applied to his uncle. That Frederick was in earnest is shown by the instruction he sent at the same time to his minister at Versailles, Knyphausen, to give advice to the same effect. He believed, as he wrote to Knyphausen, that by turning aggressor France would release him from his obligations to her under the 1741 treaty. Rouillé, the French foreign minister, unobligingly replied that France would appreciate it if her Prussian ally assumed the task himself and on his own. Frederick excused himself by citing his defence commitments against Russia, Austria and Saxony.[48]

Naturally rumours of Prussia and France 'concerting measures of a dangerous tendency' reached George II at Hanover.[49] In the prevailing situation—Britain and France set on a collision course, the Old System as good as shattered—an obvious step was to try to tackle the root of the evil by approaching Frederick himself. Frederick, himself troubled by the implications for Prussia of the impending Anglo-French war, eased the step by hinting at his willingness to meet George II while passing through Hanover on his way to his western dominions.[50]

On 6 July 1755 Philippine Charlotte, Frederick's sister and Duchess of Brunswick-Wolfenbüttel, arrived in Hanover on a visit with her two eldest daughters—'unexpectedly', as Holdernesse wrote to Robinson.[51] Her eldest daughter, it was felt, might do very well as a Princess of Wales—hence the visit. Another reason for interest was that Duke Charles of Brunswick-Wolfenbüttel stood second only to the Landgrave of Hesse-Cassel as a troop jobber, and he would soon have 4,000 men for hire on the expiry of a French–Prussian contract. Münchhausen took charge, while Madame von Münchhausen presented the young ladies informally to George II. While the king played at flirting with the Princess Amalia, Münchhausen sounded out the duchess on her Prussian brother's inclinations. On 11 July he reported to Newcastle that her reply had been 'so positive that I am nearly tempted to make something of it, at least at the present moment' (*si positivement, que je suis presque tenté, d'y faire quelque fonds, au moin dans le moment present*). A fortnight later, on 26 July,

Münchhausen advanced one step further. Frederick might be persuaded to adopt 'an inactivity in favour of' Hanover. The rulers of Brunswick-Wolfenbüttel and Hesse-Cassel—allied by blood, marriage and treaty—might offer their good offices with regard to Frederick, and the king had already approached them on this matter. The results were still to be seen. It was all very cautious.[52]

Newcastle took up Münchhausen's suggestion of 11 July. He supplied the strategic context: 'The King of Prussia fears above all things Russia and the treaty we may sign with her.' Hence 'It might have been possible to obtain a Neutrality …'. Here too the circumspection is remarkable. (By the end of August Kaunitz too had a hunch that 'the two brothers Münchhausen' were interested in an 'Inactivity' rather than a 'Neutrality', probably in contrast to the British ministers.)[53] Newcastle stressed that it was Münchhausen who had given him the idea of an understanding with Frederick, and that he, in turn, now imparted his amplification to no one else, not even to Holdernesse whom Münchhausen might, however, make party to the scheme if he wished.[54] It may be assumed that Newcastle really had discussed the matter with no other person, except Hardwicke, his *alter ego*. Münchhausen promptly admitted Holdernesse into the affair, in a subordinate capacity (see below).

Indeed, at first glance the scheme was attractive. It solved the problem of Hanoverian security at a price of '£100 to £130,000 p.a. only'—Newcastle did not omit this point from his letter. The neutralization of Germany would also conserve British resources for the war at sea and beyond the seas—a national interest much in keeping with public opinion. However, Newcastle, while adjudging Frederick to a nicety, disregarded the implications concerning Russia and France if such an understanding was reached with Prussia. The case of Russia has been stated in the context of the Petersburg convention (see above). As for France, the neutralization of Germany (and the protection of Hanover) would be attained only if Versailles adhered to the unenterprising spirit which had prevailed there of late, or if Prussia and Russia were both willing to make war on France in the defence of Hanover—whatever the letter of their treaty obligations. These were dangerous assumptions to make, and as it turned out they were wrong. Hardwicke indeed had the insight to suspect that a British–Prussian *entente* might hurl France and Russia into just that precipitate action which it was designed to prevent. But, having stated his doubts, Hardwicke acquiesced.[55]

Münchhausen accepted Newcastle's reasoning.[56] From then until the beginning of December 1755 Hanover was again the advance headquarters from which the Continental policy of Britain was conducted, with Münchhausen in charge of operations. The king was reconciled to the idea of an alliance with his nephew, and with his nephew very much an equal; the march of events carried conviction. Also, George II, rapidly aging, was losing his old pugnacity. Holdernesse in this matter was no more than an executive of Münchhausen, just as he was an executive of Newcastle in Whitehall, and he realized it without rancour.[57] The Duke of Brunswick assumed the role of go-between which Münchhausen had assigned to him.

George II left Hanover on 8 September 1755, never to return.

The road to the Convention of Westminster has often been described.[58] Frederick refused to undertake quietening the fears of George II for Hanover until his fear of Russia overrode every other consideration.[59] At the same time the one really cogent reason why he should not have tied himself to Britain—for fear of driving the French into Kaunitz's outstretched arms—does not seem to have occurred to him. When Holdernesse, finally back in London, showed the Prussian chargé d'affaires, Louis

Michell, the text of the Petersburg convention, Frederick at last unequivocally ordered Michell to proceed, on 7 December.

The second Convention of Westminster[60] was signed on 16 January 1756 and ratified without delay. Though its terms in detail were hammered out in London, the Hanoverian ministers were kept in the picture. They concurred in everything, but chose to stress that the treaty which they had done so much to promote was British, and not electoral.[61] It is another example of their doctrine, almost a faith, that to stay out of mischief Hanover had to stay out of European treaties.[62]

The treaty was designed to 'maintain the tranquillity of Germany'. It bound both sides, Britain and Prussia, not to 'attack or invade, either directly or indirectly, the territories of the other'; it bound them to 'exert their utmost efforts to prevent their respective allies' from doing likewise; it also bound them to unite their forces to punish 'any foreign power which should cause troops to enter ... Germany, under any pretext whatsoever'. The treaty also disposed of the outstanding disagreements between Britain and Prussia. The British guarantee of 1745 to Frederick was endorsed on the latter's terms—covering all territories in Prussian possession and thus disposing of George II's claim to East Friesland.[63] All Prussian claims against Britain 'under any pretext whatever'—meaning the Prussian merchants' claims against the Admiralty—were bought off for £20,000. Frederick for his part undertook to pay the remainder of the Silesian debt forthwith. A secret article expressly excluded the Austrian Netherlands from the guarantee of neutrality—on the insistence of Frederick, who hoped thereby to please France.[64] It was also agreed, though not stated in the text, to restore diplomatic relations between the two countries to ministerial level.[65] Though the treaty was in the name of George II as king *and* elector, it was not signed by any Hanoverian representative. George II, like his Hanoverian ministers, explicitly considered it as between Britain and Prussia only.[66]

The British public took well to the treaty. It laid to rest a financial grievance and it appeared to defuse a dangerous situation in the unpopular Continental sector. Their common Protestant faith played a role, though the *motif* of Frederick the Protestant hero did not reach its peak until the events of 1757 gave it a superficial credibility.[67] Parliament did not deal with the treaty until May, when its text was put before it. The Commons on 11 May voted the £20,000 compensation readily enough. It seems that only Pitt opposed 'the idea of defending Hanover by subsidies'—which was hardly an apposite description of the Westminster convention.[68] But Pitt's political position at this juncture must be seen as a whole: he was struggling at a time of national peril to be accepted into the inner councils of an administration from which he had been dismissed a few months earlier; he had to guard his public image as a dauntless defender of 'British' over 'German' interests, but neither could he insult the king or antagonize the ministry beyond the possibility of instant reconciliation.

The Hanover ministers were jubilant. Even Münchhausen was optimistic for once that Frederick had acted in good faith. The ministers shared George II's view that it was not only the Prussian danger that had been averted, but that France as well would be deterred from aggression in Germany. At the same time they were anxious to maintain the pretence that they themselves had little to do with the Convention; it was a British affair.[69]

One other thought arises in retrospect: had Newcastle realized—what Hardwicke fleetingly suspected—that the Anglo-Prussian treaty would drive France into the arms of Austria and thus make a Continental war all the more probable, might he not have become all the more eager for the convention as causing a major French diversion from the theatre that mattered most to Britain—the seas and the colonies? But Newcastle did not think along such lines. He feared a Continental war as an evil in itself, and in any case he was not mentally equipped to act on grandiose speculations of this sort.

When the tsaritsa became convinced that a neutrality was about to be signed between Britain and Prussia, she made a declaration to Williams that she regarded the Petersburg convention as binding Russia only against Prussia.[70] Apart from the momentous European implications, this meant from the Hanoverian viewpoint that the Westminster convention remained useful only in the case—now unlikely—that France attacked Hanover in concert with Prussia.

On 1 May 1756 the French government, outraged by what it considered Frederick's faithlessness and impudence, gave in at last to Austrian representations and concluded the first, defensive, Treaty of Versailles.[71] The 'Reversal of Alliances' was a fact. It was not a reversal of enmities, however, with Britain still opposed to France, and Austria to Prussia. In any event the former Habsburg–Bourbon rivalry had been in the melting pot ever since the Comte de Luc's mission to Vienna in the last year of Louis XIV.

On 17 May 1756, after Admiral Byng's failure to relieve Minorca, Britain declared war on France. It was the long-expected consummation of two years' undeclared hostilities in North America and the West Indies, and on the high seas—all of which figure prominently in the declaration. Hanover was to be prominent in paying the bill.

* * *

For much of 1756, from the passing of the euphoria engendered by the Westminster convention until the thickening suspicion of Frederick's impending eruption, the rela-tions between Hanover and Britain were determined by the question of the 'German troops'.

When the reports of French invasion plans started to accumulate, the British government at the end of January 1756 officially requested the Dutch authorities to fulfil their obligations under the alliance of 1678, and to despatch to England 6,000 infantry at their expense. The Dutch excuses—no straight refusal—arrived during March.[72] They ought to have taken nobody by surprise. The political and military decay of Holland had been a byword in the courts of Europe since 1748 at the latest.

But an alternative still had to be found. An appeal to the manhood of the British nation was not in the nature of George II, or his then ministers, or the bulk of the Commons—to the disgust of Pitt, genuine if exaggerated for effect. The 8,000 Hessians, just retained under contract, were the solution that naturally presented itself. The response of Parliament was overwhelming; on 23 March 1756 the Commons voted their thanks *nem. con.* [73] Newcastle and Fox immediately decided to bring over at British expense a similar number of Hanoverian troops, actually 9,000—twelve battalions of infantry and five companies of artillery. The gain to the defence of the kingdom was obvious, on paper at least. Also, the tables would be neatly turned on the enemies of the Hanoverian connection.[74] The king was agreeable; Hanover for once seemed reasonably secure, in the wake of the Petersburg and Westminster conventions. Parliament acquiesced, though not quite as enthusiastically as one week before in the case of the Hessians. 'His Majesty's electoral troops' were, after all, more of a political problem than mere mercenaries.[75]

Once the politics had been dealt with, the administration worked unusually fast. By the last third of May the Hessians were in their quarters in Hampshire and Sussex, the Hanoverians in Kent. The passage of the entire Hanoverian contingent from Stade to Chatham, in twenty-one British transports, took six days, proof that physical communications could be good even before the age of steam. The Hessians were commanded by Prince Isenburg, who was to fall at Bergen in 1759, under the command of Prince Ferdinand. The Hanoverians were under the commanding officer of the army, General von Sommerfeldt.[76] They arrived almost to the day of the British declaration of war on France.[77]

Münchhausen and his colleagues raised no objections. It was a prime point of their policy to prove to Britain that they could render vital help. Indeed, Münchhausen's letter to Newcastle and Holdernesse on the eve of embarkation makes pathetic reading in its joyful effusion until one remembers that their correspondence was habitually on fulsome terms.[78] However, as the fear of invasion receded in Britain, the Hanoverian ministers became nervous lest the presence of their troops should cause annoyance to 'the Nation' rather than assuage its needs.[79] That they adjudged the English public correctly is shown by the Maidstone incident, where a Hanoverian private was rashly convicted of stealing two handkerchieves and dealt 300 lashes. His commanding officer, Count Kielmansegge, who tried to have him released, had to leave England.[80]

As war in Europe and, in particular, a Prussian offensive became likely in July 1756, and as information of French plans to invade Hanover multiplied, the Hanoverian ministers schemed to have the German troops returned from England. They did not press the issue with the king directly. The king's right to dispose over the army was unchallengeable and he guarded it jealously, but their urgent and repeated requests for expensive alternative measures rendered necessary, so they explained, by the absence of part of the army, clearly point one way.[81] They gained their point, though less through their own pull than because of general developments.

On 29 August 1756 Frederick invaded Saxony, and Germany was at war. On 9 November 1756 the king informed the Hanoverian ministers of his decision to send the 'German corps' back in readiness for a French invasion.[82] This time six months passed between the order and its full implementation. The Hanoverian troops had to pass a miserable winter, though the king tried to alleviate their hardships. An 'Act to make provision for the quartering of the foreign troops in his Majesty's service, now in this kingdom' on equal terms with British troops was an attempt to ease their situation, and it was passed in the Commons without opposition on 16 December 1755.[83] George II might have been more successful if he had spent some of his private funds to provide the German troops with better billets. But in eighteenth century England more than his parsimony militated against such conduct. (The king's concern for the comfort of his Hanoverian soldiers is shown, *inter alia*, in the interest which he took in their home mail facilities.)[84]

By the middle of May 1757 all the German troops were back on the Weser, in time for the battle of Hastenbeck.

* * *

It is easy to analyse in retrospect the misconceptions of the Hanoverian policy-makers. It is harder to find fault. The fundamental flaw in the position of Hanover was her exposure to every enemy of the King of Great Britain as the apple of his eye, at once cherished and weak. They had probably overrated—out of fear, antipathy, and some slowness to adapt—Frederick's readiness to assault Hanover in any circumstances. Hence their sustained endeavour for a British–Russian alliance, when such an alliance became less of an insurance, and more of an imponderable risk to Hanover, than could have been conceived in 1746. Hence their energetic action in 1755 for a British–Prussian alliance, with insufficient attention paid to what the French government might do in consequence. The fumblings of the British government during much of 1756 left them with no hope of salvation through leadership from that quarter, and they did their utmost to put their country on secure ground. Yet their utmost was feeble, with Europe on the brink of a general war, and they knew it only too well.

Notes

1. Khevenhüller to Münchhausen, Nov 1748 (?), *HHStA*, England, K. 95; Münchhausen to Newcastle, 4 May 1749 (N.S.); Newcastle to Münchhausen, 3 Mar 1749 (O.S.); Cal. Br. 24, England, 1740. Khevenhüller's letter of thanks to Münchhausen is in the name of the empress, 29 Mar 1749, Add. MSS 32816, f. 297.
2. Three articles in English covering this affair are D. B. Horn, 'The Origins of the Proposed Election of a King of the Romans, 1748-50', *EHR*, XLII (1927), 361-370; D. B. Horn, 'The Cabinet Controversy on Subsidy Treaties in Time of Peace', *EHR*, XLV (1930), 463-466; R. Browning 'The Duke of Newcastle and the Imperial Election Plan, 1749-1754', *J. of British Studies*, VII (1967–68), 28–47. Mediger, 439-443, complements their findings on the Hanoverian side.
3. Browning, Reed, *The Duke of Newcastle*, New Haven, 1975, 34, suggests that the idea may have originated with the Hanoverian ministry, since a letter they sent to the younger Münchhausen in April 1749, translated and passed on to Newcastle, contains the expression 'la future élection'. But the context makes it probable that the reference is to the election of the Duke of Cumberland as coadjutor and ultimately successor of the Archbishop of Cologne as Bishop of Osnabrück (Add. MSS, 32816, f. 312). See also the *acta* of Baron Vorster, Austrian minister at Hanover, for 13 Aug 1750, *HHStA*, Staatskanzlei. Hannover, Fasz. 27. 'Poet, wit and diplomatist' is the sub-title of Williams's biography by the Earl of Ilchester and Mrs Langford-Brooke, London, 1928.
4. For letters of acknowledgment from the Emperor and Maria Theresa to George II, the 'originator' of 'the whole affair', dated 9 Oct 1750, see Cal. Br. 24, Oesterreich, 4493. The letters flow over with expressions of gratitude and are empty of political content.
5. Newcastle to Keith, 21 July 1750, Add. MSS 32722, f. 239.
6. *Geheime Räte* to Newcastle, 29 Jan 1751; Steinberg to Newcastle, 1 Feb 1751; Newcastle to Münchhausen, 1 Feb 1751; Add. MSS 32826, ff. 102-103, 119-120, 206-207.
7. Cal. Br. 24, Oesterreich, 4497; Cal. Br. 24, England, 1741; Hann. 92, XLV, Nr. 13, vol. I, *passim*.
8. The finances of Hanover in the eighteenth century still await the labours of an historian with the qualifications of a chartered accountant and a taste for detective work; George II was as secretive a man of business as he was grasping. The Hanoverian War Chancery accounts (Hann. 46, 78-79, 81c) give only a partial picture. For intriguing glimpses into the technique of remittances from England to Hanover, see Hann. 92, XXIX, II, 1, vol. II. Lehzen, *Hannovers Staatshaushalt*, Hanover, 1853-55, II, 27-28, states that the assets of the *Schatulle* in 1756 amounted to 9,447,900 ⅔ thaler—not quite £2 million. By the time of George II's death during the Seven Years War this treasure was depleted. (See below, pp. 129).
9. For the text of the treaty, see Hann. 10, Köln, Nr. 2.

10. Cal. Br. 24, England, 1741; also Browning, *op. cit.*, 165.
11. Vorster to Court Chancellor Count Ulfeld, 24 July 1751 (*HHStA*, Staatskanzlei Hannover, Fasz. 6), representative of several.
12. In a letter to Prince Louis of Brunswick, a field-marshal in the Dutch service and elder brother of Prince Ferdinand, 19 Nov 1750, Hann. 91, Münchhausen I, Nr. 20. Prince Louis was a particular confidant of Münchhausen.
13. Vorster to Ulfeld, 18 Sept 1751, *HHStA*, Staatskanzlei Hannover, Fasz. 6.
14. Add. MSS 32821, ff. 281-288, 297, 476-477.
15. For an edited collection of Prussian publications concerning her claims to East Friesland, see *Preussische Staatsschriften, 1740-1745*, 363-432.
16. The quotation appears in a Prussian pamphlet published as early as 1745 (*Preussische Staatsschriften, 1740-1745*, 368). It concerns a legal point and obviously does not deny Hanoverian rights as such; but its implication is clear. As an aside it is worth mentioning that another claimant to East Friesland was Countess Kaunitz-Rittberg, the mother of the Austrian statesman. While it is absurd to suppose that Kaunitz's attitude to Frederick was determined by this claim, it cannot have sweetened his feelings either.
17. *Pol. Corr.*, IX, 200, 227. For Frederick's attitude in the affair, see *Pol. Corr.* IX, 225-228, 334-338. The standard treatment is still Sir Ernest Satow, *The Silesian Loan and Frederick the Great*, Oxford, 1915.
18. Newcastle, at Hanover, to Holdernesse, 21 Sept 1752, S.P., Regencies, 43/49.
19. For quotations and pertinent observations, see Mediger, 447-450; the relevant files were destroyed in World War II.
20. George II and P. A. von Münchhausen to *Geheime Räte*, 16, 39 Jan 1753, Hann. 92, LXXV, 16[a].
21. *Geheime Räte*, to George II, 6 Feb 1753, *ibid.*
22. George II to *Geheime Räte*, 20 Feb, 13 Mar 1753, *ibid.* Lifelong slavery as a description of Prussian army service had already been used by Maria Theresa in 1744 (Arneth, II, 442).
23. See R. Koser, 'Preussen und Russland im Jahrzehnt vor dem siebenjährigen Kriege', *Preussische Jahrbücher*, XLVII (1881), 473-4.
24. *Pol. Corr.* IX, 358-359, 376, 382, 450; George II to *Geheime Räte*, 27 Mar 1753, Hann. 92, LXXV, No. 16[a].
25. For the text of the treaty, see Martens, I, *Autriche*, 145-178.
26. Maria Theresa to Zöhrern, 31 Jan 1749, *HHStA*, England, K. 97.
27. For the memorandum of March 1749 (and Kaunitz's haughty reaffirmation of 8 May), see *HHStA*, Vorträge, K. 62. Kaunitz's own summing up is given in Arneth, *op. cit.*, IV, 535-536.
28. For the text of the Accession treaty and its appendant declarations, see Pribram, II, 53-57. For an attempt as late as 1753 to induce George II to accept Separate Article No. 4 'as Elector', see the draft of a treaty in R. Khevenhüller-Metsch and H. Schlitter (eds.), *Tagebuch des Fürsten Johann Khevenhüller-Metsch*, Vienna, Leipzig, 1908-1925, V, 358-360 (note 124). For the draft of a Quintuple Defence Treaty to include George II as both king and elector, Austria, Russia and Saxony-Poland, also of 1753, see *HHStA*, Vorträge, K. 72, and Pribram, II, 70-74. The originator of both concepts is Bartenstein, whose voice in foreign affairs was stilled before the year was out. It seems that neither of the concepts was brought to British or Hanoverian knowledge.
29. Mediger, 450; the relevant Hanoverian files were destroyed in World War II. For the measures already ordered by the secretaries of state—representations to the major powers, including France, regarding the risk inherent in Frederick's stoppage of the Silesian loan repayments—see Newcastle to Yorke, 13 Feb 1753, S.P., Foreign, 84/462; Newcastle to Keith, 13 Feb 1753, *ibid.*, 80/191; Newcastle to Dickens, 13 Feb (referred to in letter of 9 Mar) 1753, *ibid.*, 91/57.
30. Mediger, 452-453. The originals were destroyed in the Second World War.
31. S.P., Foreign, 91/57.

32. Hann. 92, LXXV, 16[a].
33. Newcastle to Dickens, S.P., Foreign, 91/57. This phase of British–Russian negotiations is treated in detail by Mediger, 453 *et seq.*, with stress on the Russian angle.
34. Hardwicke to Newcastle, 9 Aug 1755, Yorke, *Hardwicke*, II, 231-232.
35. E.g. Münchhausen to Newcastle, 7 Aug 1753, Add. MSS 32846, f. 35; 9 Aug 1754, Add. MSS 32850, f. 63; Münchhausen to his brother, 28 Jan 1755, Hann. 92, LXXV, Nr. 16[b]. In this letter Münchhausen also advocates alliances to be concluded by the king 'as elector'. The context makes it clear that he had in mind agreements with Austria and Imperial *Stände* only.
36. Holdernesse to Williams, 11 Apr 1755, S.P., Foreign, 91/60.
37. For the text of the convention, see Martens, *Angleterre*, 184, 191-200.
38. For the text of the treaty, see Jenkinson, III, 47-53. For the making of the treaty, *Hessisches Staatsarchiv Marburg*, 4 f, England, 258.
39. Holdernesse to Robinson, 21 May 1755, S.P., Regencies, 43/53. The files at Marburg (note 38, above) give a fascinating and, to us, unedifying insight into the landgrave's business skill.
40. Meeting of the Lords Justices, 22 July 1755, S.P., Regencies, 43/125; Russell (ed.), *Correspondence ... Bedford*, II, 166; Browning, *Newcastle*, 220, 222. As to the constitutional aspect Newcastle must have remembered the attack by Lyttelton and Pitt in the Commons in 1744, on a payment of £40,000 made to the Austrian commander in the Low Countries without previous parliamentary sanction. Their motion was defeated, but their point went home. (*P.H.*, XIII, 698-702.)
41. Newcastle to Holdernesse, 11 July 1755, transmitting a confidential account of Sir John Barnard's views which Newcastle regards as representative of 'opinion at large', Add. MSS 32857, ff. 42-46. City 'opinion at large', of which Barnard was indeed representative in the reign of George II, was often suspicious of ministerial policies, without being thereby Tory in the conventional sense. See Lucy Sutherland, 'The City of London in Eighteenth-Century Politics', in Aubrey Newman (ed.), *Lucy Sutherland: Politics and Finance in the Eighteenth Century*, London, 1984, 41-66.
42. London, 1756. See also Add. MSS 41355.
43. *A Letter* [*Second*, etc., up to *Sixth*] *to the People of England* ... , J. Scott, London, 1755. (*Second, Third Letter*, Scott, 1756; *Fourth Letter*, M. Collier, 1756; *Fifth, Sixth Letter*, J. Morgan, 1757; all published in London.)
44. *J.H.C.*, XXVII, 399; *P.H.*, XV, 616-664.
45. For the Austrian 'ultimatum' to Britain as resolved at the State Conference of 15 June 1755, and its underlying reflections, see *HHStA*, Vorträge, K. 77, under 17 June. 'Ultimatum' is Kaunitz's expression; it refers to the unyielding tenor of the Austrian message, not to a time limit. For the subsequent British decision to put an end to the negotiations, in harshest terms, see Holdernesse to Keith, Hanover, 6 Aug 1755, S.P., Foreign, 80/196. When Kaunitz was informed by Keith he 'seemed ... mortified [and] turned the discourse immediately' (Keith to Holdernesse, 27 Aug 1755, *ibid.*). Actually Kaunitz was relieved that Austria was thus excused from taking part in the looming war between Britain and France (Kaunitz to Colloredo at Hanover, 27 Aug 1755, *HHStA*, England, K. 197). Keith's reports between April and August 1755 bear witness to his inadequacy when facing Kaunitz. Arneth (*op. cit.*. IV, 382-387) denies that Kaunitz intended to wreck what was left of the alliance with Britain. But there can be no doubt that Kaunitz deliberately put the alliance under an all but intolerable strain.
46. E.g. his appeal to Count J. J. Khevenhüller of 14 April 1755 in which he confesses to his impotence to avert the break, *HHStA*, Staatskanzlei Hannover, Fasz. 27.
47. Holdernesse to Newcastle, 6 July 1755, Add. MSS 32856, ff. 539-541; Münchhausen to Newcastle, 4 July 1755, *ibid.*, ff. 470-472; Newcastle to Holdernesse, 18, 25 July 1755, Add. MSS 32857, ff. 159-188, 354-363; Newcastle to Münchhausen, 18 July 1755, *ibid.*, ff. 198-203; Hann. 91, Münchhausen I, Nr. 22; also Mediger, 501-503; Ward, *op. cit.*, 173-174.

48. La Touche's report of 5 April 1755, quoted in Koser, *König Friedrich der Grosse*, I, 572-573; Frederick to Knyphausen, 5 Apr, 6 May 1755; Knyphausen to Frederick, 25 April 1755 (*Pol. Corr.*, XI, 105-106, 143-145).
49. Münchhausen to Khevenhüller, 10 Mar, 14 Apr 1755, *HHStA*, England, K. 107, Staatskanzlei Hannover, Fasz. 27; Holdernesse to Robinson, 18 May 1755, S.P., Regencies, 43/53.
50. On this, see also Patrick F. Doran, *Andrew Mitchell and Anglo-Prussian Diplomatic Relations During the Seven Years War*, New York, London, 1986; 22-23; also n.59 below.
51. 9 July 1755, S.P., Regencies, 43/55. The visit was not unexpected, of course, but it was genuinely conceived as a *Brautschau*, a match-making inspection. For illuminating details of the visit see Anna Wendland, 'Eine Brautschau in Herrenhausen', *Hannoversche Geschichtsblätter*, Neue Folge, IV, 3, 1937. Though the capital of the duchy had just been transferred to the town of Brunswick, the state continued to be called for some time Brunswick-Wolfenbüttel.
52. Hann. 91, Münchhausen I, Nr. 22. The letter of 26 July is signed by both Münchhausen and Steinberg, but Münchhausen's authorship is unmistakable. Münchhausen seems to have cogitated turning towards Frederick for some days prior to the arrival of the duchess at Herrenhausen.
53. Kaunitz to Colloredo, 27 Aug 1755, *HHStA*, England, K. 107, replying to: Colloredo to Maria Theresa, 6 Aug 1755, *ibid.*, K. 106.
54. 25 July 1755, Add. MSS 32857, ff. 348-353; Hann. 91, Münchhausen I, Nr. 22. By that time the idea of an accommodation with Frederick, chiefly for the security of Hanover, had already occurred to Newcastle, but until Münchhausen's initiative he still saw it in the context of the Old System—as he had done during the Legge mission of 1748 (see pp. 72-73 above).
55. Hardwicke to Newcastle, 28 July 1755, Add. MSS 32857, ff. 397-398; 9 Aug 1755, Add. MSS 32858, f. 74.
56. Münchhausen to Newcastle, 2 Aug 1755, Hann. 91, *ibid.*
57. E.g. 'I am persuaded our friends the Münchhausens [Philip was with the king in Hanover] will not keep it [the progress of the negotiations] secret from me ... ' (Holdernesse to Newcastle, 30 July 1755, Add. MSS 32857, f. 452.) As late as mid-August Holdernesse told the Austrian envoy Count Colloredo 'on his honour' that Britain had no dealings with Frederick regarding a 'concert', and would have none. The Hanoverian ministers might indeed be interested, and follow up an aside from Frederick's sister, the Duchess of Brunswick. But even if they tried to play a lone hand, the British ministry would restrain them. At any rate, he, Holdernesse, knew nothing of Hanoverian attempts in this direction—and surely the king would have kept him informed! Colloredo believed him. (Colloredo to Maria Theresa, 17 Aug 1755, *HHStA*, England, K. 106.) Holdernesse was of course equivocating, to put it mildly. He had just returned from Brunswick, where he had gone, not on the royal match business as Colloredo believed, but with Münchhausen's briefing to the duke, for Frederick. But the tenor of Hodernesse's effusion to Colloredo—and Colloredo's trustfulness—indicate a man who was playing second fiddle without resentment.
58. Waddington, *Louis XV et le renversement des alliances*, Paris, 1896, is still fundamental. Its modern complement is Braubach, *Versailles und Wien von Ludwig XIV bis Kaunitz*, Bonn, 1952. Koser, *König Friedrich der Grosse*, I, 578-583, gives a concise correlation of the Russian–British and the Prussian–British negotiations, from Frederick's angle. The Hanoverian role is lightly sketched by Ward, *op. cit.*, 176-179, and detailed in Mediger, 503-509, 564-572. Herbert Kaplan, *Russia and the Outbreak of the Seven Years War*, Berkeley and Los Angeles, 1968, is lucid and informative, though the author underemphasizes the part of the Hanoverian ministers. Frederick himself later wrote, though with little emphasis, that it was the Petersburg convention which made him conclude a treaty with Britain. (*Histoire de la guerre de sept ans, Oeuvres,* IV, 36.)

59. *Pol. Corr.*, XI, 418-420. I do not think my judgment is invalidated by the curious *pas de deux* of June 1755 between Frederick and George II concerning their possible meeting at Hanover. It came to nothing, because neither of the two was really interested in meeting.
60. Properly 'of Whitehall', as the convention was indeed referred to by the Hanoverian ministers for some time to come.
61. *Geheime Räte* to George II, 30 Dec 1755, Hann. 92, LXXII, Nr. 3.) Diede had his doubts; as usual, his dissent was on legal rather than political grounds.
62. For the text of the 1756 Convention of Westminster, see Jenkinson, III, 55-60.
63. Cf. *Pol. Corr.*, V, 183, 207, 215.
64. The Austrian Netherlands were part of the Empire, but not of 'Germany' in common parlance.
65. *Pol. Corr.*, XII, 4, 10-11.
66. George II to George Friedrich von Steinberg at Vienna, 18 May 1756, Hann. 92, LXXII, Nr. 3.
67. See Schlenke, *op. cit.*, 225-226; also by the same author, 'England blickt nach Europa: Das konfessionelle Argument in der englischen Politik um die Mitte des 18. Jahrhunderts', *Aspekte der deutsch-britischen Beziehungen im Laufe der Jahrhunderte*, London, 1978, 24-25.
68. *J.H.C.*, XXVII, 602-608; *P.H.*, XV, 704.
69. Münchhausen to Newcastle, 30 Dec 1755, Add. MSS 32861, ff. 498-501 (two letters); George II to *Geheime Räte*, 16 Jan 1756; *Geheime Räte* to George II, 23 Jan 1756, Hann. 92, LXXII, Nr. 3; Waddington, *op. cit.*, 233.
70. Williams to Holdernesse, 8 Feb 1756, S.P., Foreign, 91/62; also Kaplan, *op. cit.*, 41-45.
71. For the text, see Wenck, III, 139-147.
72. Holdernesse to Yorke, 30 Jan 1756, S.P., Foreign, 84/472; Yorke to Holdernesse, 16, 19, 23 Mar 1756, S.P., Foreign, 84/473. For the text of the 1678 treaty, see Jenkinson, I, 213-214.
73. *J.H.C.*, XXVII, 539-540.
74. 'Hanover treaties and Hanover troops are popular throughout every country,' Thomas Potter to Pitt, 4 June 1756, W. S. Taylor, H. J. Pringle (eds.), *Correspondence of William Pitt, Earl of Chatham*, London, vol. I, 1838, 161.
75. *J.H.L.*, XXVIII, 547-548; 552; *P.H.*, 702-703. According to the latter source, a hostile motion was defeated by 259 against 92.
76. Sichart, *op. cit.*, III, pt. 1, 229-232, gives a wealth of detail. See also Hassell, *Die schlesischen Kriege und das Kurfürstenthum Hannover*, Hanover, 1879, 163-164.
77. See also Savory, 'Jeffery Amherst conducts the Hessians to England', *J. of the Society for Army Historical Research*, XLIX (1971), 152-181.
78. Münchhausen to Newcastle, 6 Apr 1756, Add. MSS 32864, f. 159; to Holdernesse, same date, S.P., 100/17.
79. The files of the German Chancery contain a particularly poignant example. The British agent responsible for the embarkation of the troops at Stade was charged with grave dereliction of duty. The younger Münchhausen asked the indulgence of his colleagues at the 'Government' at Stade (i.e. Bremen-Verden) not to proceed with the complaints: everything had to be done to prevent 'the growth of aversion, let alone hatred [*abgeneigt oder gar gehässig zu werden*]' against the Hanoverian corps in England. (P. A. von Münchhausen to Government of Stade, 4 June 1756, Hann. 92, LXXII, Nr. 5.)
80. For the incident, see H. Walpole, *Memoires of the Last Ten Years of George II*, London, 1822, II, 85. Kielmansegge was related by marriage to the Countess of Darlington (d. 1725), the half-sister of George I. It is another sidelight on the embarrassments the first Hanoverian kings might have to cope with. See also *The Gentleman's Magazine*, 1756, 448, 475; *The London Magazine*, 1756, 505; 1760, 519-20, for contemporary agitation.
81. E.g. *Geheime Räte* to George II, 16, 23 July, 17 Aug 1756, Hann. 92, LXXII, Nr. 10.
82. Hann. 92, LXXII, Nr. 5.
83. *Statutes at Large*, VII, London, 1764, 4; *J.H.C.* XXVII, 635. The Act is filed prominently

in the Hessian archives (Marburg, 4 f, England, 271).

84. Philip von Münchhausen to General Sommerfeldt, 8 June 1756, Hann. 92, LXXII, No. 5. For much administrative detail regarding these troops' stay in England, see Royal Archives, Windsor, Cumberland Papers microfilm edition, British Library, boxes 47-49.

Chapter 5
The Seven Years War to the death of George II

The Seven Years War is the climax of the period under review for Hanover and Britain, as well as for other countries in Europe. And yet it is an anti-climax regarding the central problems of this work. The contradiction is such only at first glance, for the cataclysmic crisis was to leave the Hanoverian policy-makers bereft of significant power to influence their country's fate. Perhaps their heart was fainter than it need have been, but they were not cut out by background or training to cope with the terrors that engulfed them. Initially they tried to keep Hanover out of the vortex, by trying to establish a 'Neutrality', covenanted or merely understood. Once this hope was gone, they sank into despondency. Variations of approach to the crisis between the king and his Hanoverian ministers, and between the ministers among themselves, are discernible, and the changing fortunes of the war made their impact on them too. But, given spurts of scheming and moments of optimism, their mood was basically one of gloom. While there was no longer a 'British relationship' in an active sense, the impending death of George II was much feared at Hanover.[1] This was not surprising, as the heir apparent's view of 'that horrid electorate which has always lived upon the very vitals of this poor country'[2] is unlikely to have remained unknown at Hanover. However, when death came to the old king it proved a blessing in disguise. The reported aversion of George III to the land of his ancestors deprived Hanover of the negative importance which had been her bane for twenty years.

When the Hanoverian ministers received the news of Frederick's invasion of Saxony on 29 August they knew that a German war was certain. They despatched a number of reports assessing the situation to the king embodying some forty pages,[3] and they decided on their own responsibility to complete putting the army on a war footing—a daring step in view of the expenditure involved. (George II promptly reproved them, though more in sorrow than in anger.)[4] Most of their concern, however, was directed at the implications of the Westminister convention in the situation in which they now found themselves. No unanimity was obtained. Schwicheldt, always extreme in his anti-Prussian sentiment, held that the convention was defensive, and not offensive, and by attacking Saxony Frederick had rendered it inoperative, though he conceded that it might be reactivated if France invaded Hanover, or Russia Prussia. The majority of the ministers, however, took a line that bears Münchhausen's imprint. The convention was the only 'cover' (*Bedeckung*) Hanover had, and its validity ought therefore to be upheld. Moreover, the ministers felt that, while Hanover should not alienate Frederick, France on no account ought to be provoked either. Hanover had to avoid both being classified as the active accessary of an aggressor (which Frederick evidently was) and being associated with his eventual overthrow. Out of all these pitfalls, the conclusion reached by the ministers was to shun all military cooperation with Frederick except in the event of a French invasion, when massive Prussian protection would become essential. It will be seen that for practical purposes Schwicheldt and his colleagues were not far apart: until the French—and for that matter, the Russian—invasions materialized, the ministers all did their best not to associate with Frederick.

What is particularly striking in these reports is that at this moment of truth none of the ministers gave a thought to Britain, in whose power lay the capacity to make or break Hanover. Such neglect on their part may have been a reflection on three years of Newcastle's leadership.[5] However, it was a passing lapse.

If the Hanoverian ministers could afford, psychologically at least, to disregard Britain under the stress of the hour, the king in London could not. While he passionately shared his Hanoverian ministers' objective that the war had to be kept from Hanover, his diplomatic priorities differed. He no longer found distasteful the idea of active cooperation with Prussia in time of war, provided Frederick engaged effectively to share in the burden of Hanoverian defence. For one, old age and experience prevented him from going against what had by then become official British policy. And secondly, neither old age nor experience made him abandon the hope of acquiring territory for Hanover by Frederick's grace. (For this, see above, chapters I and III.) And so he tried to turn a deaf ear to appeals from the Emperor that he ought, as elector, to assist the Empire in avenging the injuries which Frederick had wrought, and when this became impossible, he replied in studiously noncommittal terms, with a bias towards Prussia.[6]

When the first excitement over Frederick's invasion of Saxony had abated, Münchhausen sent a memorandum on the state of affairs to his brother in London.[7] It combines historical analysis with an appraisal of the prevailing situation, enjoins special pleading to be used with the British ministers, and—in effect—emerges as the author's political *apologia pro vita sua*. The guideline of his thoughts, never put into so many words, but discernible in every sequence, is that the war has to be kept away from Hanover—and that he, Münchhausen, will fail to do so. The gist of his argument runs thus: ever since the peace treaties of Westphalia (1648) and of the Pyrenees (1659) the power and ambition of France had been the chief menace to the liberty and independence of Europe. It was the Old System of alliances, based not on altruism but on the enlightened self-interest of the partners, which had held the French menace in check. Now the Old System had broken down because *Klugheit* had given way to *Hass*. If only properly understood the Convention of Westminster was still in keeping with the Old System, for Silesia was of no importance to the balance of power and Austria had no right to expect Britain to dissipate her resources on that account. Furthermore, the neutralization of Germany freed British resources at sea and overseas, thereby weakening France, the enemy of Austria too. Though the empress, in her hatred of Prussia, had thrown herself into the arms of France, measures had to be undertaken that would show Austria the difficulties and dangers of such a policy.

With regard to the Protestant powers of Denmark and Sweden, though alliances with them were desirable, efforts in that direction were likely to be wasted: Denmark was friendly, but concerned with her own immediate gains; Sweden was weak and in the tow of France. Protestant delegations at the Diet should be encouraged in the hope of stultifying the projected Imperial measures against Prussia that threatened to involve Hanover—though 'votes remain at all times very weakly means'.

What Hanover had to aim for was an army at least 40,000 strong before the coming spring. An army such as this would also be to the British advantage, for Britain now had an opportunity of gathering under her wing those states willing to take up arms for their own freedom, and she would lose her credit for many years if she were to fail to seize the opportunity. As for Hanover, a strong army might discourage France from risking mighty forces merely to attempt the destruction of Hanover. On the other hand, if France had reason to believe that she could have her revenge on Hanover without a special effort—through the auxiliaries she sent to the empress—then undoubtedly she would do so, whatever the Austrians intended.

Münchhausen concludes: 'Hence we and the Protestant lands around us are exposed to the hardest of fates in the coming spring. England sees the most natural of her allies ruined along with the king of Prussia, and she will remain without a single treaty partner on the Continent. She should easily be able to foresee what will soon await her within her own borders.' The 'most natural of her allies', as the text makes clear, are Hanover and 'the Protestant lands around us'—the latter evidently Brunswick-Wolfenbüttel, Saxe-Gotha (the native country of Augusta, the dowager Princess of Wales!), Schaumburg-Lippe and Hesse-Cassel, all significant as troop suppliers for England in that hour of need.

It is the summing up of a good and wise man whose world is falling apart; a man who is neither very strong-minded nor well suited to snatching victory from the jaws of defeat. As in duty bound, Münchhausen offered what advice he could, and it is sensible advice. The conclusion shows that he did not believe in its efficacy.

* * *

This missive, it must be remembered, was written when a man was at the head of the British ministry whose relations with Münchhausen were close on both the personal and the political level. However, on 11 November 1756 Newcastle resigned. On 4 December William Pitt became secretary of state for the Southern Department. The Duke of Devonshire, First Lord of the Treasury, was a figurehead, and Pitt was in effect policy-maker.

Even earlier another extraneous factor was imposed on the relations between Hanover and Britain, of a kind not previously known: a British diplomatist in a key position who took a violent dislike to the Hanoverian ministers and all they stood for. On 11 May 1756 Mr (after 1764 Sir) Andrew Mitchell presented himself at Potsdam as British minister. He came in the wake of a succession of failures; his appointment proved a reversal with a vengeance. Mitchell immediately fell under the spell of Frederick and remained so for the greater part of the war—often critical, but steadfast in his loyalty. There is no other example in eighteenth century Britain of a senior representative abroad who identified his country's interests to such an extent with those of the ruler to whom he was sent. Mitchell naturally adopted Frederick's aversion for 'these ignorant and presumptuous magistrates'[8] at Hanover—their unending deliberations, their distrust of radical solutions, their proneness to panic, their ignorance of military affairs, their distaste for the Prussian alliance; above all, their 'great duplicity'. Moreover, Mitchell believed Münchhausen was trying to undermine his position in England. Whatever the Hanoverians did or abstained from doing was likely to rouse Mitchell's suspicion or anger. He denounced them to his superiors and to Frederick; he complained to Münchhausen. His position was all the more difficult since he had George II's 'strict command constantly [to] acquaint M. de

Münchhausen at Hanover with everything in which the affairs of the Empire in general, or those of His Majesty's Electorate in particular, are concerned ...'.[9] Mitchell's dislike became obsessive during a stay at Hanover in February 1757 when he tried, and failed, to convince Münchhausen of 'the candour with which the King of Prussia had acted [and] the attention he had had to the king's [i.e. George II's] interest ... only in order to save Hanover from being invaded [in 1756]'.[10]

It seems that Münchhausen was fundamentally unconscious of Mitchell's antipathy. Until the appointment of Cumberland to the command of the Army of Observation in April 1757 (see below)—when Münchhausen's sense of personal responsibility for the fate of Hanover was necessarily blunted to some extent—he thought it his duty to put upon the the disobliging Mitchell commissions at Berlin. Nor was George II disturbed by Mitchell's complaints beyond pointedly urging close cooperation between Mitchell and the Hanoverian ministers; more often the king was evasive. So what might have become a malign influence remained no more than an irritant to the relations between the two ministries. But British indifference to Mitchell's grievances also shows how unimportant Hanover was growing on the wider scene.[11]

* * *

The change of ministry in Britain occasioned a brief correspondence between Newcastle and Münchhausen that is of interest. In the first letter Newcastle mainly restricts himself to a notification of his (and Hardwicke's) resignation, rather self-pitying in style and none too loyal to his successors. Two months later he had evidently recovered his panache. More significantly, he turns out to be in accord with Pitt's emerging concepts of Continental diplomacy. 'Simple onlooker that I am', Newcastle offers Münchhausen his opinion on affairs, in strict confidence, though he realizes, as he writes, that he cannot expect Münchhausen's approval. His main point is that Austria ought to be written off, and Frederick ought to be kept loyal to Britain at all costs. 'If it appears to the king of Prussia that he has nothing to hope from this [i.e. our] side, he will immediately make his peace with France, the first article of which will be his abandoning the king and his electorate.' Then France will patch up a peace between Prussia and Austria, and fall upon Hanover. To prevent this calamity the closest concert with Prussia is needed. In particular a joint Army of Observation ought to be set up in Westphalia to which Frederick would—hopefully—contribute 10,000 men. Münchhausen differed from Newcastle with unwonted plainness, though in the most courteous terms. He had never presumed to judge the interests of Britain but he was, he implied, a judge of Hanoverian interests, and he felt that an overt declaration in favour of Frederick would mean charging Frederick with the defence of Hanover, a task for which he had no forces at his disposal.[12]

Pitt's disdain for Hanover was a byword, though Newcastle somewhat ambiguously held out the hope that office might qualify his attitude.[13] A warning from Philip von Münchhausen that 'His Majesty was occupied to the utmost with English entanglements at home'[14] could not have raised the elder brother's morale. From November the Hanoverian files are full of deliberations in which the listless pessimism of the reports of 3 September is consolidated. The sense of passivity can only be explained by the conviction of the ministers that whatever happened (*widerfahren*) to Hanover, England would not be induced to conclude a peace disadvantageous to herself.[15] Voices were not lacking in the *Geheimes Ratskollegium* that Britain was positively interested in a war on Hanoverian soil so as to make France divide her resources. Only two active principles breathe animation into these depressing pages. The first was the need to strengthen the army, and the ministers did what they could.[16] Their second principle was that any involvement with Frederick should be reduced to the absolute minimum. If the Westminister convention demanded such involvement—and most of the ministers believed that it did—then self-preservation had to come before treaty observance. In any case Prussia had committed aggression against Saxony, and she had committed it in spite of repeated warnings from George II to Frederick, and from Münchhausen to Podewils. This conscience-saving argument appears again and again.[17]

It was a move by Vienna that gave the Hanoverian Privy Council a new sense of direction. On 4 January 1757 the Hanoverian envoy there, Georg Friedrich von Steinberg—a son of the *Geheimer Rat*—received an offer from Kaunitz, responding to cautious enquiries from Hanover. Austria was prepared to sign a convention of neutrality with Hanover—on conditions: George II 'as elector' had solemnly to bind himself to give 'no aid whatever' to Frederick, 'either in money or in troops, either directly or indirectly'; and he had also to 'accord to the Empress and her allies all sureties, facilities and just and reasonable conditions which should [*doivent*] follow' from the convention. By an unofficial stipulation the allied armies should be allowed 'innocent passage' through Hanover—obviously on their way to invade Prussia from the west. The wording of the offer was blunt to the point of discourtesy.[18] Even though Steinberg at Vienna and his superiors at home received the idea with relief, Münchhausen still kept his head: French rights of passage through Hanover, as he knew, would of a certainty draw the Prussian army into the country and turn it into a battlefield. Moreover, anything like collusion between Hanover and France would utterly ruin any prospect of British aid.[19]

In sum, the Hanoverian ministers preferred a mere declaration of neutrality to a formal convention, provided that Frederick could be kept in the picture *pari passu* with the negotiations, to forestall his anger. The exception among them was again Schwicheldt, who seems to have delighted in the thought of adding insult to Frederick's injury.

To assuage their anxiety, the ministers prepared memoranda for Frederick and Podewils, which pictured the neutrality as a measure taken for the greater security of Prussia. They wanted, so they claimed, to have the Prussian territories in the west included in the neutrality. Frederick was scornful in his total rejection of the project.[20] Predictably, the British ministry, which in the context meant Pitt, also opposed the neutrality uncompromisingly: Frederick's certain ill will was no price to be considered in exchange for the possible safety of Hanover.[21] George II, on his part, agreed to the principle of a 'Neutrality' for Hanover with Austria, but even in the first months of 1757 he knew that he could not treat Pitt as in 1741 he had treated Walpole and his colleagues.

After months of intense exchange between all the courts concerned, the Austrian minister in London, Count Colloredo, delivered an 'ultimatum' of French composition to the younger Münchhausen on 27 April 1757. This stated that Austria and France would accept the neutrality only if they might use Hanover as a base of operations against Prussia, on terms which turned half the electorate (south of the river Aller) into occupied territory and robbed the remainder of the capacity to defend itself. Colloredo did not contact any British minister. George II rejected the offer out of hand: honour, justice and regard for his dignity did not permit him thus to betray an ally.[22] While his indignation was undoubtedly genuine—and the conditions were humiliating indeed—another factor proved decisive. Admiral Byng had just died aboard the *Monarque*, shot by sentence of a court martial for 'not doing his utmost'. With the nation in ferment, and Protestant Frederick's popularity rising rapidly, acceptance of a 'Neutrality' of the sort offered was impossible. Philip von Münchhausen put the matter succinctly when he wrote to his brother that 'a neutrality pact, at a time when English enthusiasm for Prussia had reached a peak, would have engendered a conspiracy that might have cost His Majesty crown and sceptre'.[23]

The Hanoverian ministers were bitterly sorry. In spite of the clear royal decision, and the British ministry's attitude which lay behind it, Münchhausen tried in his Imperial correspondence 'to keep the door open'.[24] But for the moment Münchhausen did not dare to engage in pursuing the course further.

Hesse-Cassel and Brunswick-Wolfenbüttel had been kept in the general picture throughout the negotiations. Like the Hanoverian ministers, the rulers of both states accepted the king's decision, though the files leave no doubt that they would have preferred a neutrality.[25]

* * *

In the meantime the British ministry had acted to ease the burden on Hanover by obtaining from Parliament a grant of £200,000 for her defence. The occasion of the request was Pitt's first address to the Commons as senior minister of the crown, on 18 February 1757, and though he was jeered for his apparent inconsistency, he was not deflected from his purpose. He knew that Frederick had to receive proof that Britain was in earnest in the wish for cooperation, and that Hanover was Prussia's bastion in the west.[26] But money was not troops, and moreover the sum was paltry at a time when the Hanoverian coffers were draining with frightening speed.[27]

Another problem was the selection of a commander-in-chief for the 'Army of Observation' to be formed in Germany. Not even the Hanoverian ministers seriously considered a Hanoverian general, highly acceptable as such a choice would have been to them on political and social grounds.[28] The king would have preferred Prince Louis of Brunswick, the Dutch commander-in-chief. Prince Louis refused, and his younger brother, Prince Ferdinand, became an obvious choice, with the additional advantage of being a trainee of Frederick's. Frederick, however, was not ready at that stage to forgo the services of one of his best younger generals, and suggested the Duke of Cumberland, George II's surviving son, who had been considered in London as an alternative candidate even before. In the circumstances his appointment was logical. There was no reason to consider Cumberland an outstanding commander, but after the death in 1750 of Marshal Saxe the French had no outstanding commander either. Cumberland was certainly a professional soldier with much experience in the field and he was a believer in the Prussian drill which made the Prussian army tactically superior to any other. Frederick may have wanted to flatter George II, but it seems that the chief reason for his proposal was that only Cumberland would not become the Hanoverian ministers' dupe.[29] The Hanoverians, on their part, showed loyal enthusiasm for the king's son and were relieved that no Prussian general was appointed at a time when their aversion to cooperation with Prussia was at one of its periodic peaks. The political scene in England was favourable, and Cumberland was duly appointed. But before Cumberland agreed to take up his command Pitt had to be dismissed as secretary of state, as Cumberland refused to contemplate receiving Pitt's directions.[30] It is a curious incidental of 'Hanoverian–British relations'. Cumberland left London on 9 April 1757 to take up his command, while intelligence reports claimed that 100,000 Frenchmen were ready to advance east.

After the trough of depression at Hanover, early summer saw a certain recovery of spirits that can partly be explained in psychological terms. War was certain, and the Hanoverian army with its Hessian and other auxiliaries was as prepared as could be hoped for; even the German troops previously in England were back home in time. The Duke of Cumberland generated a confidence which subsequent events did little to justify; but the *Geheime Räte* were civilians to the bone, and very ready to expect the best from the elector's son. The fortunes of war too smiled on Frederick, and therefore on Hanover. Frederick's costly victory before Prague, on 6 May 1757, seemed to forecast an Austrian military collapse. A spectacular raid of Prussian 'free bands' into south Germany brought Bavaria to the brink of deserting Austria. Münchhausen momentarily became convinced that a fighting alliance with Prussia was a good thing after all.[31]

The battle of Kolin of 18 June 1757—the first, and politically the farthest reaching, of Frederick's military defeats—put an abrupt end to this euphoria. Münchhausen's report of his endeavour to retrieve the offer of an alliance already despatched to Berlin would be amusing but for the fate of peoples involved.[32] Though the document was recovered, Münchhausen sank back into despondency. Predictably Frederick not merely announced that no major contribution to the defence of Hanover could now be expected from him; he also recalled his six battalions—the former garrison of Wesel —already serving with the Army of Observation.

The news that reached Hanover from Britain was disheartening too. The 'ministerial squabbles', the 'internal dissensions', the sleep into which the English nation seemed to have fallen, all offered golden opportunities to France. With the Newcastle–Pitt ministry firmly in the saddle by July 1757 Münchhausen gave vent to another cry from the heart: '[Indeed] the King of Prussia must risk all [after the defeat of Kolin] ... However, [Münchhausen] cannot understand why we should, for love of the King of Prussia, ruin ourselves with him and refuse to consider a neutrality ... Mr Pitt would not send us 20,000 to 30,000 Englishmen. Even if he did, we would remain the weaker party, and our country the theatre of war. We should also have to fear the ban of the Empire as accessory breakers of the peace ...' And again: 'Nobody acts nowadays by political rules; all are ruled by passion.'

It is worth noting that at that early date Münchhausen was putting the onus for decisions concerning Hanover on Pitt, not on Newcastle, the First Lord of the Treasury, nor on Holdernesse, the secretary of state for the north (and as such traditionally responsible for German affairs). Then Philip reported that the new team now thought 'seriously and unitedly of the most vigorous measures' concerning the war—an early testimonial to Britain's greatest war ministry until 1940. The elder brother responded that 'the main matter indeed depends on English advice and decisions'—not a new thought.[33] Already on 5 July 1757 Münchhausen had mused on a possible future 'Neutrality', clearly with the view of making the idea acceptable to the king and whoever was in charge at Whitehall: 'Whatever is agreed to [concerning a neutrality] will not hinder us from countering with operations which go beyond any that we will put into words now—when there is hope of success; we shall then be able to advance the common cause [with Prussia] better than can be done at present.'[34] It reads like an anticipation of the Convention of Kloster Zeven and its subsequent breach (see below).

Late in April the two armies started to march and counter-march, the French under Marshal d'Estrées, the Army of Observation under Cumberland, who took over from the Hanoverian general Zastrow at the beginning of May. Though the movements of both generals have been condemned as sluggish and inept, they were probably not below the operational standards of the eighteenth century, between the War of the Spanish Succession and the French Revolutionary wars (very gifted commanders excepted). Moreover, the Army of Observation was a patchwork with a nominal strength of 47,000 at best, opposed to 75,000 French at the lowest count.[35] Here at any rate is a valid reason not to blame Cumberland for his dilatory strategy, even though his performance—tactics and logistics—already at that early stage leave much room for criticism. Furthermore Münchhausen strongly encouraged Cumberland to take no risks.[36]

On 11 July 1757, the Danish and French governments concluded a 'convention' of neutrality for Bremen-Verden, the Hanoverian territory which bordered on Holstein—virtually a Danish possession—to the north. The convention was humiliating to Hanover in that it did not cover the Army of Observation should it retire into Bremen-Verden, and did not give immunity to the Hanoverian army magazines there. George II was no party to the negotiations and rejected the convention for himself as an insult.[37]

Cumberland's relations with his father's Hanoverian ministers deserve passing notice, if only for the light they shed on his personality. He was in constant contact with Münchhausen, who was the senior member of the Privy Council; Steinberg and Schwicheldt were either at his headquarters or else entrusted with special assignments for his army. Cumberland's correspondence with them is businesslike and courteous on the whole. Yet all was not well. The ministers, as was their custom, on their own accord submitted to Cumberland situation reports, with suggestions for policy, thereby offending Cumberland's *amour propre*. At his son's request, George II wrote to his Hanoverian ministry not to molest Cumberland with such *Vorträge*, but to concentrate instead on the execution of his instructions.[38] It is inconceivable that George II would have given his ministers such a dressing-down with regard to his own relations with them. Münchhausen, at any rate, disregarded the order after the disaster of Kolin, and it seems Cumberland acquiesced. We do not know whether the Hanoverian ministers took offence at the time, but in any case they were later to learn from the king's will that George II 'categorically' (*ausdrücklich*) expected Cumberland to follow the advice of his Hanoverian ministers should he become guardian of a king who was a minor, if that advice was unanimous.[39]

By mid-July 1757 d'Estrées had occupied Hesse-Cassel and the southern tip of Hanover with Göttingen. More important strategically, he had crossed the Weser without meeting determined opposition. On 26 July the two armies clashed at Hastenbeck, south-east of Hameln. In a day's heavy fighting the Hanoverians and their allies were forced out of their defensive positions. It was no glorious victory for the French. Indeed, it had been touch-and-go as to which of the two commanders would be the first to realize in the dust of battle that his adversary was on the point of retreating.[40] Strategically, however, Hastenbeck was decisive. Greater generals than

Cumberland might have hesitated to risk another field battle against an enemy twice as strong, in what was largely open country. The point is that Cumberland immediately wrote off the campaign as lost.

George II professed to leave the decision concerning the line of retreat in the hands of Cumberland.[41] Cumberland then proceeded in accordance with the contingent plan of operations of 1753 (see above, pp. 85) and his own 'Instructions' of 30 March 1757 (see below)—he withdrew northward under the guns of Stade, where the lower Elbe safeguarded his communications with Britain. During the spell of optimism at Hanover in April and May 1757, when close cooperation with Frederick seemed to most of the ministers for once a promising proposition, Münchhausen had guardedly recommended to Cumberland a line of retreat eastward in case of need, into conjunction with the Prussian army.[42] The king had reproved him and his colleagues for this forwardness with unusual harshness (see above). Now, however, after Frederick's defeat at Kolin on 18 June had made them see his ruin as certain, their anxiety to isolate Hanover from Prussia made them fall in with Cumberland's strategic considerations. But the Observation Army's retreat to the north, however warranted conceptually in the circumstances, was carried out in unnecessary haste, and hence in disorder, and hence with great loss of substance and morale. The French, under a new commander, the Duc de Richelieu, occupied the town of Hanover on 9 August. The archives and treasury had been sent north even before Hastenbeck, first to Stade and thence to Glückstadt, in Holstein, under Danish protection. Most of the leading families seem to have fled shortly afterwards. Of the ministers, Steinberg was with Cumberland, whom he cannot have helped from the point of view of morale. Diede, Schwicheldt and Behr, under standing orders for this contingency, preceded the retreating army to Stade. Münchhausen, Bussche and Hake stayed behind in French-occupied Hanover. The Hanoverian delegate who negotiated the surrender of the capital was Friedrich Karl von Hardenberg, George II's envoy to Versailles in the neutrality negotiations of 1741/42 (see above, pp. 35-47). The king's choice for this of all tasks looks like a strange blunder, but it probably made no difference to the outcome.

Cumberland's part in the subsequent Convention of Kloster Zeven (see below) must be examined from two points of view: firstly it bears on British–Hanoverian relations and, secondly, it throws light on the relationship between George II and his son. On balance it must be concluded that George II did treat Cumberland unfairly, as historians have generally agreed since. However, the matter is more complex than has usually been acknowledged.

The king's 'Instructions' to Cumberland when he assumed command of the Army of Observation is dated 30 March 1757 and counter-initialled by the younger Münchhausen.[43] Its spirit is decidedly defensive and takes in two possibilities: should it transpire that the French army is bound for Bohemia (that is, leaving Hanover unmolested in the main), then the king was not of the intent (*Meinung*) that his army should advance in their direction and defy them (*die Spitze bieten*). In case of a French attack on the electorate, however, all that was humanly possible should be done for its defence—at all times with a view to keeping open the retreat to Stade; in the direst emergency the army should go there, take up position and 'hold on until it becomes clear how circumstances develop' (*so lange zu halten, bis sich ergibt, wie die Konjunkturen weiter laufen*).

It is no wonder that these orders with their implied desertion of Prussia were kept from Pitt, who was about to be dismissed in any case.[44] On the other hand, it is fairly clear that the instruction was not meant to cover a surrender such as the Convention of Kloster Zeven virtually became. On the eve of Hastenbeck, when things were already looking much worse than on Cumberland's departure from England, George II replied to Münchhausen's thinly disguised appeal of 5 July for a neutrality (see above, p. 110) with a firm negative which repeated the operative clauses of the instruction almost word for word.[45] The phrase 'holding on until it becomes clear how circumstances develop' must therefore be understood in its plain sense.

Then came the news of Hastenbeck and the knowledge that the French war machine was inexorably taking hold of Hanover. George II was shaken to his innermost core. No help could be expected from Prussia: Frederick himself had said so within two days of the defeat at Kolin,[46] even if the military situation had not spoken for itself. Pitt, back in office *and* in power, was adamant that British troops for Hanover were out of the question.[47] He knew, of course, that this meant the end, for practical purposes, of the Army of Observation and the submission of Hanover to the French, and he accepted the situation.[48] George's despair found its outlet in a spate of letters he and Philip von Münchhausen sent to Cumberland, to the 'jetzt zu Stade befindlichen Geheimen Räte samt und sonders', and to the Danish government on 11 August 1757.[49] Their gist is an authorization for Cumberland to conclude 'einen Partikulier-Frieden' with the French on behalf of Hanover, and a plea for Danish mediation. Of these letters those of Philip von Münchhausen's to the Danish minister Count Bernstorff are the clearest and most articulate. George II 'as elector' Münchhausen explained, has no 'feud' (*Fehde*) with either France or the empress. He was therefore willing to conclude a separate peace 'on fair terms' (*auf billige Conditiones*). These were held to be: the Army of Observation to be dispersed and the Hanoverian troops to return to their permanent quarters, the auxiliaries to be sent home; George II to assist nobody whomsoever while the 'troubles' in Germany continued; the French to evacuate the territory of Hanover and her German allies; the allies to be included in the 'separate peace'. George II could not be expected to render aid against Prussia, and he would undertake to keep Frederick informed of the negotiations. The young Münchhausen also implored Bernstorff to obtain an interim order to the French generals 'to spare the innocent subjects [of Hanover] so far as possible'.

Perhaps not surprisingly, the instructions of George II to Cumberland and his Hanoverian ministers, while not actually contradicting the letters to Copenhagen, carry a spirit altogether different. They are an urgent request to conclude a 'separate peace' preferably, and if not a peace, then a 'neutrality or a convention'. The elaborate 'fair conditions' are replaced by a defeatist formula: the articles are to be signed while 'my army has *not as yet* been destroyed, and the enemy is *not as yet* fully master of my German lands' (my italics). The only stipulation is that Frederick is to be kept informed of all steps in the negotiations, and every effort made to persuade him of their necessity. Full powers signed by the king were attached for Cumberland to conclude with the French whatever conditions he might obtain. All the letters to Cumberland are couched in terms of strongest confidence. The letters to the ministers order one of them—unnamed—to join the rather ineffectual Steinberg as adviser at Cumberland's headquarters.

At the same time the younger Steinberg in Vienna was instructed to implore the good offices of Maria Theresa for a separate peace between Hanover and France.[50]

Of the ministers at Stade, Diede was senior. However, Schwicheldt presided over the War Chancery and it was he who joined Cumberland. The point may have historical significance. Diede had the virtues of his faults: he was somewhat heavy and hesitant, but he was morally courageous and of intellectual integrity. Schwicheldt, on the other hand, was mercurial and eager to leave his mark, while he was temperamentally unfit to stand up to royalty. He was also burning to get Hanover out of the hated connection with Prussia. Cumberland was predisposed to throw in his hand; with Steinberg and Schwicheldt by his side capitulation was a foregone conclusion.

As the weeks went by, and Cumberland vainly tried to soften Richelieu's conditions, George II regained some of his composure.[51] Several factors came into play; the passing of the first shock of defeat; the political atmosphere in England, where the new ministry was getting into its stride. The fear of Frederick's anger and capacity for retribution was also a balancing factor. But George II did not reverse his instructions. It is the mood of his letters that changes. There is a new stress on the king's confidence—perhaps an overstress—that his son would not sign a disadvantageous deal; particularly no deal that 'might be aimed at ruining' the army. At the same time George II tried to insure Hanover with Britain for the sacrifice he was about to make as elector, in a British war. Philip von Münchhausen put the case in a memorandum to the British ministry of 16 September. The king initialled the copy which remained at the German Chancery.[52] The document begins with an oblique apology for the king: 'once having opened' negotiations for a 'reasonable accommodation' concerning his German possessions 'and those of his friends', he cannot break off without 'legitimate or obvious' (*apparantes*) reasons. However, as such reasons are likely to emerge 'it is natural as well as just' that the king should know what to expect from Britain 'if he sacrifices for her sake the well-being and deliverance of his electorate, by seizing the first opportunity … to break off the negotiations in question'. Would Britain guarantee the king's German possessions to the full when a general peace was made? Would Britain take upon herself the charge of the king's German troops during the emergency—not just during the present occupation of Hanover? A speedy and precise reply to the memorandum would be appreciated.

The following day, 17 September 1757, the news of the Kloster Zeven convention burst upon George II.

Cumberland's negotiations with Richelieu during the weeks that preceded the convention repeat in one important aspect the battle of Hastenbeck: both were a contest of will and nerve, and Cumberland lost again. There is no doubt that the French army was in a bad state, and Richelieu could not have forced on his adversary the harsh conditions for which he held out—and Richelieu knew it. But Cumberland was not inclined to run risks, and the Danish go-between, Count Lynar, further lowered his morale.

The elder Münchhausen, at Hanover behind the French lines, was precluded from taking part in the proceedings. Later he preened himself on being innocent of the convention.[53] It rather looks like sheer luck.

On 8, 9 and 10 September 1757 Richelieu and Cumberland signed the convention, Richelieu at Kloster Zeven, Cumberland at Bremervörde, fifteen miles to the north.[54] It was a Hanoverian capitulation. The Army of Observation was disbanded: the Hanoverian army was to retire into Lauenburg, across the Elbe, except for a few regiments which remained at Stade; the allied contingents were to be dismissed to their respective countries. Of the stipulations to Bernstorff—security and evacuation—nothing.

The news of the convention left George II shattered. 'Never havc I felt like this' is the opening of his rebuke to Steinberg and Schwicheldt at Stade. He continues, 'the matter was considered in your presence, and you counselled acceptance. How you could do so is entirely beyond my comprehension.'[55] This particular censure is unreasonable, considering the circumstances, but it shows the king's underlying trust in his Hanoverian ministers' effectiveness. Cumberland the king recalled in a letter of deadly hurt, though he phrased his instructions courteously.[56] In both letters the king maintained that his authorization to conclude a separate peace rested on the understanding that the peace would entail a French evacuation of Hanover and safeguards for the king's allies. Though this is no untruth, it is a misrepresentation inasmuch as it ignores the spirit in which he wrote after Hastenbeck. And inasmuch as his reproaches now are based on his reviving spirits in early September they ignore the difficulties of communication, enormously increased by warfare and enemy occupation. When Cumberland was back in London his father had persuaded himself into a rage—'here is my son who has ruined me and disgraced himself'. George II's 'arrant political cowardice' is one explanation, without doubt. Another may have been his rapid aging, which made him forget the mood of his instructions to Cumberland after Hastenbeck.[57] Cumberland accepted it all with unwavering dignity. Three years later he had the satisfaction of learning that George II repented of his treatment before his death.[58]

The news of the convention, and its possible impact on the British public, also caused George II to ask his Hanoverian ministers for another opinion on the advisability of breaking the personal union. (See below, pp. 134–135.)

On one possible cause of a bad conscience George II may be absolved. He did not betray a loyal ally. During these very months Frederick was trying hard to make his own peace with France—even renew his alliance with France—without informing Mitchell, let alone the Hanoverian ministers. 'Rumours' reached Münchhausen, who communicated them to Newcastle.[59] But Rossbach had been fought the previous day, and Frederick's contemplated treachery became irrelevant, in the light of his major victory on the battlefield.

Eleven weeks passed between the signing of the Kloster Zeven convention and its repudiation by Cumberland's successor, Prince Ferdinand of Brunswick. George II made yet one more attempt, through his Hanoverian minister at Vienna, to find out whether the French might not be induced to evacuate Hanover; he did not mention a 'separate peace' any longer.[60] Ratifying the convention was by now a political impossibility and was never considered in London.

The decision in London to renew hostilities in Germany as soon as feasible was not matched by a similar resolve at Hanover and Stade. The country was groaning under French exactions, official and private.[61] Indeed, the trauma, after generations of freedom from invasion, was to leave its imprint on popular feeling towards Britain. (See also below, p. 130.) But for the time being the Hanoverian ministers considered another bout of warfare the ultimate catastrophe. They said so, in the face of their master's renewed pugnacity and pressure from the British ministry which urged him on.

Münchhausen, at Stade by royal order since 26 October, put diplomatic and administrative preparations into effect for the resumption of fighting. He did so with a heavy heart which he disguised neither to George II nor to his colleagues.[62]

By now the British ministry was ready to answer the younger Münchhausen's memorandum of 16 September 1757 (see above). The reply naturally took account of the changed situation. On 7 October the Hanoverian minister was summoned to a meeting of the Cabinet Council: Lord Granville (Carteret), Lord President of the Council; the Duke of Newcastle, First Lord of the Treasury, the 'prime minister'; Lord Holdernesse, Secretary of State for the Northern Department; Lord Anson, First Lord of the Admiralty; Lord Mansfield, Lord Chief Justice of the King's Bench; Lord Ligonier, commander-in-chief of the army; Mr Pitt. Philip von Münchhausen has our sympathy if he was a bit awed. The message was brief:[63] 'The king's servants do not conceive themselves anyways founded to offer their humble advice to his Majesty with regard to the safety and welfare of his electoral dominions. But in case his Majesty as elector shall, on the advice of his electoral ministers, judge proper to consider the convention concerning his Majesty's Army of Observation as broken and annulled, and in consequence thereof shall put the said troops again into activity—their Lordships are humbly of opinion that, the electoral revenues being entirely cut off, the pay and charge of the said troops ought, in justice and in honour, be supplied from hence [i.e. Britain], from the day that they shall recommence the operations of war against the forces of France, in concert with the King of Prussia.' To make doubly sure, Newcastle, the acknowledged confidant of the elder Münchhausen, wrote in similar vein to his friend 'nowise by order of His Majesty', and even added an explicit warning: no reactivation—no aid.[64] Notwithstanding his friendliness and courtesy, the diction reads like Pitt's—which it may have been. Münchhausen replied—deferentially and unconvinced.[65]

Two events finally made Münchhausen and his colleagues take heart. The earlier was the news that Prince Ferdinand of Brunswick was to take command of the Army of Observation. He was still unknown as an independent commander. But he was a Guelph and he was Frederick's choice, trained and tried under his eyes. The second event was the battle of Rossbach, which Frederick won over the French and Imperial armies on 5 November. Tactically it was the most showy of Frederick's victories. Partly for this reason and partly because of the national animosity against the French, it became at once his most popular victory among the Germans, and has remained so into our own times.[66] The *Geheime Räte* were satisfied at last and may have shared the elation—Schwicheldt again excepted.[67]

On 28 November 1757 the armistice convention officially came to its end with a letter from Prince Ferdinand to the Duc de Richelieu. On 26 November the ministers issued a manifesto, without the king's previous consent, which justified the step to the public. Since Prince Ferdinand did not permit its publication until he himself had written to Richelieu, it seems that they predated its publication by two days. The justification, in German and in French, lists a variety of contraventions of the Kloster Zeven convention by the French government, army commander and lower echelons. It complains that the French occupation clearly intended 'entirely to ruin the army and the country'. The 'allies' are mentioned in a context which obviously refers to the German states—Hesse-Cassel and Wolfenbüttel above all. Of Britain there is no hint—not unexpectedly. George II meticulously appears 'as elector'. The draft of the manifesto is signed by all the ministers then at Stade. Soon after, on 30 November, they published their order to all officials to obey and assist Prince Ferdinand in the pursuit of the war, above Münchhausen's signature.[68]

Henceforth Britain covered most of the charges of the Hanoverian army during the war. She never covered them in their entirety, quite apart from the indirect burdens that continued to fall upon Hanover. Of French oppression indeed the country was soon rid. The new commander lived up to all hopes. On 28 February 1758 the French army evacuated the town of Hanover. By the end of March the electorate was free of the enemy. It remained so—except for the southern tip with Göttingen—for the remainder of the war.[69]

At the renewal of hostilities the Hanoverian ministers had asked their colleague Philip von Münchhausen to enquire of the king how they should act in case of a future disaster—presumably without the knowledge of Prince Ferdinand.[70] Their anxiety is understandable, but it proved unnecessary.

The period that spans the renewal of hostilities in western Germany at the end of 1757 and the death of George II on 25 October 1760 is the era of Pitt in his glory. In his concept of the war, 'His Majesty's forces in Germany'—no longer an 'Army of Observation'—performed a vital function, dissipating the French war effort and protecting Frederick's western flank. To enable these forces to do this, several conditions had to be fulfilled. First—they 'should be looked upon entirely as an *English army* to be directed by the king through the channel of his English secretary of state—who should be answerable to this country'.[71] Then the army needed an efficient commander, and Prince Ferdinand served admirably. A considerable stiffening of British manpower became essential, and this must have been a difficult decision for Pitt to take. But with French reverses at sea, and the turnout of a militia which gave a feeling of institutionalized security, the matter was tackled. From the summer of 1758 onward a British national contingent was built up within the army in Germany which by 1761 counted about a quarter of its effectives—18,000 out of 77,000.[72] The army needed the long-term security provided by a cooperative House of Commons and an enthusiastic and affluent British public—their presence is a measure of Pitt's statecraft. Last but not least a king was required in London who acquiesced in Pitt's concept of global war, and a ministry at Hanover that was loyal and pliant. But with the army in Germany practically in British pay, its commander a Prussian general merely seconded to the British (not the Hanoverian) service, and the Hanoverian chests utterly exhausted, this matter was no issue.[73]

Even so Pitt demanded that copies of all correspondence between the elder Münchhausen and Ferdinand were sent to the ministry in London, and that Ferdinand's official reports to George II passed through Holdernesse, as secretary of state for the Northern Department, and not through the younger Münchhausen at the *Deutsche Kanzlei*.[74] The provision was not scrupulously kept; in any case it made no difference to the new relationship between Hanover and Whitehall.

With these essentials of strategy settled there remained little scope for 'Hanoverian–British relations'. Münchhausen remained in charge at Hanover. His relations with Prince Ferdinand were correct but not confidential. He felt that he was not in the picture as regards Ferdinand's conduct of the war, though he showed no resentment.[75] Otherwise his letters to his brother abound with references to the British national interest as embodied in global warfare; he did not enlarge on the subject *ex officio* to outsiders. His official contacts with the British government went either through his brother or through Holdernesse. Occasionally he exchanged confidences with Newcastle. They shed some light on their mood; neither could influence major trends, though for different reasons. Münchhausen never wrote to Pitt, it seems.[76]

Münchhausen's overriding concern remained the need for peace. He never lived down the French occupation. He was haunted by the spectre of its return. Every victory of Prince Ferdinand—and these were the years of Crefeld, Minden and Warburg—received an acknowledgment that seems to reflect a nervous twitch. Every reverse, even an alarmist letter from a senior officer writing behind the C-in-C's back, sent him into despair.[77] The same pessimism pervades Münchhausen's assessments of Fredrick's fortunes, though here it was only the repercussions on Hanover that interested him. The war continued 'to eat up the country' ('*manger le pays*'—almost a technical term); the curse of the British commissariat differed only in kind from that of the enemy, not in degree.[78] He somewhat diffidently requested monetary compensation for Hanover from Newcastle—over and above the charges for the army, mostly borne by Britain. These requests were put directly through his brother, but he achieved nothing, except, perhaps, the payment of his and his colleagues' salaries from the British exchequer.[79] Nor did his requests for a speedy peace settlement rouse an echo at Whitehall.

Against this background Münchhausen's negotiations with the Prussian ministers for territorial gains at the projected peace are even more incongruous than on earlier occasions. This particular stage—the last—in pursuit of his master's pet ambition begins in the second half of 1756, when Frederick again tried to lure his uncle into more active cooperation with him. George II was as eager as before, but with Pitt at the helm a Hanoverian *Siegfrieden* just was not on the cards. The interim solution that presented itself was to conduct secret negotiations with Frederick and his ministers behind the back of the British ministry, as well as keeping in the dark the Prussian envoy in London, Knyphausen, recently transferred from Paris; he was considered too unreliable by George II to be let into the secret. On these terms Münchhausen corresponded with Podewils and Podewils's successor Finckenstein (Hyndford's 'little spy' of 1743; see above, p. 58), under orders from his king. He did so with much cavilling, and constantly tried to cut down the king's appetite, which was inordinate, as always when the theme of territorial aggrandizement arose: Osnabrück and parts of Münster to the west; Paderborn, Hildesheim and the Eichsfeld to the south. With this provision Münchhausen certainly represented his master in his Prussian correspondence as best he could. As to the British ministry, they were kept out of the secret while it mattered—though it was only the scruples of one of their own appointees which stopped their being prematurely informed in a way most prejudicial to their Hanoverian colleagues. As early as 2 July 1758 Frederick, during the honeymoon period following the British–Prussian treaty of 11 April, gave Mitchell the gist of his Hanoverian negotiations, with stress on the greed for land of the Hanoverian ministers. At the same time Frederick enjoined on Mitchell secrecy on his 'word of honour', 'as [Frederick] would not willingly be the occasion of a moment's uneasiness to the King [George II] ...'. It is incredible that Frederick should have expected Mitchell to keep his word; indeed, a case can be made out that it was Mitchell's plain duty instantly to report home. But it seems Mitchell kept quiet for almost half a year, and when he at last informed Newcastle his conscience hurt him for having put his patriotic duty before his pledge to the King of Prussia.[80]

The negotiations between Hanover and Berlin broke down when Frederick, six weeks after his indiscretion to Mitchell, peremptorily demanded that the British ministry be put in the picture.[81] Münchhausen presented this demand to George II as proof of Frederick's bad faith—that Frederick merely thought to temporize—and asked for further instructions. He was more explicit to his brother. To start with, he wrote, 'British interests and ours are at variance, with other contrarieties that arise from it.' Münchhausen believed that at heart Frederick wanted the negotiations to fail, 'whether from the multitude of [Hanoverian] demands, a point on which I have given my diverging opinion [to George II] several times, or for other reasons, I cannot know'.[82] The consternation in which Münchhausen clothed the letter ('I felt as if I were tumbling from the skies') has an exaggerated ring. It was certainly mixed with relief that here was a way out of an unrewarding business. He was right. George II rarely failed to respond to an argument based on the demerits of his nephew's character, and he allowed the negotiations to fizzle out for the time being. Also, of course, he may not have felt like facing Pitt's wrath. Not that he abandoned his desires. Until his death he would on occasion advance feelers regarding territorial gains to Hanover at the general peace. Whether these were made to Newcastle in person, or to foreign diplomatists with injunctions to strict secrecy (and promptly reported to Newcastle in turn), the British ministers—Pitt, Hardwicke and Newcastle himself—remained adamant in their rejection.[83]

* * *

Immediately after the death of George II on 25 October 1760 Münchhausen wrote a series of letters to his brother in which he summed up the current situation of Hanover, together with reflections on the past and on the future.[84] These letters include his epitaph on his master and, less directly, his opinion on Hanover's relationship with Britain. Their abstract may therefore serve as a conclusion to the narrative part of this work.

'Before the war His late Majesty had the joy of knowing that his countries were the happiest in Germany.' The war brought indescribable suffering, what with the oppression of the French when in occupation, and the 'indescribably wicked [*unbeschreiblich böse*] English commissariat', inefficient indeed, but even more fraudulent than inefficient.[85] All the treasuries were depleted as a result, and the country was deeply in debt, after a depreciation of the currency and a resultant lack of small coin. Then the country suffered from ruthless foraging, often indistinguishable from looting and robbery; the insatiable rapacity of both armies for draft animals and carts had put an end to the cultivation of large tracts of farmland. The military situation was equally gloomy, for though Prince Ferdinand had the writer's confidence, the army was starved of men, and 'mit Geld allein lässt sich kein Krieg führen'. The very disasters which had befallen France overseas and on the oceans forced her into concentrating her resources in Germany, while Frederick himself was at his last gasp.

In these circumstances it was the stern duty of His Majesty's German ministers to press for peace, lest the country fall into total ruin. To get peace, even territorial sacrifices on a rough basis of *uti possidetis* were warranted: Prussia to cede Silesia, Hanover Göttingen. (The University of Göttingen was the childless Münchhausen's true daughter—as the king in a moment of insight had thus referred to it.[86] That Münchhausen was prepared to abandon Göttingen for the sake of peace is true proof of his anguish. It is, however, likely that in this case Münchhausen would have transferred the university elsewhere.) 'We shall have reason to thank God if we obtain peace' without paying in land; to try to hold out for acquisitions was inexcusable. 'The king of blessed memory would have been a truly great regent had he not always tried to obtain for his German lands a few miserable bailiwicks and villages, in wars on which the weal and woe of all Europe depended. Nor did he get them. But he lost the glory, greater than all victories, that the general good was his only aim.'[87]

It is a shattering obituary from a sterling servant and friend.

The need to act was all the more pressing (thus Münchhausen) as the situation was favourable, with France tired and ready to forgo territorial acquisitions in Germany. Surely Frederick would agree to such an outcome, but if he did not—and Münchhausen does not sound optimistic—then he had no right to draw Hanover into his own perdition.

Peace obtained, the obvious task was reconstruction. The foremost measure to be taken was troop reduction, 'not in the way officers are minded, but according to sensible rules based on a true policy'—another remarkable statement of Münchhausen's political philosophy.[88] It would indeed be best to discharge the entire rank and file of the army—to save money, but also 'for the domestic happiness of the land'. Still, so radical a measure would hurt the reputation of Hanover in the Empire. Münchhausen offers no way out of the dilemma. Positive economic assistance from outside was also needed, both in money and in goods. The aid should in fairness come from Britain, 'since the war was waged for the sake not of the royal German lands, but of the [British] crown'.

The part of Britain in these letters is elusive. Britain is always there, though she is not often named. The gist is plain. Just as the war had brought Hanover close to destruction, so it had brought Britain wealth beyond measure. It was for Britain alone to decide which of her conquests to keep at the peace, and which to return. The French navy—a menace to Britain, not to Hanover—was 'ruined' for twenty to thirty years to come. The writer was very conscious that he and his colleagues had no say in the determination of British policy; they were not informed of decisions taken; they were unclear even as to the situation in the field. All this was so obvious that 'I [Münchhausen] would on no account recommend to incur through useless representations and complaints nothing but hatred'. But the British ministry ought to consider whether the downfall of Hanover in the coming campaign of 1761—if peace was not obtained before then—would make France more pliable at the conference table. And it might be well if *mon cher frère* talked these things over with 'Milord Bute'—to that extent did Münchhausen at Hanover assess the seat of influence in London after six weeks of the new reign.[89]

At no point is there a critique of the connection between Hanover and Britain as such, not even by implication.

* * *

The death of George II is as significant an event in the relations of Hanover and Britain as can be found in the writing of histories outside biographies proper. Münchhausen and his colleagues realized its overriding importance, as we have seen, and as was only natural. Not being provided with the gift of prophecy, it was also natural for them to exaggerate the danger which the death of George II posed for Hanover. They could not know that within two years Frederick, their ally against their will, in whose probable ruin they tended to see the ruin of Hanover, would emerge from the war unbeaten, and indeed a victor politically and morally. Nor could they divine that George III would take his electoral duties more seriously than they had, with some reason, dared to hope. But before these points receive the attention necessary to round off the present study, further discussion concerning the period under review is necessary.

Notes

1. 'When I just consider the possibility that our dear king might die … I cease to think and see such an abyss for the country …' (Münchhausen to his brother, 30 June 1758, Hann. 92, LXXII, Nr. 45, vol. I).
2. Prince of Wales to Bute, 5 Aug 1759, quoted in R. Sedgwick (ed.), *Letters from George III to Lord Bute*, London, 1939, 28.
3. *Geheime Räte* to George II, 3 Sept 1756, Hann. 92, LXXII, Nr. 10. Formally these reports were a response to messages from the king of 17 and 20 August which, as often, were essentially requests for guidance clothed as orders. At that date Frederick's impending action was seen in London as a dangerous possibility, but not a certainty. Mediger (646-649) analyses the Hanoverian *vota* in detail.
4. George II to *Geheime Räte*, 14 Sept 1756, *ibid.*
5. E.g. 'Newcastle's proposal [of September 1756, to raise an army for the defence of Hanover] was nothing more than a placebo to alleviate the king's anxiety for his electoral lands'. (Doran, *op. cit.*, 100.)
6. E.g. Colloredo to Maria Theresa, 19 Nov 1756, *HHStA*, England, K. 108; George II to Francis I, 5 Nov 1756, *HHStA*, England, Hofkorrespondenz, K. 4.
7. 7 Oct 1756, Hann. 91, Münchhausen I, Nr. 30. Münchhausen virtually repeats his analysis, *mutatis mutandis*, in a memorandum he drew up on 8 September 1757, during Hanover's darkest hours (Hann. 92, LXXII, Nr. 12, vol. I).
8. *Histoire de la guerre de sept ans*, *Oeuvres,* IV, 121.
9. Holdernesse to Mitchell, 7 Dec 1756, Add. MSS 6813, f. 162.
10. 'Short account … of the negotiations at Brunswick and Hanover in February 1757' by Mitchell, Add. MSS 6870, ff. 66-89.
11. The above is based on the Mitchell Papers in the British Library, in particular those for 1757. Doran, *op. cit.*, is indispensable on the relationship between Mitchell and Frederick.
12. Newcastle to Münchhausen, 26 Nov 1756, 25 Jan 1757; Münchhausen to Newcastle, undated draft (early January 1757?), Hann. 91, Münchhausen I, Nr. 24; I have not found Münchhausen's letter in the Newcastle papers at the British Library and it is possible that he decided not to send it.
13. Letter of 25 Jan 1757 (see preceding note).
14. Dated 28 Dec 1756, Hann. 91, Münchhausen I, Nr. 31.
15. Münchhausen to his brother, 25 Jan 1757, Hann. 92, LXVI, Nr. 13.
16. For details, see Sichart, *op. cit.*, II, 83-84. Hassell (*op. cit.*, 256) truly remarks that, whatever their shortcomings, the Hanoverian ministers of 1756 did more to prepare their country for the coming storm than did their successors in 1803 and 1866 for the assaults engineered by Napoleon and Bismarck.
17. Hann. 91, Münchhausen I, Nr. 30; Hann. 92, LXVI, Nr. 13; Hann. 92, LXXII, Nr. 5[a].
18. Robert Meyer, *Die Neutralitätsverhandlungen des Kurfürstentums Hannover beim Ausbruch des siebenjährigen Krieges* (Kiel, 1912), is still useful, if somewhat narrow. Meyer used neither British nor Austrian sources. Mediger (655-666) is detailed and incisive; my own interpretation differs from his on some points. The biography of Count Schmettau (Friedrich Graf von Schmettau, *Lebensgeschichte des Grafen Schmettau von seinem Sohn*, Berlin, 1806, 320-334) sheds light on the dilatory Hanoverian diplomacy as seen by a suffering observer. Schmettau was Frederick's special envoy at Hanover during these months. See also Schmettau's complaint to Mitchell from Hanover, 20 Feb 1757, RA CP

(M), 49/53. For the text of Kaunitz's offer, including the passages which he apparently merely read out to Steinberg, *HHStA*, Staatskanzlei Hannover, Fasz. 9.

19. Münchhausen to G. F. von Steinberg, 7 Mar 1757, Cal. Br. 24, Oesterreich, Nr. 4510.
20. Frederick to Podewils, 29 Mar 1757, *Pol. Corr.*, XIV, 434.
21. On Pitt's attitude to the neutrality project in the wider context, see Doran, *op. cit.*, 112-113.
22. For the 'ultimatum' (which was an 'ultimate' proposal, not expressly limited in time), see RA CP (M), 50/119. For a British official view of the offer, see Holdernesse to Mitchell, 29 Apr 1757, *ibid.*, 50/118. For Colloredo's reports on the failure of his task, to Kaunitz of 29 April and 3 May 1757, and to Count Starhemberg, the Austrian ambassador at Versailles, of 29 April 1757, as well as for his last appeal to Philip von Münchhausen of 27 Apr 1757, see *HHStA*, England, K. 110. Colloredo's reports do more honour to his devotion than to his perspicuity. He ignored the pressures on George II and instead blamed Münchhausen's supposed incompetence and prejudice. As to responsibility for the neutrality terms, it seems that Vienna was essentially as answerable as Versailles for their harshness. Kaunitz may have applied more sugar-coating to spare the feelings of George II, no more. (See the minutes of the conference between Kaunitz and other Austrian personages with Lieutenant-General d'Estrées, the future victor of Hastenbeck, at Vienna, 28 Feb 1757, *HHStA*, Vorträge, K. 80.)
23. 2 Aug 1757, Hann. 91, Münchhausen I, Nr. 31. British enthusiasm for Frederick was to reach new peaks after the battles of Rossbach and Leuthen, but Philip wrote after the glorious, and jolting, defeat at Kolin. See also Schlenke, *op. cit.*, 230-234.
24. Münchhausen to his brother, 12, 15 Apr 1757, *ibid.* His lamentation in the earlier letter is typical of many and evokes those of Newcastle to Hardwicke: 'Mon cher frère habe ich Ursache um Vergebung zu bitten, dass ich so oft gegen meinen Vorsatz handle, und Dieselbe mit den hiesigen traurigen Umständen unterhalte, obgleich dieses solche weder ändern noch bessern kann. Ich weiss zu meiner Entschuldigung nichts als dieses anzuführen, dass ich mich erleichtert finde, wenn ich mein über die Gefahr worin wir uns befinden höchstbekümmertes Herz in Dero Schoss ausgeschüttet habe, und ich hoffe, dass Sie mir diesen Trost verstatten werden ...' But then Münchhausen had more cause to lament than Newcastle, and he had no thought, so far as we know, of his personal fate.
25. Cal. Br. 24, Wolfenbüttel, Nr. 8273; *Hessisches Staatsarchiv Marburg*, 4 f, England, Nr. 272.
26. *J. H. C.*, XXVII, 713, 724; Basil Williams, *The Life of William Pitt*, 305-306.
27. By mid-June 1757 the advances made by the Schatullkasse to the Kriegsgewölbe alone amounted to 2·9 million thaler—about £500,000 ('Pro Memoria' for George II of 22 June 1757, Hann. 92, LXXVII, Nr. 38). And this before the French had crossed the Weser, or serious fighting taken place (see below).
28. Westphalen, Prince Ferdinand's confidential secretary, frequently refers to the Hanoverian generals' incompetence. Savory (see below) does not share Westphalen's flat condemnation, but the generals were not cut out to be commanders-in-chief in a world war.
29. Mitchell to Holdernesse, 16 Mar 1757, Add. MSS 6806, f. 101; Frederick to George II, 22 Mar 1757, Hann. 92, LXXXII, Nr. 12. I am obliged to Professor Mediger for salient points on this matter.
30. B. Williams, *Pitt*, I, 311.
31. For Frederick's futile efforts in the Seven Years War to achieve a covenant under his leadership between the Protestant states of Germany, see Hermann Meyer, *Der Plan eines evangelischen Fürstenbundes im siebenjährigen Kriege*, Celle, 1893, and G. B. Volz, 'Friedrichs des Grossen Plan einer Losreissung Preussens von Deutschland', *Historische Zeitschrift*, CXXII (1920), 267-277. For Münchhausen's correspondence on the 'Union' with the Hessian-Cassel minister Friedrich August von Hardenberg, see Hann. 91, Münchhausen I, Nr. 29.
32. Münchhausen to George II, 23 June 1757, Hann. 92, LXXXII, Nr. 12.
33. Münchhausen to Philip, 5, 26 July; Philip to Münchhausen, 17 July 1757; Hann. 91,

Münchhausen I, Nr. 31.
34. *Ibid.*
35. Cumberland commanded 27,000 Hanoverian and 19,600 German auxiliaries from Brunswick-Wolfenbüttel, Hesse-Cassel, Saxe-Gotha and Schaumburg-Lippe. A breakdown is given in the 'Instruction' for Cumberland (see below). A strong Prussian contingent with the Observation Army would of course have been of supreme importance. But this Frederick refused to consider even before the battle of Kolin, unless the British ministry assured him of Russian neutrality—which it was in no position to do.
36. RA CP (M), 53/43, 53/50.
37. P. A. von Münchhausen to Cumberland, 23 July 1757, RA CP (M), 54/262, to the Danish minister, Bernstorff, 11 Aug 1757, RA CP (M), 55/99.
38. George II to Cumberland, 27 May 1757, referring to the memoranda of the Hanoverian ministers of 29 Apr and 7 May 1757, *ibid.*, 51/287, 50/163, 50/247.
39. The will of 3 Apr 1751, Cal. Or. 3, Abt. I, Nr. 35, K. 5.
40. For a detailed description of the battle, see Sichart, *op. cit.*, III/1, 253-276.
41. Holdernesse to Cumberland, 16 Sept 1757, Add. MSS 6815, f. 76.
42. *Geheime Räte* to Cumberland, 29 Apr, 7 May 1757, Hann. 92, LXXI, Nr. 17^{dl}, vol. IV.
43. Hann. 92, LXXII, Nr. 11, vol. I (1). E. Charteris, *William Augustus Duke of Cumberland and the Seven Years War*, London, n.d. [1925], gives a slightly different version of the Instruction (322-327) translated into English from a copy in the Cumberland Papers.
44. The evidence that Pitt was ignorant of the Instruction is circumstantial but, to my mind, irrefutable.
45. 'Pro Memoria' signed by George II on 19 July 1757 and despatched to Hanover, Hann. 92, LXXII, Nr. 11, vol. II (2).
46. Frederick to George II, 20 June 1757, *Pol. Corr.*, XV, 175; Mitchell to Holdernesse (quoting Frederick), 28 June 1757, *ibid.*, 193.
47. Pitt to Cumberland, 29 July 1757, quoted in Hassell, *op. cit.*, 380; Pitt to George Grenville, 11 Aug 1757, quoted in Doran, *op. cit.*, 151.
48. Pitt to Sir Benjamin Keene, British ambassador to Spain, 23 Aug 1757, RA CP (M), 56/101-102. It is in this letter that Pitt offers to restore Gibraltar to Spain in return for Spanish aid in the reconquest of Minorca. Pitt's indifference to the fate of Hanover in August probably helps to explain the generosity he showed to Cumberland, his political enemy, when Cumberland returned in October, beaten and disgraced.
49. Hann. 92, LXXII, Nr. 12, vol. I; RA CP (M), 55/94, 55/95, 55/99.
50. Philip von Münchhausen to the elder Steinberg, 9 Aug 1757, Hann. 92, LXXII, Nr. 12, vol. I; the younger Steinberg's note for Kaunitz of 12 Sept 1757, *HHStA*, Staatskanzlei Hannover, Fasz. 9. Cumberland informed Mitchell confidentially of the appeal to Vienna; Mitchell immediately passed the news to Eichel, Frederick's confidential secretary (!). Eichel then told Mitchell that the elder Steinberg had in this case put Berlin in the picture, at the behest of George II. (Mitchell's 'Journal' for 1757, entry of 30 Aug; *Memoirs and Papers of Sir Andrew Mitchell, K.B.*, Andrew Bisset ed., London, 1850, I, 364.)
51. George II to Cumberland, 7, 16 Sept 1757, Hann. 92, LXXII, Nr. 12, vols. I, II; RA CP (M), 56/80.
52. Hann. 92, LXXII, Nr. 13, vol. II.
53. Münchhausen to Mitchell, 18 Sept 1757, Add. MSS 32875, f. 118; Münchhausen to Newcastle, 28 Mar 1758, Hann. 91, Münchhausen I, Nr. 36. For Münchhausen's actual mood at the time, see his memorandum of 8 Sept 1757, the day Richelieu signed the convention, for a justification of his policies. (Hann. 92, LXXII, Nr. 12, vol. 1.) Though Münchhausen does not refer to the convention, it is permissible to infer from what he does say that he would have advocated submission.
54. For the convention, see Hann. 10, Frankreich, Nr. 2. Hanoverian sources refer to the 'Convention of Bremervörde'.
55. 20 Sept 1757, Hann. 92, LXXII, Nr. 12, vol. II.

56. 20 Sept 1757, *ibid.*
57. P. von Münchhausen in his letters to his brother in late 1757 complains of the king's deteriorating health (*loc. cit.*).
58. The third, and last, codicil to the testament of George II, of 15 Sept 1759, Hann. Br. 9, Domestica, Nr. 98[c], K. G. In the second codicil of 6 Oct 1757, under the full impact of Kloster Zeven, George II had annulled the apanage originally devised to Cumberland, in favour of the Prince of Wales and Hanoverian public objectives, 'for valid reasons' (*aus bewegenden Ursachen*). The third codicil 'explicitly' declared that those sound reasons had never been any but the state of British and Hanoverian finance; and hence in this codicil the king made alternative provision for the Duke, 'who had always behaved as a good and dear son, in token of Our paternal love' (*welcher sich jederzeit als ein guter und lieber Sohn gegen Uns betragen haben, als ein Zeichen Unsrer väterlichen Liebe und Zuneigung*). When the testament was opened, Cumberland insisted that this passage be read out twice.
59. *Pol. Corr.*, XV, 300-301, 336-337, 362-364. Münchhausen to Newcastle, 6 Nov 1757, Hann. 91, Münchhausen I, Nr. 36.
60. George II to G. F. von Steinberg, 20 Sept 1757, quoted by Hassel, *op. cit.*, app. 26.
61. Hassell, *op. cit.*, 431-433, gives a brief but telling description. For a flood of harrowing detail, see Hann. 9e, Nrs. 7-12, 24, 26; Hann. 92, LXXII, Nr. 17, vols. I, II. These volumes should one day form the basis of a case study of what military occupation meant for the population in the 'civilized' eighteenth century.
62. The most significant exchanges are: George II to *Geheime Räte* at Stade, 5, 11, 14 Oct 1757; *Geheime Räte* (including separate *vota* and annexes) to George II, 17, 19, 30 Oct 1757; Hann. 92, LXXII, Nr. 12, vol. II. The king's three letters were delivered at Stade by Philip von Münchhausen in person, sent there the better to convince his colleagues (George II's instruction to P. von Münchhausen of 18 Oct 1757, *ibid.*). His colleagues promptly convinced him. The decision to renew hostilities of course lay with neither.
63. Hann. 92, LXXII, Nr. 12, vol. II.
64. Newcastle to Münchhausen, 10 Oct 1757, Hann. 91, Münchhausen I, Nr. 36.
65. Münchhausen to Newcastle, 6 Nov 1757, *ibid.*
66. 'Und kommt der grosse Friedrich dann und klopft nur auf die Hosen, dann läuft die ganze Reichsarmee, Panduren und Franzosen'—elderly Germans will remember the jingle from their nursery. See also Goethe—no German nationalist—in *Dichtung und Wahrheit*, Part I, Book 3.
67. Münchhausen to Secretary J. E. Mejer at Stade [?], 8 Nov 1757; 'this happy news [of the battle] will change [or "renew"] all, here too'. Hann. 92, LXXII, Nr. 12, vol. III. For Schwicheldt's dissenting *votum* principally in favour of a separate peace, 9 Feb 1758, see Hann. 92, LXXII, Nr. 13.
68. Cal. Br. 24, Wolfenbüttel, 8274; Hann. 9e, Nr. 214.
69. The classic description of the war in west Germany remains Christian H. Ph. von Westphalen, *Geschichte der Feldzüge des Herzogs von Braunschweig-Lüneburg*, Berlin, 1859-1872, 6 vols. Westphalen was Prince Ferdinand's confidential secretary and friend. For a modern treatment in English, Sir Reginald Savory, *His Britannic Majesty's Army in Germany During the Seven Years War*, Oxford, 1966.
70. 'Pro Memoria' initialled by all the ministers at Stade except Philip von Münchhausen, 28 Nov 1757, Hann. 9e, Nr. 214. I have not found a reply.
71. Pitt as quoted in Newcastle's 'Heads for Mylord Hardwicke', 16 Feb 1758, Add. MSS 32997, ff. 342-343.
72. Savory, *op. cit.*, 311.
73. The king agreed without reservation to Pitt's demand quoted above (Add. MSS 32997, f. 346). He also agreed on a later occasion that 'the army should advance according to the motions of the enemy', i.e. not according to a narrow interpretation of Hanoverian security needs. (Newcastle to Pitt, 24 Mar 1758, Add. MSS 32878, f. 330.)
74. Doran, *op. cit.*, 158.

75. E.g. Münchhausen to his brother, 11 Jan 1761, Hann. 91, Münchhausen I, Nr. 73. There are many instances, unobtrusive but unambiguous.
76. The correspondence between Prince Ferdinand and Pitt (Chatham MSS, PRO/30/8/90) bears on the conduct of the war, and not on 'Hanoverian–British relations'. The notes which Philip von Münchhausen occasionally wrote to Pitt (Chatham MSS, PRO/30/8/80) are of technical content.
77. Münchhausen to his brother, 11 Aug 1758, shakily written in his own hand, vents his 'consternation' which robs him 'at this moment of the power to write or think'. He had just received a defeatist note from Adjutant-General von Reden. (Hann. 92, LXVI, Nr. 13.) (Reden, as Professor Mediger informs me, was incited by the hereditary Prince of Brunswick, Ferdinand's nephew.)
78. For a typical complaint by P. von Münchhausen to Newcastle 'by the express order of the king', on the remissness of the British commissariat, 28 Oct 1759. P.R.O., Treasury Papers, T/64, 96, pp. 248-250. The German novelist Wilhelm Raabe recaptures what the war meant to the common people of Hanover and Brunswick, in his stories *Die Innerste*, *Das Odfeld* and *Hastenbeck*, written late in the nineteenth century. Raabe's ancestors had lived through the war, and the memories had not died out when he was a boy at Holzminden, on the upper Weser. Characteristically, the French treated the University of Göttingen—not, it appears, the town—with the consideration due to an abode of learning and polite society (see J. S. Pütter, *Selbstbiographie*, Göttingen, 1798, 2 vols., I, 370-371; also, H. Wellenreuther, 'Göttingen und England im achtzehnten Jahrhundert', *250 Jahre Vorlesungen an der Georgia-Augusta 1734-1984*, Göttingen, 1985, 36-37, 44).
79. According to Kenneth L. Ellis, 'The Administrative Connections between Britain and Hanover', *J. of the Society of Archivists*, III (1969), 557. It is impossible to get a precise picture of the moneys which passed from Britain to Hanover during the war, as many of the transactions were settled between Newcastle and P. von Münchhausen informally. (See the letters between George III and Lord North of August 1775, Sir J. Fortescue ed., *The Correspondence of King George the Third from 1760 to December 1783*, London, 1927-28, 6 vols; III, 237-239.) On the close cooperation of Newcastle and P. von Münchhausen in financial matters during the war, see Taylor, Pringle eds., *Correspondence of William Pitt*, London, 1838-40, 4 vols; I, 303-304, 306; also Treasury Papers, T/1 375 *et seq.*
80. Mitchell's 'Journal' for 1758, entry of 2 July, Bisset, *op. cit.*, II, 33; entry of 8 July, *op. cit.*, II, 35; Mitchell to Newcastle, 11 Dec 1758, *op. cit.*, I, 472-474.
81. Finckenstein to Münchhausen, 1 Aug 1758, Hann. 92, LXXXII, Nr. 12.
82. Münchhausen to George II, 7, 10 Aug 1758, *ibid.*; Münchhausen to his brother, 7 Aug 1758, *ibid.*
83. For a direct appeal the king made to Newcastle, Newcastle to Hardwicke, 21 Nov 1759, Hardwicke to Newcastle, same day, Add. MSS 32899, ff. 6-7, 13-14. For an approach to Count Viry, the Sardinian minister, through Philip von Münchhausen, see Newcastle's 'Most Secret' memo., 22 Nov 1759, ff. 35-36.
84. Hann. 91, Münchhausen I, Nr. 73. The first letter is dated 23 October 1760; possibly this is an error. The last letter used here is of 17 January 1761. Münchhausen's treatment justifies presenting his arguments as of one date.
85. For a less emotional but equally negative assessment of the British commissariat, see Westphalen, *op. cit.*, I, 119-121. Savory, *op. cit.*, 303-305, quotes Ferdinand in the same sense. The case for the British Treasury and, to some extent, for the commissariat is put by R. Browning, 'The Duke of Newcastle and the Financial Management of the Seven Years War in Germany', *J. Soc. Army Historical Research*, XLIX (1971), 20-35.
86. F. Frensdorff, *Allgemeine Deutsche Biographie*, XXII, 737.
87. Münchhausen was no master of the written word. Therefore his language, terse and pregnant for once, should be set out here: 'Der hochselige König wäre ein recht grosser Regent gewesen, wenn er in Kriegen, bei denen es auf das Wohl und Wehe des ganzen Europa ankam, nicht allemal gesucht hätte, einige elende Ämter und Dörfer für seine

Deutschen Lande abzubekommen. Er hat sie doch nicht erhalten, sich aber einem Ruhm entzogen, der grösser als alle Siege gewesen sein würde: nämlich dass das allgemeine Wohl sein einziger Zweck gewesen wäre.'

88. One is reminded of Clemenceau's quip that war is too important a business to be left to the generals—except that Münchhausen did not mean to be sarcastic.
89. The letter of 12 Dec 1760.

Chapter 6
Economic and cultural aspects

Economic themes play a minor role in the relations of Hanover and Britain in the middle of the eighteenth century.[1]

There were British apologists for the personal union who said that Hanover was an asset to the British economy. There was the lure of a preferential market: British manufactures and colonial re-exports, for Hanoverian raw materials under politically advantageous conditions. In addition claims were made of what today would be called a geopolitical character.[2] Hanover had a coastline on the North Sea, and access to two major river systems reaching into the heart of Germany—the Weser and the Elbe. Cogent as the case is on paper, it was never translated into reality.

One fallacy of the 'geopolitical' argument is that the coast of Hanover was ill adapted to economic development, through the nature of the seaboard *and* its close hinterland. In addition, the mouths of the Weser and the Elbe were dominated by Bremen and Hamburg, Imperial cities—that is, practically sovereign. Lastly, the Weser and the Elbe were not 'Hanoverian' rivers; essentially they were her frontiers to the west and north-east.

However, the basic reason for the insignificance of the economic nexus is the backwardness of the electorate, which had little to offer the expanding economy of Britain. (For a brief sketch of the economy of Hanover, see above, 'Introduction'.) A complementary factor of great importance is the diffidence and distrust of the authorities, amply supported from below. George II indeed, like his father, showed some enterprise. As was natural he sought to interest his Hanoverian ministers in undertakings which involved British subjects and capital. But his efforts were sporadic and he failed to overcome the inertia, and occasionally the hostility, of the Hanoverian authorities. Münchhausen showed some signs of rising above his colleagues in this field too. Yet he, like them, was socially conservative and politically timid, and he did not endeavour to change the prevailing current. The fear of antagonizing powerful outsiders—Hamburg, Holland, the East India Company—was a significant political factor in their reckoning as well.

There was of course trade between Hanover and Britain: raw linen from Hanover in declining quantities, 'colonial' produce from Britain. It cannot have been significant.[3] For one, Hanover's external trade remained insignificant altogether. Secondly, Britain gave Hanover no favoured treatment, while the Hanoverian ministers seem to have made no conspicuous efforts to protect their producers from British goods. On the contrary, they protested strenuously to Whitehall against the imputation that they might be doing so[4]—yet another facet of their overriding concern not to arouse British animosities.

Attempts were made to develop both Harburg and Stade, Hanover's ports on the lower Elbe (Stade actually on the Schwinge, a short tributary of the Elbe). Elaborate projects included the development of better harbour facilities and the foundation of overseas trading companies.[5] British commercial and financial circles were willing to invest in such schemes which had the blessing of the king. An Englische Manufactur-Compagnie was established at Harburg; but all this activity came to naught. The ministers at Hanover, the noble *Landdrosten*, and the burghers seemed united in quiet obstructionism.

Occasional initiatives strove to create the framework for a monetary economy: a central bank; the issue of paper money; legislation regulating mortages, loans on collateral, bills of exchange. The tutelage or inspiration was usually British. They all petered out before they entered the practical stage. In mitigation of the ministers' attitude it can be said that their views did represent a solid consensus of the economic community in the electorate.

Even agriculture, overwhelmingly Hanover's main 'industry', failed to prove an avenue for mutual cooperation before the reign of George III. It is true that even before the Seven Years War English ways and innovations were not unknown, and since its publication in 1750 the learned supplement of the *Hannoverische Anzeigen* paid admiring attention to English agricultural practices. But it was not until the closing decade of the century that English influence can be proved on an appreciable scale.[6]

It is an entirely different question whether Hanover profited—or perhaps lost—from the personal union in purely financial terms. In Britain the popular prejudice is pungently expressed by Bolingbroke: '... we shall throw the small remainder of our wealth ... into the German gulf which cries "give, give" and is never satisfied'.[7] In Hanover, at a later date, the claim that large revenues had regularly gone to Britain was a facet of the resentment felt after the inglorious surrender to Bonaparte in 1803.[8] The claim is unfounded. (George II laid down in his will of 3 April 1751—a fortnight after the death of Frederick Prince of Wales—that 'for ever ... none of our German treasured moneys and revenues shall be drawn hither [to Britain], but they shall be used solely for the good of Our Electoral and other German lands'.[9] This solemn injunction undoubtedly represented practice until that date, and was observed even after. In the same paragraph the king decreed that 'for ever ... no Englishman shall be put over Our German lands, as deputy, or governor, or under whatever other name'.)

As already stated, no detailed balance sheet can be offered regarding the assertion that Hanover derived substantial benefit from the personal union; the state of accounting is entirely insufficient. But a general picture, drawn from a variety of sources, may be put forward with confidence.

George II did amass a great fortune in Hanover from regular remittances between his accession and 1756. The recipients were the *Kriegsgewölbe*—the special fund of the War Chancery—and his privy purse (the *Schatulle*). Neither set of transactions was kept secret from the Hanoverian ministers; the king definitely did not take his British ministers into his confidence any more than he could help. The origin of the money in the main was savings from the Civil List. Surpluses of the Hanoverian troop subsidies came a poor second.[10] The total involved over these twenty-nine years can only be guessed; £3 million may be near the mark.

These remittances did not benefit Hanover economically to any marked degree. The king 'treasured' most of the money (disregarding army expenditure, for which the subsidies were intended). Occasionally he lent certain sums to the Board (the *Kammer*) against interest in anticipation of state revenue or to make up a deficit.

The money thus accumulated in Hanover was spent during the first two years of the Seven Years War. The most detailed account we have, in a secondary source, credits the *Schatulle* with almost 9·5 million thaler at the start of the war, and 670,000 thaler at the death of the king.[11] The same source says that between 1727 and 1761 George I, II and III (*sic*) remitted to the *Kriegsgewölbe* out of their private means almost 12 million thaler.[12] Also at the king's death his privy purse in London was found to contain 17,000 guineas only.[13] It is difficult to arrive at anything like hard facts from all this. But it seems that the king's cry of anguish in 1758 that by then the defence of Hanover had cost him two and a half million pounds, 'the saving of thirty years',[14] is near the truth. And much as the dissipation of his wealth must have hurt this avaricious man, the evidence indicates that once the enemy was in sight he never hesitated to give in his country's defence.

* * *

Hanoverian influence on English civilization can be disposed of at once: there was no such influence before the 1760s.[15] The British climate of opinion was unfavourable, and Hanover had as yet little to offer. George II with his personal foibles and political handicaps was marginally an impediment to the role of Hanover as a conduit for German culture. (It can be argued that his patronage did Handel more harm than good.) Later in the century, however, a change of attitude took place: German philosophy and literature, and the German language as their vehicle, acquired prestige among the educated class in England and Scotland. Göttingen took something of the place that Leyden had occupied in the past, as a university where earnest young Englishmen and Scots might spend some years with profit to their intellect and morals. As an additional boon to the status seeker, George III sent three of his sons to Göttingen. But in 1760 all this lay in the future.

On the Hanoverian side the picture is somewhat different. To start with, the elector's subjects were undoubtedly proud of his elevation, and inclined to bask in reflected glory. That holders of electoral offices were often styled 'Königlich-gross-britannisch Kurfürstlich-braunschweig-lüneburgisch'—no doubt to their and their families' immense satisfaction—is at once the symbol of this reflection and the limit of its application. It needs no stressing that British law was not cognizant of these honours.

On a more sober level, knowledge of the English language seems to have been more widespread in Hanover than elsewhere in Germany (except at Hamburg and Bremen), though it did not remotely approach French. Again, Göttingen was effective, with its stock of English books and its English tutors. Moreover, so far as it went, the diffusion of English reached the upper bourgeoisie and the recent nobility, including, naturally, the 'secretariocracy'. It did not extend to the ancient nobility. Of George II's Hanoverian ministers only Steinberg, Philip von Münchhausen and Schwicheldt seem to have been able to translate from English; the former two, of course, spent many years of their lives in England.

Periodical publications which got into their stride in the 1750s devoted to things English an appreciable part of their space and attention, though not inordinately so. The editorial mood was uniformly one of approval and emulation.

Here is the starting point of the *Englandverehrung*, of admiration for English history, law, society, language, literature, economics, and in particular for the British constitution. It was widespread—if not deep searching—in Germany in the last third of the eighteenth century, and it centred largely on Göttingen.[16] A remnant of this admiration persisted in Hanover far into the nineteenth century.[17] It may not be entirely extinct in today's Land Niedersachsen.[18]

Did those who held to an *Englandverehrung* have their opponents too? As we have seen, ever since Frederick's eruption on to the European scene and up to the Seven Years War there was a feeling within the Privy Council that the British connection exposed Hanover to horrible dangers, without Hanover being able to remove their cause. There is no evidence that this feeling penetrated into circles outside the Privy Council.

Here too the Seven Years War brought a change, though it was slow, by no means pervasive, and in itself unproductive of political action. Suffice it to say that at least some minds advanced from a sense of British culpability for the disaster of the war to a more general grievance against British selfishness, cupidity and arrogance. These voices were first heard in public during the French Revolution, and became more insistent after the French occupation of 1803.[19] The material and spiritual misery of the following ten years brought another reversal. The return of the personal union in 1813, with the expulsion of the French, was welcomed with a relief that seems to have been spontaneous and universal.

Notes

1. Two modern monographs bear directly on this theme: Klaus Puster, *Möglichkeiten und Verfehlungen merkantiler Politik im Kurfürstentum Hannover unter Berücksichtigung des Einflusses der Personalunion mit dem Königreich Grossbritannien*, Hamburg, 1966, and Otto Ulbricht, *Englische Landwirtschaft in Kurhannover in der zweiten Hälfte des 18. Jahrhunderts*, Berlin, 1980. In the following I have drawn freely on both works.
2. Such arguments feature prominently in Malachy Postlethwayt, *Great Britain's True System*, 1757.
3. I have not discovered satisfactory statistics. Sir Charles Whitworth (*State of the Trade of Great Britain*) and Elizabeth B. Schumpeter (*English Overseas Trade Statistics*) do not mention Hanover separately. Much that related to commerce and customs was destroyed in the Hanoverian archives during World War II. Also, whatever overseas trade there was largely used outlets outside Hanover—Bremen chiefly for exports, and Hamburg for imports. This is another factor unconducive to quantitative enquiry.
4. Memorandum by *Geheime Räte*, 20 Apr 1756, transmitted to Newcastle. The memorandum denies the complaints of Yorkshire clothiers that the Hanoverian authorities discriminated against English woollens (Add. MSS 32864, ff. 351-352). Yet in 1769 the ministers compelled the *Regierung* of Bremen-Verden to license the brewing of 'English ale and porter beer' at Stade, against local opposition. A rider added that the initiative deserved encouragement rather than obstruction. (Niedersächsisches Staatsarchiv Stade, Rep. 31, Tit. 41^{l}, Nr. 3.) Ale, after all, was less of a British staple export than broadcloth.
5. For Stade, see also Weise, 'Stader Fernhandelspläne seit den Zeiten der Merchant Adventurers und ihre Beziehungen zu Hamburg', *Hamburger Wirtschaftschronik*, 1950, 13-30.
6. For an illuminating forerunner, see Otto Ulbricht, '... Hinüber ...' (bibliography).
7. Letter to Lord Marchmont, 9 June 1741, *A Selection from the Papers of the Earls of Marchmont* (G.H. Rose ed.), 3 vols., London, 1831; II, 258.
8. Thus Seumnich, *Ueber die Verbindung des Churfürstenthums Hannover mit England*, Hamburg, 1803: '... the king receives a million thalers annually [from Hanover] ... for the conduct of parliamentary elections' (11). K. Seumnich, doctor of law, was a Hanoverian.

9. Cal. Or., Des. 3, Abt. I, Nr. 35, K.G.
10. For this, see Brauer, *op. cit.*, 185-190.
11. W. Lehzen, *Hannover's Staatshaushalt*, Hanover, 1853-55; II, 27-28. The exchange rate of the thaler varied between five and six to the pound.
12. *Ibid.*, 126. A recent introduction to this theme is Mediger, 'Vorbemerkung' to Hann. 46, Kriegsgewölbe.
13. Hann. 9, Domestica, Nr. 98c, K.G.
14. Walpole, Horace, *Memoires of the Last Ten Years of the Reign of George the Second*, London, 1822; II, 457-458.
15. For German—as distinct from Hanoverian—cultural impacts on England at that time, see G. N. Davis, *German Thought and Culture in England 1700-1770*, Chapel Hill, 1969. Leibniz made some impression, but he was a lone star—and he died in 1716.
16. Franz Uhle-Wettler, *Staatsdenken und Englandverehrung bei den frühen Göttinger Historikern* (thesis Marburg, 1956) is an important monograph on the role played by Göttingen.
17. 'Ever since Hanover came into closer contact with England through the elevation of her dynasty to the British throne, the adjective "English" has stood for excellence only'—Albert Hüne, *Geschichte des Königreichs Hannover und Herzogthums Braunschweig*, Hanover, 1824-1830; II, 540. Further examples in Röhrbein, von Rohr, *Hannover im Glanz und Schatten des britischen Weltreiches*, Hanover, 1977.
18. The *Land* of Niedersachsen, established with the consent of the British military administration in 1946, has as its heart the former electorate of Hanover, with the addition of Brunswick-'Wolfenbüttel' and, among other territories, the chief prizes which were so dear to George II, and which remained always beyond his grasp—Hildesheim, Osnabrück, East Friesland. With some fancy we have here his belated victory over Frederick of Prussia.
19. The subject is amply surveyed in Carl Haase, 'Obrigkeit und öffentliche Meinung in Kurhannover 1789-1803', *Niedersächsisches Jahrbuch für Landesgeschichte*, XXXIX (1967), 192-294; and Reinhold Oberschelp, 'Kurhannover im Spiegel von Flugschriften des Jahres 1803', *ibid.*, XLIX (1977), 209-247.

Chapter 7
The 'opinions' of the Hanoverian ministers, 1744 and 1757

It is of obvious importance for the theme of this work to know how the Hanoverian ministers viewed the real import of the personal union, and it is indeed fortunate that on two occasions, in 1744 and in 1757, George II asked the Hanoverian *Geheimes Ratskollegium* to give their opinion on this issue.[1] Since the resulting labours of the *Geheime Räte* were bulky as well as searching, whereas their result in political terms was nil (and clearly expected to be nil by the authors)—the opinions are best treated separately.

The idea of dissolving the personal union between Hanover and Great Britain was nearly as old as the personal union itself. Early in 1716 George I wrote his testament, with the draft of an explanatory codicil added in 1720, in which he provided for the separation of the two dignities *after* the reigns of his son, the future George II, and his grandson, the future Frederick Prince of Wales (whose succession to both the British crown and the Hanoverian electorship the testator regarded as 'settled—*eine ausgemachte Sache, bei welcher es sein Verbleiben hat*').[2] Thereafter the British crown should go to the firstborn, the electorship to the second, and their respective descendants after them. During the first two reigns Hanover should have a permanent governor (*Statthalter*), since the king would obviously reside in London. The king's reason for providing for the ultimate dissolution of the personal union, as it appears in the testament, was regard for Hanover and the electoral office, as Hanover would 'as it were, turn into a dependency of the crown of Great Britain which ... would be very disadvantageous in many ways to the welfare of those [German] countries'. Apparently this disadvantage would not count so long as the king in London was born, and had been brought up, in Hanover. In 1721 George I received, at his request, a Hanoverian opinion on the testament and codicil drawn up in the main by his chief Hanoverian adviser, Baron Andreas Gottlieb von Bernstorff. The opinion accepted the king's decision and its underlying reasoning, though it questioned the advisability of appointing a *Statthalter*. Two years earlier George I had submitted the testament to the scrutiny of an English legal committee, who were sceptical.[3]

At his accession George II suppressed his father's testament, which thus lost any political effect it might have had otherwise. However, this does not mean that the new king decisively rejected the concept of separation.[4] That separation was generally popular with public opinion in England under George II, and occasionally wildly popular, has been related earlier in this work, and has only an indirect bearing on the present chapter except as the occasion of the king's request to his Hanoverian ministers.

The first occasion arose when the campaign against Hanover and Carteret was at its height in England. George II then wrote to his Hanoverian ministers on 13 January

1744 that Parliament might perhaps discuss the separation of the crowns under his descendants. And as there could be no doubt that this change could be lawfully carried out in Britain by an Act of Parliament, the *Geheime Räte* were required to give their opinion on the German side of the problem. The instruction is matter-of-fact, with a hint in favour of separation. In turn the ministers worked quickly. Their collective reply is dated 7 February 1744, with a supplement of 3 March. Contrary to the gist of their instruction the ministers devoted most of their effort to a political analysis. For this they received the mildest of royal rebukes.

The prevailing sentiment of the replies—the collective one and the three separate opinions of Münchhausen, Diede and Lenthe—was that a separation was inadvisable on political as well as juridical grounds. As to the juridical question, the Prince of Wales could of course renounce his own right of succession to the German lands and the electoral dignity, as well as that of his descendants. The difficulty was whether such renunciation was constitutionally the last word. Room was left for doubt by the Imperial constitution as embodied in the Golden Bull of 1356; by the precedents in the subsequent history of the Empire; by the inheritance laws, testaments and dynastic agreements binding the Guelph house; even by the oath of allegiance sworn by George II's own electoral subjects.[5]

As to the political question, the Hanoverian ministers saw an interdependence of British and Hanoverian interests. They again insisted on their incompetence sufficiently to judge British interests. Still, they opined that the personal union with Hanover was a major asset in Britain's perennial rivalry with France. In this conflict it was a vital interest of Britain to maintain the balance of power and the *systema imperii*. The 'joining of crown and electorate in one person' greatly facilitated these objectives—diplomatically and strategically, as well as commercially and psychologically.

Then the ministers proceeded to deal with possible objections to their reasoning. The most interesting of these is that the personal union involved Britain in quarrels not of her concern, but in answer to this objection the Hanoverians contended that Britain's interests committed her to Continental involvement in any case. 'A wise government' (*eine weise Regierung*, which may also be understood as 'wise governing') could avoid 'all clashes' (*alle Contrarität*). However, 'assuming, though not granting, that such an impression arose, affairs could be managed in such a way as to make the lesser [interest] yield to the greater'—that is, Britain would see to it that her own needs were secured first. 'In this connection the events of 1741 well merit to be cited as an example of Your Majesty's setting aside the impression of accepting advantages from Prussia or France with regard to Your Majesty's German interests, so that the English common system might be pursued [rather than that of Hanover].' (Evidently the *Geheime Räte* regarded their bypassing of British interests in the neutrality issue as the mere corollary of British callousness concerning the security of Hanover. George II certainly cannot be said to have subordinated his Hanoverian to his British interests while the danger to Hanover was at its height.)

The Hanoverian ministers' opinion gives little space to the *Hanoverian* stake in preserving the personal union. 'Politics' were outside their brief, of course. But it also seems that this aspect needed no particular pleading. They and their master understood the power of Britain as a necessary safeguard, in the long run, from the 'violence and injustice' which Prussia and France were liable to inflict on Hanover, and which Hanover could not withstand unaided. That George II in his dual capacity was also 'a tutelary deity of German liberty and the Protestant religion' followed, according to the Hanoverian ministers, from all that had been said before.

The opinions delivered in 1757 differ from those of 1744 in their greater volume, diversity and sophistication. This is probably due less to a maturing process than to the change in circumstances. All the same, the qualified disenchantment with the British connection which is one of the strands in the later opinions was to remain a feature of the Hanoverian attitude after 1760. The point should not be overstressed. It never became the dominant strand, though it gradually percolated downward in Hanoverian society from then on. To that extent the lesson of the war—not merely of the French occupation—left its imprint.

On 27 September 1757 Philip von Münchhausen wrote to his brother in French-occupied Hanover, in cypher. The idea of separating the two crowns under the king's successors had again arisen, the younger Münchhausen said. 'Those who claim to wish the German lands well allege *inter alia* that, once a king reigns over Britain who is English-born and bred, and whose knowledge of the electorate amounts to little or nothing, the latter may fare ill.' It was believed that there would be no difficulty in passing the necessary legislation in Parliament; moreover, the matter might even be brought up at the start of the coming session, in November. The king therefore once more requested his Hanoverian ministers to give their opinion on the feasibility and the desirability of a separation as soon as possible.

The 1757 instruction strikingly differed from that of 1744. It was much more specific and pointedly asked that the consequences for Hanover be stated and analysed. Most important, its justification was no longer the present hostility of British opinion, but the dangers to Hanover after the death of George II, already well over seventy. The oblique reference to the future George III with his English background and reputed anti-Hanoverian prejudices may be taken at face value: here was a factor of prime significance which had already given the Hanoverian ministers much cause for anxiety. What goes unmentioned in the letter is the French occupation of Hanover in a British war, and the king's dismay at the Convention of Kloster Zeven. There was no need: the addressees lived amidst the former, and knew only too well about the latter.

The elder Münchhausen signed his opinion on 12 October 1757, shortly before he left Hanover for Stade. His views can be summarized in one sentence: the union was a good thing for Hanover so long as the English wanted it, but it spelt ruin for Hanover, once they did not. In the former case Britain would give Hanover effective protection against her enemies, 'even though the impending fall, or at least the considerable weakening, of the King of Prussia will remove one mighty and fearsome neighbour'. (And this from the Hanoverian chief minister at a time when Frederick was the Continental mainstay of British war policy!) In the latter case Hanover would draw upon herself the attentions of all those countries primarily interested in hurting Britain, without the benefit of any British exertions on Hanover's behalf. Even if such a catastrophe were avoided, the British ministers of a future sovereign might choose to exploit Hanover grievously for the sake of Britain, 'though one must not doubt the excellent sentiments (*besten Gesinnung*) of the heir to the throne'. On the other hand, if the separation were to be carried out on the assumption that Britain was *not* interested in the personal union, actual good might result therefrom for Hanover. For one, the elector could marshal his resources—political as well as military—and give them over to Hanoverian considerations. Moreover, 'it seems to me that the [British] nation would then be more inclined to help protect these countries'—when, that is, their allegiance could no longer be taken for granted.

Münchhausen saw no legal or constitutional barriers to the separation so far as the Empire and the Guelph countries were concerned.

How did Münchhausen really feel? Reading between the lines it is clear that he still believed the union to be serviceable so long as George II lived; in any case, as long as he lived a separation was not a practical proposition, so the union had better be made to serve. But in 1757 the king was very old, and, in the final analysis and not without some trepidation, Münchhausen seems to have considered a separation of the crowns as desirable for Hanover in the future. If so, he probably changed his mind at a later stage, in view of his excellent relations with King George III.

Against this truly formidable vote, the other opinions can be briefly discussed.

Steinberg, the oldest minister after Münchhausen (and to die within two years), mainly considers it hard on Hanover that a separation at this stage should free Britain from her obligation to extricate Hanover from the mire in which she had landed her. Schwicheldt, in the most systematic of the opinions, believes that the union should be preserved if the Old System—the alliance between Britain and Austria—was to be restored. If it was not, then Hanover would have to turn to Austria, and the union ought to be dissolved. Behr, the youngest of the ministers, also gave the shortest opinion and the least equivocal: the union had to stay. Hake, like Behr a junior member of the Privy Council, by and large prefers the union to continue, though he has grave doubts as to British good will and reliability under a new reign. Busche, with a wealth of diplomatic experience at Dresden and Vienna, rather mistrusts British intentions too, but remains on the fence. Diede, in the most impressive opinion after Münchhausen's, hesitantly favours keeping the union. His analysis of Hanover's needs once the war is over was to leave an unmistakable imprint on Münchhausen's own cogitations as revealed to his brother three years later (see above). It is of interest for the working of the Privy Council that its secretary, J.E. Mejer, elder brother of the Chancery secretary in London, added his own opinion. Though Mejer lists the benefits of a separation, he thinks that they are definitely outweighed by the risks that a break-up would entail.

In contrast to the former occasion, in 1757 there was no collegiate opinion—in itself a significant deviation from the norm.

George II acknowledged the opinions on 29 November 1757 without further comment. It seems that he was content to let the future run its course. In 1744 he had explicitly said that a separation would not take place in his own lifetime.[6] With yet stronger reason this held good in 1757. His testament with its codicils, written between 1751 and 1759, clearly assumes that the personal union stays in force.[7]

Notes

1. The bulk of the opinions is collected in Hann. 92, II, Nr. 8; a lesser number were destroyed in World War II. Richard Drögereit analyses the material in his 'Das Testament König Georgs I. und die Frage der Personalunion zwischen England und Hannover', *Niedersächsisches Jahrbuch für Landesgeschichte*, XIV (1937), 94-199 (henceforth Drögereit).
2. In this paragraph I have mainly used Drögereit and the more recent research of Professor R.M. Hatton (*George I, Elector and King*, 157-169). It seems Drögereit had no access to

primary sources in England. For the text of the testament and its codicil, see Drögereit, 180-199.

3. British Library, Stowe MSS, 249, for the deliberations of this committee.
4. On George II's occasional flirting with the idea of separation before 1740, see Lord Hervey, *Some Materials Towards Memoirs of the Reign of King George II* (R. Sedgwick ed.), III, 795-802, 855-857. It appears the king was swayed by the hope of establishing the Duke of Cumberland as elector. Queen Caroline, according to Hervey, opposed separation as an unwarranted diminution of the king's heritage.
5. I have relied on Drögereit for the three separate opinions of 1744 and for Secretary Mejer's opinion of 1757, all of which were lost in the war.
6. George II to *Geheime Räte*, 7 Feb 1744, Hann. 92, III A, Nr. 8.
7. Calenberger Originalarchiv, 3, I, Nr. 35, K.G.

Conclusions

It is a commonplace that the 'union' between Hanover and Britain after 1714 was personal, being vested in a hereditary prince, in conformance with the succession laws of each state. Otherwise Hanover and Britain were entirely independent of each other—in nationhood, constitution and international law.

All this is true, of course. But it is easy to overlook the significance of what the personal union entailed. The period under review was the heyday of the monarchical age in Europe. A common ruler of otherwise 'independent' states might properly turn his hold into a union in a very real sense—politically and even constitutionally. It was the political will of the English nation that gives the accepted axiom of the two countries' separate identities its historical truth.

Besides the 'merely personal' character of the union, and the British determination to keep the union as inoperative as possible on the political plane, additional factors determined the relationship between the two states.

First of all, so far as administration and domestic politics—in the widest sense—were concerned, Britain and Hanover went their own ways. This is not a self-evident result of the constitutional situation. Given the Hanoverian propensities of George II on the one hand, and Britain's superiority in resources on the other, it might reasonably have been otherwise.

For one, George II's love of Hanover, and his devotion to her interests, never made him tamper with the British constitution as he understood it—and it was a subject that certainly exercised him throughout his reign. '*Nach der hiesigen Verfassung … unmöglich*', 'according to the constitution of this country … impossible', runs like a thread through his correspondence with the *Geheime Räte*, and they never, not once so far as can be ascertained, dared to question his judgment.

On the other hand, it is tempting to probe into his practice by the way in which he attempted, or refused to attempt, to promote Hanoverian interests while in England. Evasion and, better, the withholding of information were expedient up to a point—chiefly in Continental diplomacy, and with great circumspection in money matters. The king attempted no confrontation with what the Whig consensus of mid-century regarded as constitutional custom; no confrontation, that is, beyond petulance and incivility towards the ministers of the crown, once these had thwarted his wishes with their official advice. On broader issues of political rather than constitutional significance the same fundamental caution held good, though here the king's general disrespect for public opinion appears as making him go further in accepting risks for the sake of Hanover. It is difficult to pontificate on the motives of so unintrospective a person as George II. Yet it is clear across the centuries that temperamental pusillanimity ('political cowardice'), shrewd calculation and an ingrained sense of honour and duty all come in; the proportions cannot be determined.

George II's Hanoverian entourage in London had no say in British matters. Partly this was accidental: Steinberg and the younger Münchhausen lacked both the personality and the wish to bend British affairs to Hanoverian desires; the Hanoverian servants in England of George I had been of sterner stuff. Then there was Lady Yarmouth, a patriotic Hanoverian, and a partisan of Frederick in the Seven Years War. George II in his old age greatly depended on her for his comfort, and she endeavoured to smoothe matters with him for people who were of her way of feeling. British ministers certainly considered the advisability of using her as a channel to the king.[1] But all this hardly amounts to meddling in British affairs. As for the ministers in Hanover, they were neither equipped nor ambitious enough to get involved in British politics. In the rare cases when Münchhausen discussed British interests with outsiders, George II ordered him to desist, in as sharp a tone as he ever adopted towards him.

As for meddling in Hanoverian affairs, British ministers neither knew nor cared. Carteret is a special case, in this as in so much else. He knew, and he might have cared for, Hanover's concerns but he had other irons in the fire.

Foreign observers were well aware that British policy could not be managed by using Hanoverian agencies, nor vice versa.[2]

Again, though the personal union was not legally indissoluble, for practical purposes all parties assumed it to be a fact of life for the indefinite future. There is the famous interchange between Walpole and Speaker Onslow in 1741.[3] Walpole told Onslow that George II intended to ask for legislation to separate the two crowns some time in the future, and Onslow replied that that would be a 'message from heaven'. Late in 1759 Pitt, Hardwicke and Newcastle reacted in like manner, again when George II suggested legislation to this effect.[4] But whereas in the earlier episode Walpole's and Onslow's scepticism is merely suggested, in 1759 Hardwicke and Newcastle put their disbelief in the feasibility of the separation into words. There can be no doubt that the dislike of the union, together with a shrugging acceptance of its permanence, was shared by all ministers during the reign of George II, while the stresses of war brought their discomfort into the open. As far as the Hanoverian ministers are concerned, their analysis of 'separation' clearly did not transgress the limits of an intellectual exercise.

Thirdly, while British public opinion at all levels overwhelmingly disliked the Hanoverian connection, with only an occasional dedicated supporter, there was a middle-of-the-road consensus which was not blindly hostile to Hanover. It can be summed up thus: Britain had brought over her kings from Hanover in order to secure the Revolution settlement. Though this had its risks and drawbacks, it was a bargain. The sovereigns—George I and George II—by and large stood by it. At the same time they loved the land of their birth and were deeply concerned for its welfare. This too was a fact of life, neither unnatural nor despicable. Hence an obligation rested on Britain with respect to Hanover, politics and expediency apart. Britain was bound to do her reasonable best not to let Hanover come to grief because her elector doubled as king of Great Britain. By the middle of the century it was not a trump card for George II and his Hanoverian ministers to play—there were so many other considerations that were more important to an Englishman with a stake in politics. But it was a card nevertheless, and they played it for all it was worth.[5]

Fourthly, against British ignorance of Hanover must be set Hanoverian ignorance of Britain. It was ignorance of a different kind, for the Hanoverian ministers and their clever secretaries cared a great deal about what happened in Britain. They were all too clear as to the importance for Hanover of the good will, or otherwise, of the cabinet, of Parliament, and even of public opinion. But if they knew much of what went on, their understanding did not go deep. They knew that 'the Nation' feared and hated France for the harm France might do to British trade. But they lacked the empathy to realize what 'trade' meant to the nation apart from mere money-making. They knew towards the end of 1744 that the Pelhams were intriguing against Granville and likely to force him out of the ministry, and of Granville's failure to form an administration fifteen months later, and they commiserated with 'our dearest king'; but the nature of the forces at work were beyond their grasp.[6] These instances can serve for many such.

Finally, the Hanoverian ministers had one supreme concern, one overriding anxiety: the security of Hanover. Again, this is not self-evident. Their supreme concern might have been their master's 'Grandeur und Wohlfahrt'—Münchhausen's expression. It might have been the aggrandizement of Hanover at her neighbours' expense. It might have been their own status, or their careers, or their fortunes. The question whether a minister's prime duty lay with his prince or with his country did give Münchhausen qualms. He concluded that it lay with his prince, as indeed he must—in accordance with his background, if not with his plain oath of office. But it is significant that he felt the need to argue the point within his breast, and his life's work shows a deep-felt concern for his adopted country. As for personal gain, the ministers were human, in all conscience, but they lacked the spur to selfish ambition: socially, they were at the top from birth; politically, they had reached the summit. Money-grubbing was not part of the mental climate of Hanover—and their official incomes were very good. The experience of generations assured the ministers that they had little to fear from court intrigue, interlopers, or royal arbitrariness. They were rational too; they knew that Hanover was weak in a world where Frederick of Prussia set the pace, and they were frightened. Any change, they feared, was dangerous, and likely to be for the worse. Whatever their accountability to the elector, they felt responsible for the safety of Hanover. They did not always carry this burden with courage, dignity, or even good sense, but they never for a moment dismissed it from their mind.

These points are essential for an understanding of what governed the Hanoverian ministers' attitude in their dealings with Britain, in which, first and last, they made every effort for British interests to coincide as nearly as possible with those of Hanover. At one end of the scale lay straightforward conformance to British policy, a precondition for which was that there should indeed be a 'British policy', personified in a minister who knew his mind and kept the Hanoverians on their toes. Carteret's secretaryship from 1742 to 1744 fits into this slot. (Pitt's secretaryships do not, for reasons summed up below.)

Then the ministers might try to persuade their British colleagues that a policy they thought good for Hanover was also good for Britain. An obvious target for this approach was a man like Newcastle who, they felt, as did others, was open to persuasion. The ten-year effort of the Hanoverian ministers to draw Britain into a great-power defence alliance because of the Prussian threat was a major instance of such endeavour.

Then the ministers constantly tried to prove that Hanover could be 'of use' to Britain. Münchhausen's part in the King of the Romans project is a specific example of this line. The ostentatious support for the despatch of Hanoverian troops to

England early in 1756—when for once Hanover herself seemed reasonably secure from invasion—is another major instance. Minor instances abound and are sometimes pathetic in their poignancy. When Britain had drifted into war with Spain in 1739, in her usual state of unpreparedness, George II with the cooperation of the *Geheime Räte* pressed on the British ministry muskets from his brand-new factory at Hertzberg, not as a free gift, to be sure, but on what he considered very reasonable terms. When Whitehall was unenthusiastic he was genuinely hurt. Thereupon the Lords Justices relented, and bought the muskets.[7] All through the Forty-five the Hanoverian ministry acted as a news collection agency covering the German seaboard and delivering intelligence which in retrospect does not look bad at all. It seems these services were unsolicited, and acknowledged from London with hardly more than a patronizing nod.[8] In this crisis, too, the king's Hanoverian war treasury advanced 90,000 thalers (about £15,000) in order to secure the service of 5,000 Bavarian auxiliaries, until the authorities in London should be ready to act; the transaction was of course a Hanoverian as much as a British concern.[9] During the Seven Years War, at least one British sea captain was officially assisted by the Hanoverian authorities in recruiting—though not in pressing—for the Royal Navy.[10] All this amounted to a conscious eagerness to prove that the Hanoverian 'alliance', as it was significantly called, was worthwhile to the major partner.

In one specialized field Hanover served Britain beyond the need for self-advertisement. Ernest Augustus, the first Elector of Hanover, and his elder brother the Duke of Celle (the father-in-law of George I) had evolved a first-rate postal intelligence, with surveillance offices straddling the post routes to Celle, Gifhorn and Nienburg. With regard to speed, technical dexterity, and deciphering, this service belonged to the best in Europe. After 1714 it was at the disposal of the British secretaries of state. Perhaps not all of it, for the intercepted mail passed from Hanover through the German Chancery and, at least in the reign of George II, was scrutinized by the king in person before it was read by British eyes. Cooperation extended to training and the loan of specialists, with Whitehall an eager taker. It is difficult to judge the benefit to Britain in diplomatic terms, since both sides kept all references to this matter out of their diplomatic correspondence. For mail passing north to the line Nienburg–Celle–Gifhorn it must have been considerable. South of it the Thurn und Taxis postal administration, politically under Austrian influence, was unsafe from the British–Hanoverian viewpoint. More prosaically, British ministers at home freely used the services of the *Deutsche Kanzlei* for their correspondence with the Continent, so far as was geographically convenient.[11]

Then there remained the Hanoverian appeal to the British sense of duty and honour. It was a last resort, and it became more necessary in default of other approaches as the years passed. Hanover's case comprised more than mere calls on British compassion. Hanover, the case went, was exposed to danger and hardship because Britain's enemies could strike through her at British interests or, at least, take revenge, for whatever reason, on the king of Britain. It was a British interest to protect Hanover, because—besides all else—national honour is ever linked to national interest. It was not a forlorn appeal, for it touched a chord that did exist in the British public consciousness. But it was not a strong chord, and when the storm broke, it got lost.

Situations did develop in which the interests of Hanover and Britain were so patently opposed that not even a pretence of mutuality could be kept up by the Hanoverian ministers. No matter that this was unfortunate—such eventualities did happen, and then Hanover had to follow her own path. The fact was acknowledged and put on paper, though hardly for British consumption.[12] But what was never said is that even so extreme a contingency had a limitation: the British ministry, or the British minister who mattered, had to acquiesce in the Hanoverians going their separate way. If this acquiescence was not forthcoming, the Hanoverian ministers never summoned up the determination to push on regardless of risk (or advise the king to do so). It is the greatest blemish in their collective personality, though surely the excuses for this timidity are good. The Hanoverian neutrality of 1741-1742 is a valid example of this aspect of the relationship with Britain: the agreement with Fleury was made although it went squarely against the British national interest as perceived at the time. When Carteret put his foot down, the agreement was abandoned—with much circumspection and no little duplicity. (The flaw in this example is that by the time Carteret superseded Harrington in February 1742 the most acute sense of crisis at Hanover had passed. But it had not passed altogether, and from what we know of Carteret's relations with the Hanoverian ministers, and their atttitude to him, it is difficult to imagine that they would have pursued a line in the teeth of his opposition, under any circumstances.)

The first year of the Seven Years War is a negative indication of the same fact: the Hanoverian ministers were then eager to find another 'Neutrality' to save their country from the ravages of invasion and occupation. It was the British 'No' which paralysed them, and they faced the impending catastrophe in despair and a feeling of utter helplessness. Again the example is not perfect inasmuch as it does not take into account George II. Yet the flaw here is slight. George II too would have dearly liked a neutrality for Hanover, at whatever cost to British strategy and prestige; but he was in London, and his sense of what he might attempt at his peril was sharper than his Hanoverian ministers'.

This leads us to George II himself. He loved Hanover, and he did not love England. He knew it, everybody knew it, and he knew that everybody knew. At the same time his British crown was dear to him—it was the major part of his inheritance, of his wealth, and of his consequence in the world. He was not stupid: he had a vivid appreciation that up to a point he might indulge his love for Hanover, but if he were to transgress beyond it, he ran real risks. And he did not often err in his estimate as to where the point lay. In a way difficult to define he was also a man of honour who wanted to do his duty by Britain. As for his Hanoverian ministers, he could indeed order them about, and rebuke them when they were remiss. On the other hand, they might manage him—George II has emerged in the history books as a king to be managed, so long as it was cleverly done and with a proper show of deference. But their relationship was more complex than this picture leads us to believe. For one, when we speak of Queen Caroline, Sir Robert Walpole, or the Hanoverian ministers, the last word on George II's 'capacity of being managed' will never be said; there is a case for arguing that somewhere along the line it was he who fooled them.[13]

Also, with one important exception, to be treated below, the Hanoverian ministers' need to 'manage' the king seldom went beyond the rules of phrasing: commands on his part, and proposals on theirs. The ministers and the king had so much in common. Their respective social outlook and economic interests, if not identical, were by then adjusted to each other without friction. Politically, they had the welfare or, if that sounds too emotional, the advantage of Hanover as their basic objective, with the concomitant awe of the power of Britain to do good and inflict evil. Then there is the human factor. The student of history who is conditioned to the British ministers' complaints of their master's incivility and choler can only marvel at the gentleness George II displayed towards their Hanoverian colleagues. Expressions like 'Eure gewohnte Prudenz' and 'Meine sonderbare [besondere] Liebe', 'Euch ... stets beigetan' are no mere *politesse* when a man as blunt and short-tempered as George II used them week in, year out. As for the Hanoverian ministers, they may occasionally have smiled or sighed behind the king's back; but there can be no doubt that they cared for him as a man.[14] Furthermore, the Hanoverian ministers had a certain latitude in defining policy towards Britain that was denied to the king—because they owed Britain no allegiance, and because they lived at a distance. This distinction too added vitality to their partnership with the king, so far as relations with Britain were concerned.

The one area of lingering disharmony between George II and his Hanoverian ministers over a fundamental issue—where their 'management' of him might well have shown historic consequences—was that of aggrandizement. The king schemed for the acquisition of land and people; it was to him a matter of vast importance except when circumstances were plainly unfavourable. That the ministers were less committed is certain. Generally they were cool, suspicious, and even obstructive—except when circumstances were plainly favourable. Yet they had grown up in the faith that the grandeur and glory of their master were the sense of their service, and that in 'matters of war and peace' his will was law. But they were also 'patriots'—the term actually appears in the correspondence between the brothers Münchhausen, with its attendant dilemma spelled out. Also, the king was beyond the sea most of the time; the ministers knew how much store he set on their concurrence and that, though obstinate, he was not really strong. The topic runs throughout this study; it is the author's notion that beneath the smoothness of their relationship a contest was going on much of the time, well known to the ministers if less so to the king, and that the ministers, led and represented by Münchhausen, left their imprint.[15]

There was a workaday level where Britain was useful to Hanover—with exceptions, legitimately so. After 1714 Hanover successively reduced her diplomatic representation abroad. Within the Empire the gaps were often filled by special emissaries. On the European scale, however, and particularly when dealing with the great powers, it was common under George II to make use of the British foreign service for Hanoverian purposes. There was nothing underhand about such a practice provided the objective was not in itself underhand, as in the Hyndford intrigue of 1745-47. Naturally, the Hanoverian ministers exploited the status of their powerful intercessors. The most frequent addressee was Russia—the chief supplier of grain to Hanover in years of scarcity. More colourful, though without doubt of less practical value, were the treaties which George II concluded throughout his reign with the 'King and Emperor of Morocco' and which aimed at giving his Hanoverian subjects the same protection against seizure, or rather piracy, as Britons enjoyed.[16] Another area for diplomatic assistance was Denmark, which dominated Holstein, on the northern frontier of Hanover. In a quarrel in 1738 over the bailiwick of Steinhorst—one of Münchhausen's 'miserable bailiwicks' (see p. 120)— George II went so far as to use the renewal of a British–Danish subsidies treaty as a counter;[17] but this was atypical. At the other extreme, Münchhausen, when it suited him, rejected with indignation the idea that he might bother a British diplomat with 'German business'—but this was fencing, and atypical too.[18]

* * *

Two strands make up the Hanoverian attitude to the personal union in the eighteenth century. George II was as a Hanoverian inclined to be sanguine; the union was made to serve Hanover; mishaps might be disastrous, but they were mishaps. His Hanoverian ministers were essentially pessimists: though windfalls were possible, basically the union was a snare. The discussions on the union within the Hanoverian ministry convey a sense of unreality, despite their intellectual content, which is considerable. Whatever the differences in outlook and temper, the king and his Hanoverian servants shared a streak of fatalism: the union was there to stay, and the best must be made of it, as opportunity offered or danger dictated.

This is the philosophy that welded the policy-makers of Hanover into a team. For all the mistakes they made, in anguish or greed, confusion or ignorance—and their mistakes are clearer now than they could be then—their basic failure was through no fault of their own. Nor was relief, when it came, due to their own merit.

Notes

1. 'She [Lady Yarmouth] certainly can give good or bad impressions ... ; for even the wisest man, like the cameleon, takes without knowing it more or less of the hue of what he is often upon'; Chesterfield to Newcastle, 27 Feb 1746, R. Lodge (ed.), *Private Correspondence of Chesterfield and Newcastle 1744-46*, London, 1930, 115. We do not know whether the prudish Newcastle enjoyed this Chesterfieldian gem; his reply was noncommittal.
2. 'Euer Exzellenz soll [will] ich anbei aber auch anmerken, dass die meisten, und fast alle, Entschlüssungen, welche man sowohl in Religions als andern Reichsgeschäften ergreift, nicht hier [in London], sondern in Hannover genommen werden, ... noch weniger möglich aber ist es, das britische Ministerium zu bewegen, diesfalls in eine vollkommene Erörterung der Frage einzugehen ... ' Colloredo to Kaunitz, London, 9 Apr 1756, *HHStA*, England, Berichte, K. 108. The possibility that Hanoverian ministers might sway the British ministry in *British* affairs apparently struck observers at Hanover as too absurd even for discussion. They do not seem to have been conscious of Münchhausen's and Diede's attempts to persuade the British ministry that British interests conformed to those of Hanover—which in itself is quite distinct from 'engineering' British policy.
3. Quoted by W. E. H. Lecky, *History of England in the Eighteenth Century*, London, 1901-03, II, 15, from W. Coxe, *Memoirs of the Life and Administration of Sir Robert Walpole, Earl of Orford*. According to Hervey, Walpole in 1737 professed the belief that 'in futurity', that is, after the death of George II, a separation would be of 'the greatest real benefit' for Britain, but he clearly thought it unfeasible. (Hervey, *op. cit.*, III, 800.)
4. Newcastle to Hardwicke, 21 Nov 1759, Hardwicke to Newcastle, same date, Add. MSS 32899, ff. 6-7, 13-14.
5. Horace Walpole in his enormous correspondence with Horace Mann (*Horace Walpole's Correspondence*, W. S. Lewis *et al.* eds., New Haven, 1937-1983, vols. XVII-XXVII, *passim*) gives moderate coverage to Hanoverian affairs as mirrored in British public opinion in the 1740s and 1750s, without showing particular bias either way. Mann, from his vantage point at Florence, stressed twice, in 1755 and 1760, that Britain was bound 'in honour and justice' to defend Hanover. (*Ibid.*, XX, 504; XXI, 456.)
6. *Lenthe*, 93, 254. On the latter occasion the Austrian envoy at Hanover reported home: 'The rapid change of the English ministry has been noted here indeed as nothing but an idle game.' (Jaxheim to Ulfeld, 17 Mar 1746, *HHStA*, Hofkanzlei Hannover, K. 3.)
7. Correspondence between Harrington, Newcastle, Stone and Couraud, June-July 1740, S.P., Regencies, 43/89, 90, 91, 25, 27; bills, 'Pro Memoria', 18 July, 2 Nov 1742, Hann. 91, Steinberg I, Nr. 1.

8. E.g. *Geheime Räte* to George II and Dickens, 26 Oct 1745, Hann. 92, LXXV, Nr. 7, vol. V; Jan-Mar 1746, Cal. Br. 24, England, 1740.
9. For this affair, see U. Dann, 'Moses Levi of Hanover and King George II', *Jahrbuch des Instituts für Deutsche Geschichte der Universität Tel Aviv*, X (1981), 17-27.
10. Correspondence between the electoral authorities at Stade and Hanover, 22, 25 Mar 1758, Hann. 9e, 590.
11. There is by now research in existence which touches on this fascinating subject: Schnath, *op. cit.*, II, 354-357; H. Bernhards, 'Zur Entwickelung des Postwesens in Braunschweig-Lüneburg, vornehmlich der jüngeren Linie Calenberg-Celle', *Zeitschrift des Historischen Vereins für Niedersachsen*, LXXVII (1912), 1-96. K. L. Ellis, *The Post Office in the 18th Century*, London, 1958, 63, 74, 81-82, 152; S. P. Oakley, 'The Interception of Posts in Celle, 1694-1700', R. Hatton, J. S. Bromley (eds.), *William III and Louis XIV: Essays in 1680-1720 by and for Mark A. Thomson*, Liverpool, 1968; K. L. Ellis, 'British Communications and Diplomacy in the Eighteenth Century', *Bulletin of the Institute of Historical Research*, XXI (1958), 159-167; *idem*, 'The administrative connections between Britain and Hanover', *Journal of the Society of Archivists*, III, 10 (Oct 1969), 546-566. The relevant files at the Public Record Office and the Niedersächsisches Hauptstaatsarchiv should provide material for an exhaustive monograph. The technical aspects of George II's travels between London and Hanover are covered in U. Richter-Uhlig, 'Kommunikationsprobleme zwischen London und Hannover: Die Reisen König Georgs II. von England nach Hannover 1727-1740', *Blätter für deutsche Landesgeschichte* 121 (1985), 207-227.
12. Münchhausen, *Kurtze historische Erzehlung*, 230.
13. I understand Professor Aubrey N. Newman is treating this issue in depth, in his forthcoming biography of George II.
14. Lenthe's letters to Schwicheldt (*Lenthe*, *passim*) afford many examples, all the more telling because the writer does not make much of them.
15. Professor Mediger believes that the Hanoverian ministers deferred more to the king's territorial ambitions than I will have it; it is a matter of interpreting documentary evidence. He also believes that at one conjunction, in 1745, Münchhausen and Diede conceived for Hanover a position as guardian of the German west, secured by far-flung acquisitions between the Weser and the Ems. Though this particular case is based on deduction, I think Professor Mediger is right. But it was a fleeting episode without a follow-up.
16. For texts, L. Hertslet (ed.), *Treaties and Conventions*, London, 1840, vol. I, 89-110. Contemporaneous treaties with the other Barbary states—Algiers, Tunis and Tripoli—have no 'Hanoverian' clauses; the reason may be their being vassals of the Ottoman sultan, and the British secretaries of state insisted that these agreements be restricted to bare essentials.
17. For the Steinhorst affair and its British ramifications, see Titley Papers, Egerton MSS 2685; also *Niedersächsisches Staatsarchiv*, Wolfenbüttel, Bücherei N 356.
18. For one such instance, see U. Dann, 'Zur Persönlichkeit G.A. von Münchhausens', *Niedersächsisches Jahrbuch für Landesgeschichte*, LII (1980), 311-316. D. B. Horn, *The British Diplomatic Service 1689-1789*, Oxford, 1961, p. 11, sums up the subject of British assistance from the British angle.

Epilogue
The new reign

'… once when the king [George II] was in good humour, he said to Andrié that the people here [in England] were angry at his going to Hanover, when they went all out of town to their country seats; but it was unjust, for Hanover was his country seat, and he had no other'.[1] When we realize what 'their country seats' meant to English noblemen of the eighteenth century, we also realize that George II could hardly have been more explicit about the country of his birth.

'Born and educated in this country, I glory in the name of Britain.'[2] We cannot be certain what was in the mind of George III when he inserted this sentence into Hardwicke's draft of his first speech from the throne. Some, in obsessive loathing of Bute, saw it as an obeisance to the Scots. It is more likely that the young king deliberately disavowed his grandfather's 'country seat', and this view has come to prevail with historians. The matter is of course more complex than the juxtaposition just quoted might suggest. George III never neglected his duties as elector.[3] During the abortive peace talks of 1761 he even envisaged the acquisition of Hildesheim and Osnabrück by way of a territorial 'satisfaction and indemnification appertaining to Us as elector'.[4] But surely this was no more than a flywheel running down. More significant for the future seem Philip von Münchhausen's tidings when George III had been on the throne for less than a week, that the king daily gave him proof of his love for his German lands.[5] Making every possible allowance for the young king's desire to please and for Münchhausen's wishful thinking, the letter signifies at the very least that the king cared for his image at Hanover.

But even as the years passed by, George III proved ever affable to his electoral subjects who presented themselves at Windsor, and on occasion he boasted to them of his German blood. His relations with the elder Münchhausen were excellent, though they normally corresponded in French: the king's German was rather erratic, in contrast to his grandfather's and father's. Münchhausen was practically the king's marriage broker,[6] and in 1765 he was rewarded with the style of 'Premier Ministre'—largely an honorific, for the collegiate system of government at Hanover remained intact. Like his grandfather's, the concern of George III for the administration and progress of Hanover was constant, though less than ardent. He took an interest in the not inconsiderable initiatives of Münchhausen after 1763 concerning the 'development'—as we would call it today—of the country's resources until the latter's death in 1770; and whatever was attempted afterwards, little enough in all conscience, can be traced to him rather than to Münchhausen's successors. (The amelioration of the Bremen marshlands; hesitant attempts to translate to Hanover the enclosure movement then in full swing in England; a general survey of the country; and not very effectual attempts at road building and canal digging, rate mentioning.)[7] Also, George III, like his grandfather, identified with the electorate's traditional policy of maintaining the *status quo* within Germany, rather grandiloquently known as the

'Imperial constitution'; though the expansionist yearnings of Emperor Joseph II meant that regard for the *status quo* turned Hanover from an ally—the divergent constellation of the Seven Years War was born of an exceptional need, so far as Hanover went—into an opponent of Austria. (So strong was the king's identification that for some time in 1785 he was ready to double-cross his British ministry over this issue, during the *Fürstenbund* negotiations.)[8] George III did not send his *Landeskinder* to fight in America, though they took part with distinction in the defence of Gibraltar against Spain (1779-1783). (Two Hanoverian regiments which fought in India at the same time were genuine mercenaries in the East India Company's pay.) Like his grandfather, George III provided in his testament (1765) that no 'stranger', i.e. Briton, should share in the government of Hanover.[9]

And yet the death of George II is the end of an era.

The factors that contributed to this state of affairs were most of them external to Hanover and Britain. With the end of the Seven Years War the great-power status of Prussia became part of the recognized order of Europe. Therewith Frederick lost much of his demonic image, and the Hanoverian ministers their obsessive fear. (It is true that as late as 1768 Frederick wrote in his second political testament: 'Si nous avions des brouilleries serieuses avec l'Angleterre, nous pourrions nous venger d'elle en nous emparant de l'électorat de Hanovre, pays peu préparé pour se défendre.'[10] But the point is that the European scene never induced him after 1763 to give this threat undue publicity; the 'testament' itself remained secret until the twentieth century.) French ministries—at least until the revolution radicalized and to some extent derationalized attitudes to Britain—lost interest now that the king of Britain seemed impervious on that account. In the American war France concentrated her efforts on the seas and overseas, to Britain's detriment, but to Hanover's relief. In Britain, the period of relative indifference to Continental affairs which characterized British policy after 1763 deflated the importance of Hanover as well.[11] Hanover herself played a part in the diminution of her significance: Münchhausen was in advanced old age, while his latter-day colleagues and successors sank ever deeper into parochialism, if not sloth.

But the most conspicuous factor which signifies the end of an era remains the break-up of the team. The reality of the relations between Hanover and Britain until 1760 hinged on the old king's love of, and loyalty to, Hanover. Whatever George III's sense of obligation to Hanover, he was English, and the relations between the two countries would never be the same thereafter.

Notes

1. 'The diary of Hugh Lord Marchmont', *A Selection from the Papers of the Earls of Marchmont*, ed. G. H. Rose, London, 1831, I, 53-54, under 2 Oct [1744].
2. Add. MSS 32684, f. 121; Hardwicke to Pitt, 11 Nov 1760, *Correspondence of William Pitt ...*, II, 81-82.
3. On this subject see Sigisbert Conrady, 'Die Wirksamkeit König Georgs III. für die hannoverschen Kurlande', *Niedersächsisches Jahrbuch für Landesgeschichte*, XXXIX (1967), 150-191.
4. 'Special Instruction' of 9 June 1761 for G.F. Steinberg, the electoral representative, Cal. Br. 11, 3514. I am indebted to Professor Mediger for this reference.
5. Philip von Münchhausen to his brother, 31 Oct 1760, Hann. 91, Münchhausen I, Nr. 72.

6. John Brooke, *King George III*, London, 1972, 80-83.
7. For this, in impressive detail, see Sigisbert Conrady, *op. cit.*
8. For this, see Timothy C.W. Blanning, '"That horrid electorate" or "Ma patrie Germanique"? George III, Hanover and the Fürstenbund of 1785', *Historical Journal*, XX, 2 (1977), 311-344.
9. Conrady, 169.
10. G.B. Volz (ed.), *Die politischen Testamente Friedrich's des Grossen*, Berlin, 1920, 214.
11. For a recent monograph on this subject, see Hamish M. Scott, *Anglo-Austrian Relations after the Seven Years War: Lord Stormont in Vienna, 1763-1772*, unpubl. Ph.D. thesis, London, 1978.

Biographical notes and author index

(Data concerning Hanoverians are largely taken from J. Lampe, *Aristokratie, Hofadel und Staatspatriarchat in Kurhannover*, Göttingen, 1963, vol. II. Otherwise my main stand-by has been Friedrich Hausmann (ed.), *Repertorium der diplomatischen Vertreter aller Länder seit dem Westfälischen Frieden (1648)*, Zurich; vol. II (1950), besides the national biographies.)

Dupontpietin, see Pontpietin.

Eichel, August Friedrich, 1698-1768, confidential secretary of Frederick II, p. 123.

Elizabeth Petrovna, 1709-1762, tsaritsa 1741-1762, pp. 58-59, 71, 74, 86-90, 92, 96.

Ernest Augustus, 1629-1698, duke (elector) of Brunswick-Lüneburg (Hanover) 1680-1698, elector 1692, pp. 4-5, 15-16, 140.

Ernest Augustus, 1771-1851, king of Hanover 1837-1851, p. 2.

Estrées, Louis César Le Tellier, comte d', 1695-1771, French general, pp. 111, 121.

Ferdinand of Brunswick (-Wolfenbüttel), Prince, 1721-1792, Prussian general, commander of British-Hanoverian army in Germany 1757-1763, pp. 53, 97, 109, 115-119, 122-125.

Finckenstein, Karl Wilhelm, Count Finck von, 1714-1800, Prussian diplomatist and minister, pp. 58, 64, 118.

Flemming, Karl Georg Friedrich, Baron von, 1705-1767, Saxon diplomatist and minister, p. 70.

Fleury, Hercule André, Cardinal de, 1653-1743, French first minister 1726-1743, pp. 17, 20, 35-38, 46-48.

Fox, Henry (Lord Holland), 1705-1774, British politician, secretary of state for Southern Department 1755-1756, pp. 91, 96.

Francis I, 1708-1765, Roman emperor 1745-1765, as Francis Stephan duke of Lorraine and grand duke of Tuscany. pp. 22, 35, 52, 70, 105.

Francis Stephan, see Francis I.

Frederick I, 1657-1713, as Frederick III elector of Brandenburg since 1688, as Frederick I king of ('in') Prussia 1701-1713, p. 20.

Frederick II, the Great, 1712-1786, king of Prussia 1740-1786, pp. 4, 15-34, 40, 45-46, 48-54, 56-61, 63, 67-74, 76, 80, 83-88, 90, 92-98, 104-110, 112, 116-120, 121-124, 130, 134, 138-139, 146.

Frederick, Prince of Wales, 1707-1751, eldest son of George II; born in Hanover, pp. 69-70, 77-78, 86, 128, 132-133.

Frederick William I, 1688-1740, king of Prussia 1713-1740, pp. 15-18, 23, 40.

George I, 1660-1727, as George Louis elector of Hanover 1698-1727, king of Great Britain 1714-1727, pp. 4-8, 15-16, 20, 50, 63, 85, 132, 138.

George II, 1683-1760, king of Great Britain and elector of Hanover 1727-1760, *passim.*

George III, 1738-1820, king of great Britain and elector (after 1814 king) of Hanover 1760-1820, pp. 55, 104, 129, 134, 145-147.

George V, 1819-1878, king of Hanover 1851-1866, p. 2.

George Augustus, see George II.

George Louis, see George I.

George William, 1624-1705, duke of Brunswick-Lüneburg (Celle), 1665-1705; elder brother of Elector Ernest Augustus and father-in-law of George I, pp. 4, 140.

Ginckel, Reinhard Baron Reede tot, Dutch representative at Berlin 1730-1742, p. 24.

Goethe, Johann Wolgang von, 1749-1832, p. 124.

Granville, see Carteret.

Grenville, George, 1712-1770, British politician, treasurer of the navy 1757-1762, brother-in-law of Pitt, p. 123.

Grote, Heinrich, Baron, 1675-1753, studied at Helmstedt; *Geheimer Rat* 1728, *Kammerpräsident* (and acting senior member of Privy Council) 1735, pp. 71-72, 78, 112.

Hake, Levin, Baron, 1708-1771, studied at Halle, Hanoverian service 1733, *Geheimer*

Sources

a. Unpublished archive material

Archives in Britain

British Library, London

Carteret Papers: Add. MSS 22527, 22530, 22543.
Egerton MSS: Eg. 2685-94 (Titley Papers).
Hardwicke MSS: Add. MSS 35407-8, 35452-9, 35472, 35481-2, 35593, 35839, 35870, 36119.
Hyndford MSS: Add. MSS 11380-7.
Martin Papers: Add. MSS 415355.
Mitchell MSS: Add. MSS 6804-8, 6811-18, 6863, 6870.
Newcastle Papers: Add. MSS 32700-6, 32722 32806, 32812-13, 32816, 32820-2, 32824, 32835, 32846-58, 32861, 32863-5, 32869-70, 32873-5, 32879-80, 32885, 32898-9, 32889, 32904, 32997, 33021-2, 33069.
Robinson Papers: Add. MSS 23712, 23865.
Royal letters: Add. MSS 32684.
Sloane MSS: MSS 4054-6 (Steigerthal letters 1736-1739).
Stowe MSS: Stowe 249, 483.

Cambridge University Library

Cholmondeley (Houghton) MSS: 'Correspondence', 1740-1745; 'Lists', 8.

Public Record Office, London

State Papers (Foreign): 78 (France), 80 (Germany, Empire), 81 (Germany, States), 84 (Holland), 87 (Military Expeditions), 88 (Poland/Saxony), 90 (Prussia), 91 (Russia), 100 (Foreign Ministers).
State Papers (Foreign ministers in Britain): 100 (Hanover only).
State Papers (Regencies): 43-5.
State Papers (Royal letters): 102.
State Papers (Treaty Papers, Treaties): 103, 108.
State Papers (Intercepted diplomatic correspondence): 107/46-9.
Treasury Board Papers: T 1, 375-86 (for correspondence of Ernst von Steinberg, P.A. von Münchhausen); T 64 (for correspondence T. O. Hunter–P. A. von Münchhausen, and related subjects).
Chatham Papers (PRO/30/8, First series): 50, 89, 90 (Correspondence on German affairs during Seven Years War with P.A. von Münchhausen, Prince Ferdinand and others).

Royal Archives, Windsor

Cumberland Papers (microfilm), boxes 46-57 (Correspondence, 1755-1765).
Privy Purse Accounts, RA 17107-70 (Sept 1763-1767).

Archives in the German Federal Republic

Hessisches Staatsarchiv, Marburg

Bestand 4, Abteilung f (Hesse-Cassel, Politische Akten 1567-1821, Staatenabteilung): Kurbraunschweig (Hannover), Braunschweig-Wolfenbüttel, England, Niederlande, Preussen.

Niedersächsisches Hauptstaatsarchiv, Hanover

Hann. 9d (Geheime Registratur/Oesterreichischer Erbfolgekrieg).
Hann. 9e (Geheime Registratur/Siebenjähriger Krieg).
Hann. 10 (Hannoversche Staatsverträge).
Hann. 46 (Kriegsgewölbe).
Hann. 47 (Kriegskanzlei).
Hann. 91 (Nachlässe): G.A. von Münchhausen; P.A. von Münchhausen; du Pontpietin; E. von Steinberg.
Hann. 92 (Deutsche Kanzlei).
I. Landesverfassung und höchste Behörden.
III. Domestica.
IX. Provinziallandschaften.
XXVI. Finanzwesen.
XXIX. Post-, Münz- und Lotteriesachen.
XXI. Polizei- und Städtesachen.
XXXVII. Reichssachen ...
XLV. Reichssachen und Publica
LVIII. Brandenburg-Preussen.
LIX. Hessen.
LXVI. Verschiedene Korrespondenzen.
LXXI. Oeffentliche Konjunkturen, Reichskriege und Feldzüge.
LXXII. Siebenjähriger Krieg.
LXXV. Oeffentliche Konjunkturen 1741-1783.
LXXVII. Aeltere Gesandtschaftsberichte.
LXXXII. Verschiedenes.
LXXXIV....Verträge mit fremden Mächten.
LXXXV. Personalien
Cal. Br. 11E (Reichssachen, Hannover).
Cal. Br. 24 (Aeussere Angelegenheiten): England, Holland, Oesterreich, Russland, Sachsen, Wolfenbüttel.
Nachlass B. Ch. von Behr.
Archiv des hannoverschen Königshauses (K.G.): Dep. 84, 49c; Dep. 103, IV, C; Hann. Br. 9 Domestica; Cal. Or. 3.

Niedersächsisches Staatsarchiv, Stade

Rep. 31 (Geheime Räte zu Hannover betr. Bremen-Verden).
Rep. 80 (Regierung ... in Stade).

Niedersächsisches Staatsarchiv, Wolfenbüttel
(Documents relating to Steinhorst affair, 1737-1739.)

Gutsarchiv Bodenburg
III. Familie von Steinberg, Paket 3, 6. Akte (relating to guarantees based on peace of Dresden).

Archives in Austria

Haus-, Hof- und Staatsarchiv, Vienna
Staatenabteilung, England: Berichte/Weisungen, K. 77-111.
Staatenabteilung, England: Hofkorrespondenz, K. 4.
Staatskanzlei, Hannover: Fasz. 1-9, 27 (neue Registrierung).
Vorträge, K. 61-80.

b. Published primary sources and secondary literature prior to 1814

(Treaty collections and similar compilations have not been included, with two exceptions.)

English pamphlets 1742-1748, authors unknown or uncertain: all published in London

An address to the People of Great Britain. By a Country Clergyman, 1744.
The Advantages of the Hanoverian Succession, and English Ingratitude, Freely and Impartially Considered and Examined, 1744.
An Attempt Towards a Natural History of the Hanover Rat, 1744.
A Collection of Letters Published in Old England: Or the Constitutional Journal ('Jeffrey Broadbottom, Convent Garden'), 1743?
A Compleat View of the Present Politicks of Great Britain in a Letter from a German Nobleman to his Friend at Vienna ... , 1743.
Four Letters Published in Old England: Or the Constitutional Journal (viz., of February the 25th, March the 3rd, 10th and 17th), by Jeffrey Broadbottom, of Convent Garden, 1744.
Hanoverian Politicks: In a Letter from a Gentleman at the Court of Hanover, to His Friend in England, Concerning the Present Posture of Affairs on the Continent, 1745.
The Instructions Sent by the Regency of Hanover to the Privy Counsellor De Busch, Electoral Minister of the King of Great Britain at the Court of Dresden. Together with a Letter from an Hanoverian Minister to a Member of the Parliament of Great Britain Containing a Justification of the Hanoverians, and His Sentiments on the Present Critical Conjuncture of Affairs, 1744.
King Harry IX's Speech to Both Houses of P——t, the 31st Day of November 1647, 1747?
King Harry IX's Second Speech to Both Houses of P——t, the 14th Day of May 1548, and a Letter to the Craftsman, and a Letter to Caleb D'Anvers Esq., 1748?

A Letter from Flanders, Giving an Account of the Present State of the War in the Netherlands, the Weakness of the Allies and Strength of the French … By an Old English Officer, From the Camp Near Oudenard, to His Friend at London, June 17/6, 1744, 1744.

A Letter from a Member of the Last Parliament to a New Member of the Present, Concerning the Conduct of the War with Spain: With Some Relations on the Hanover Neutrality, as far as it may Relate to, or Affect, Great Britain, 1742.

The Lords Protest On a Motion, That it is the Opinion of This House, that the Continuing the Sixteen Thousand Hanoverians in the Pay of Great Britain is Prejudicial to the True Interest of His Majesty, Useless to the Common Cause, and Dangerous to the Welfare and Tranquillity of this Nation, Die Martiis 31 Januarii 1743, 1744.

The Lords Protest, To which is Added, A List of the Members of Parliament who Voted For and Against Continuing the Hanover Troops in British Pay, January 18, 1743. Likewise the State of the National Debt, Down to Christmas 1743, 1744.

The Mysterious Congress. A Letter from Aix La Chappel, Detecting the Late Secret Negociations There: Accounting for the Extraordinary Slowness of the Operations of the Campaigns Since the Action of Dettingen: and in particular, for the Resignation of the E——l of S——r, ('Nobleman') 1743.

Observations on the Conduct of Great Britain, in Respect to Foreign Affairs, In Which … the Measures of the Present Ministry are Fully Vindicated, 1742.

The Peace Offering: An Essay. Shewing the Cession of Hanover To Be the Only Probable Means for Extinguishing the Present Rebellion … And Likewise for Lessening Our Taxes and Expence, Getting Rid of a Standing Army, Securing our Religion and Liberties, Rooting up Public Corruption, and for Confining All Future Ministers to the Pursuit of An English Interest Only … by Methuselah Whitelock, 1746.

Popular Prejudice Concerning Partiality to the Interest of Hanover … Freely Examined and Discussed, … In a Letter from an Officer at Hanover to a Hanoverian Nobleman at the Hague, Translated from the Original, 1743.

Public Discontent Accounted for, from the Conduct of Our Ministers in the Cabinet and Our Generals in the Field, 1743.

A Vindication of Our Present Royal Family Principally with Regard to Hanover … By a Friend to Hanover, To an Englishman, 1744.

English pamphlets 1755-1761, authors unknown or uncertain; published in London when not stated otherwise.

An Appeal to the Sense of the People, on the Present Posture of Affairs, 1756.

The Conduct of the Ministry Impartially Examined, and The Pamphlet Entitled Considerations of the Present German War Refuted from Its Own Principles, 1760. (See also Mauduit, below.)

A Full and Candid Answer to a Pamphlet, Entitled Considerations on the Present German War, Dublin, 1761. (See also Mauduit, below.)

The Naked Truth, No. 1, 1755.

The Occasional Patriot, or, an Enquiry into the Present Connections of Great Britain with the Continent, 1756.

Reasons in Support of the War in Germany, in Answer to Considerations on the Present German War, 1761.

Reflections upon the Present State of Affairs at Home and Abroad ... In a Letter from a Member of Parliament to a Constituent, 1755.

Hanoverian pamphlets 1803-1804, authors unknown or uncertain

Einiges zur Vertheidigung des Churfürstenthums Hannover und seiner Einwohner gegen falsche Darstellungen, n.p. 1803.
Ein paar Worte über den im Hannoverschen herrschenden Nepotismus und dessen Folgen, Von einem Hannoveraner, n.p. 1803.
Hannover, wie es war, ist und werden wird, ... Aus den Briefen des D.Bxxxxx an seinen Freund Bxxx in London, [Gotthilf F. Müller? Wolfenbüttel?], 1804.
Ich kann nicht schweigen!, n.p. 1803.
Müssen wir nicht von England getrennt werden? Verneinend beantwortet von einem Hannoveraner, [Leipzig?], 1803.
Ueber das Churfürstenthum Hannover zu Berichtigung ... und mit besonderer Rücksicht auf die Schrift des Dr. jur. Seumnich ... , 'Hannoveraner', n.p., 1803. (See also Seumnich, below.)
Ueber den Hannoverischen Adel und die Hannoverischen Sekretarien, [Burchard Christian von Spilcker?], n.p. 1803.
Ueber die Sperrung der Elbe und Weser, n.p. 1803.

Other publications

'Accounts of the Net Public Income and Expenditure of Great Britain', *Parliamentary Papers*, 1868-1869, No. 366 (XXXV).
Adelung, Johann Christoph, *Johann Christoph Adelung's pragmatische Staatsgeschichte* ... , Gotha, 1762-1769, 9 vols.; vol. III.
(Bedford,) *Correspondence of John fourth Duke of Bedford* (Lord John Russell ed.), London, 1842-1846, 3 vols.; vol. II.
Berlepsch, Friedrich Ludewig von, *Pragmatische Geschichte des Landschaftlichen Finanz- und Steuerwesens der Fürstenthümer Calenberg und Göttingen*, Frankfurt, Leipzig, 1799.
British Diplomatic Instructions 1689-1789, Vol. III, *Denmark* (J.F. Chance ed.) London, 1926.
British Diplomatic Instructions 1689-1789, Vol. VI, *France, 1727-1744* (L.G. Wickham Legg ed.), London, 1930.
British Diplomatic Instructions 1689-1789, Vol. VII, *France, 1745-1789* (L.G. Wickham Legg ed.), London, 1934.
British Diplomatic Instructions 1689-1789, Vol. V, *Sweden, 1727-1789* (J.F. Chance ed.), London, 1928.
Büsching, Anton Friedrich, *Erdbeschreibung*, 7th ed., Hamburg, 1792; Part IX, 'Der niedersächsische Kreis'.
(Campbell, John,) *The Present State of Europe* ... , London, 1750.
Chalmers, George (ed.), *A Collection of Treaties between Great Britain and Other Powers*, London, 1790, 2 vols.
(Chesterfield,) *The Case of the Hanoverian Forces in the Pay of Great Britain Impartially and Freely Examined* ... , London, 1743.

(Chesterfield,) *A Farther Vindication of the Case of the Hanover Troops; In Which the Uniform Influence of the Hanover-Rudder Is Clearly Detected and Exposed: Being a Full Answer ... to a Pamphlet, Called the Interest of Great Britain Steadily Pursued*, London, 1743.

(Chesterfield,) *The Interest of Hanover Steadily Pursued, Since the A——n. Being a Sequel to a Pamphlet, Entitled, the Interest of Great Britain Steadily Pursued ... By a Broad Bottom,* London, 1743.

(Chesterfield,) *Natural Reflexions on the Present Conduct of His Prussian Majesty ...* , London, 1744.

(Chesterfield,) *A Vindication of a Late Pamphlet Entitled, The Case of the Hanoverian Troops Considered ...* , London, 1743.

(Chesterfield–Newcastle,) *Private Correspondence of Chesterfield and Newcastle, 1744-46* (R. Lodge ed.), London, 1930.

Egmont, Diary of Viscount Percival afterwards First Earl of (R.A. Roberts ed.) Hist. MSS. Comm., 16th Report, 1920-1923, 3 vols.; vols II, III.

(Egmont,) *An Examination of the Principles and an Enquiry into the Conduct of the Two B——rs, ... in a Letter to a Member of Parliament*, London, 1749.

(Egmont,) *Faction Detected by the Evidence of Facts, Containing an Impartial View of Parties at Home and Affairs Abroad*, London, 1744.

(Egmont,) *A Second Series of Facts and Arguments: Tending to Prove, That the Abilities of the Two B——rs Are not More Extraordinary than their Virtues. In a Letter to a Member of Parliament*, London, 1749.

Frankland-Russell-Astley MSS, Hist. MSS. Comm., Vol. LII, 1900.

(Frederick II, King of Prussia,) *Oeuvres de Frédéric le Grand* (J.D.E. Preuss ed.), Berlin, 1846-1856, 30 vols.; vols. II-III, *Histoire de mon temps*, vols. IV-V, *Histoire de la guerre de sept ans.*

(Frederick II, King of Prussia,) *Die politische Correspondenz Friedrich's des Grossen* (Droysen, Duncker *et al.*, ed.), Berlin, 1879-1939, 46 vols.; vols. I-XXII.

(Frederick II, King of Prussia,) *Die Politischen Testamente Friedrich's des Grossen* (G.B. Volz ed.), Berlin, 1920.

Garden, Comte Guillaume de (ed.), *Histoire génerale des traités de paix et autres transactions principales entre toutes les puissances de l'Europe depuis la Paix de Westphalie*, Paris, n.d., 14 vols.; vol. III: 1717-1759; vol. IV: (1757) 1763-1791.

Gentleman's Magazine, The, London, 1739-1760.

(George III,) *The Correspondence of King George the Third from 1760 to December 1783* (J. W. Fortescue ed.), London, 1927-1928; 6 vols.

(George III,) *Letters from George III to Lord Bute, 1756-1766* (R. Sedgwick ed.), London, 1939.

Göttingische Zeitungen von gelehrten Sachen, 1739-1752; Göttingische Anzeigen von gelehrten Sachen, 1753-*c*. 1755.

Gundling, Nicolai Hieronymus, *Ausführlicher Discours über den vormaligen und itzigen Zustand der Teutschen Churfürsten-Staaten*, Frankfurt, Leipzig, 1747-1750, 5 parts; part V, ch. 9, 'Von Chur-Braunschweig-Hannover'.

(Hanoverian State Calendar,) *Siebenfacher Köngl. Gross-Britannisch-und-Chur-Fürstlich Braunschweig-Lüneburgischer Staats-Calender ...* . 1737-*c*. 1770.

Hannoverische Anzeigen, 1750-*c*. 1770; Supplement: *Hannoverische Gelehrte Anzeigen*, 1750-1754; *Hannoversche Nützliche Sammlungen*, 1755-1758; *Hannoverische Beiträge zum Nutzen und Vergnügen*, 1759-1762; *Hannoversches Magazin*, 1763-1792.

Hardenberg, Karl August von, 'Memorandum' of 13 January 1780, in E. von Meier, *Hannoversche Verfassungs- und Verwaltungsgeschichte 1690-1866*, II, 606-619.

(Hardwicke,) *The Life and Correspondence of Philip Yorke, Earl of Hardwicke, Lord High Chancellor of Great Britain* (P. C. Yorke ed.), Cambridge 1913, 3 vols.

Hertslet, Lewis (ed.), ... *Treaties and Conventions ... Between Great Britain and Foreign Powers ... so far as They Relate to Commerce and Navigation* ... , vol. I, London, 1840.

(Hervey, Lord,) *Some Materials Towards Memoirs of the Reign of King George II* (R. Sedgwick ed.), London, 1931, 3 vols.

Jenkinson, Charles (ed.), *A Collection of All the Treaties of Peace, Alliance and Commerce, Between Great Britain and Other Powers, from ... 1648 to ... 1783*, London, 1785, vol. II: 1713-1748; vol. III: 1750-1784.

Journals of the House of Commons, vols. XXIII-XXVIII.

Journals of the House of Lords, vols. XXI-XXX.

(Kaunitz,) 'Denkschriften des Fürsten Wenzel Kaunitz-Rittberg' (A. Baer ed.), *Archiv für österreichische Geschichte*, XLVIII (1872), 1-162.

(Khevenhüller,) *Tagebuch des Fürsten Johann-Joseph Khevenhüller-Metsch, kaiserlichen Obersthofmeisters, 1742-1776* (Khevenhüller-Metsch, Schlitter, eds.) Vienna, Leipzig, 1908-1925, 9 vols; vol. II, IV-VI.

Kielmansegge, Friedrich Graf, *Diary of a Journey to England in the Years 1761-1762* (Countess Kielmansegg tr.), London, 1902.

(Lenthe,) *Briefe des Ministers Otto Christian von Lenthe an den Geheimen Kriegsrat August Wilhelm von Schwicheldt (1743-1759)* (R. Grieser ed.), Hildesheim, 1977.

(Lichtenberg,) *Lichtenberg's Visits to England as Described in His Letters and Diaries* (M.L. Mare, W.H. Quarrell eds.), New York, London, 1969 (1938).

London Magazine, The, 1740-1760.

(Marchmont,) *A Selection from the Papers of the Earls of Marchmont* (G.H. Rose ed.), London, 1831, 3 vols; vols. I, II.

(Maria Theresa,) 'Zwei Denkschriften der Kaiserin Maria Theresia' (A. von Arneth ed.), *Archiv für österreichische Geschichte*, XLVII (1871), 267-354.

Martens, Charles de (ed.), *Recueil des principaux traités ... de l'Europe ... depuis 1761 jusqu'au présent*, vol. V (1791-1795), Göttingen, 1826.

Martens, F. de (ed.), *Recueil des traités et conventions conclus par la Russie avec les puissance étrangères*, St Petersburg, 1874-1909, 15 vols.; vols. I, V, IX-X.

(Martin, Samuel,) *Deliberate Thoughts on the System of our Late Treaties with Hesse-Cassel and Russia in regard to Hanover*, London, 1756.

(Mauduit, Israel,) *Considerations on the present German War*, London, 1760.

(Mitchell,) *Memoirs and Papers of Sir Andrew Mitchell* (A. Bisset ed.), London, 1850, 2 vols.

Moerner, Theodor von (ed.), *Kurbrandenburgs Staatsverträge von 1601-1700*, Berlin, 1867.

(Münchhausen), 'G.A. von Münchhausens Berichte über die Kaiserwahl des Jahres 1742' (F. Frensdorff ed.), *Nachrichten von der Königlichen Gesellschaft der Wissenschaften zu Göttingen, Philologisch-historische Klasse*, Göttingen, 1899.

(Münchhausen), *G.A. v. Münchhausens Berichte über seine Mission nach Berlin im Juni 1740* (F. Frensdorff ed.), Berlin, 1904.

(Münchhausen,) 'Eine Denkschrift Gerlach Adolf v. Münchhausens über die hannoversche Aussenpolitik der Jahre 1740-1742' (T. König ed.), *Niedersächsisches*

Jahrbuch für Landesgeschichte, XIV (1937), 202-232.
(Münchhausen,) 'Des Weyl. Herrn Premier-Ministers und Cammer-Praesidenten Herrn Gerlach Adolph von Münchhausen hinterlassener Unterricht von der Verfassung des churfürstl. Braunschweig-Lüneburgischen Geheimten Rath und Cammer-Collegii' (E. von Lenthe ed.), *Zeitschrift des Historischen Vereins für Niedersachsen, 1855*, 269-340.
Parliamentary History of England ... (Cobbet's), London, 1806-1820, 36 vols.; vols. XI-XV.
(Pelham,) *Memoirs of the Administration of the Rt. Hon. Henry Pelham* (W. Coxe ed.), London, 1829, 2 vols.
(Pitt,) *Correspondence of William Pitt, Earl of Chatham* (Taylor, Pringle eds.), London, 1838-1840, 4 vols; vols. I, II.
Postlethwayt, Malachy, *Britain's Commercial Interest Explained and Improved*, London, 1757, 2 vols.
Postlethwayt, Malachy, *Great Britain's True System*, London, 1757.
Preussische Staatsschriften aus der Regierungszeit Friedrichs des Grossen (Koser, Krauske eds.), Berlin, 1877-1892.
Pribram, F.A. (ed.), *Oesterreichische Staatsverträge, England*, Salzburg, Vienna, 1907-1913, 2 vols.
Pütter, Johann Stephan, *Selbstbiographie*, Göttingen, 1798, 2 vols.
Recueil des instructions données aux ambassadeurs et ministres de France depuis les traités de Westphalie jusqu'à la Révolution Française; Angleterre, tome troisième (1698-1791), vol. XXV-2 (Paul Vacher ed.) Paris, 1965.
Rousset de Missy, Jean (ed.), *Recueil historique d'actes, negociations, memoires et traités* ... , The Hague, 1728-1755, 21 vols.
Scharf, Christoph Barthold, *Der Politische Staat des Churfürstenthums Braunschweig-Lüneburg* ... , Lauenburg, 1791 (2nd ed.).
Schmauss, Johann Jacob (ed.), *Corpus juris gentium academicum*, Leipzig, 1730-1732 (?), 2 vols.; vol. II: 1696-1731.
Schmettau, Friedrich Graf, *Lebensgeschichte des Grafen von Schmettau*, Berlin, 1806, 2 vols.
Seumnich, (Dr K.), *Ueber die Verbindung des Churfürstenthums Hannover mit England und deren Folgen, über die hannoversche Verfassung und über das Verhalten der Hannoveraner bey der jetzigen Besetzung des Landes*, Hamburg, 1803.
(Shebbeare, John,) *A Sixth Letter to the People of England, on the Progress of National Ruin; in which it is Shewn that the Present Grandeur of France, and the Calamities of this Nation, Are Owing to the Influence of Hanover on the Councils of England*, London, 1757. (Also *Letters* One to Five, London, 1756-1757.).
Spittler, L.T., *Geschichte des Fürstenthums Hannover*, Göttingen, 1798, 2 vols.; vol. II.
(Stair,) *Annals and Correspondence of the Viscount and the First and Second Earls of Stair*, Edinburgh, London, 1875, 2 vols.; vol. II.
Tindal, Nicholas, *The Continuation of Mr. Rapin-Thoyras's History of England*, London, 1759; 9 vols.; vol. IX.
Treuer, Gottlieb Samuel, 'Treuer's Chur-Braunschweig-Lüneburgisches Staats-Recht' (E. von Lenthe ed.), *Zeitschrift des Historischen Vereins für Niedersachsen*, 1853, 283-359.
(Trevor,) *MSS of the Earl of Buckinghamshire*, Hist. MSS. Comm. Report XIV, Appendix 9, 1895.

Waldegrave, James, Earl of, *Memoirs from 1754 to 1758* (Lord Holland ed.?), Philadelphia, 1822.

Walpole, Horace, *Horace Walpole's Correspondence* (W.S. Lewis *et al.* eds.), New Haven, London, 1937-1983, 48 vols.

Walpole, Horace, *Memoires* (sic) *of the Last Ten Years of the Reign of King George II* (Lord Holland ed.), London, 1822; 2 vols.

(Walpole, Horatio,) *The Interest of Great Britain Steadily Pursued, In Answer to a Pamphlet Entitled 'The Case of the Hanoverian Forces Impartially and Freely Examined'*, London, 1743.

(Walpole, Horatio,) *Memoirs of Horatio, Lord Walpole ... 1678 to 1757* (W. Coxe ed.), London, 1820 (3rd ed.), 2 vols.; vol. II.

Wenck, Friedrich August Wilhelm (ed.), *Codex iuris gentium*, Leipzig, 1781-1795, 3 vols.

Westphalen, Christian Heinrich Philipp, *Geschichte der Feldzüge des Herzogs von Braunschweig-Lüneburg*, Berlin, 1859-1872, 6 vols.; vols. I-IV.

Wöchentliche hannoverische Intelligenz-Zettul und Anzeige, Hanover, 1732-1735.

Zedlers Universal-Lexicon, Leipzig, Halle, 1732-1750, 64 vols.

c. Secondary literature since 1814

(Dissertations have been identified as such only when they are unavailable in print.)

Anon., *Ein kleinstaatlicher Minister des 18. Jahrhunderts* [Friedrich August von Hardenberg], Leipzig, 1877.

Anderson, M.S., *Britain's Discovery of Russia, 1553-1815*, London, 1958.

Anderson, M.S., 'Eighteenth Century Theories of the Balance of Power', *Studies in Diplomatic History, Essays in Memory of D.B. Horn*, eds. R. Hatton, M.S. Anderson, London, 1970, 183-198.

Anderson, M.S., *Europe in the Eighteenth Century 1713-1783*, London, 1961.

Arneth, Alfred Ritter von, *Geschichte Maria Theresia's*, Vienna, 1863-1879, 10 vols.; vols. I-VI.

Baxter, Stephen B., 'The Conduct of the Seven Years War', in Stephen B. Baxter (ed.), *England's Rise to Greatness 1660-1763*, Los Angeles, 1983, 323-348.

Beer, Adolf, 'Zur Geschichte des Friedens von Aachen im Jahr 1748', *Archiv für österreichische Geschichte*, Vienna, XLVII (1871), 3-195.

Beer, Adolf, 'Holland und der österreichische Erbfolgekrieg'. *Archiv für österreichische Geschichte*, XLVI (1871), 297-418.

Beloff, Max, *The Age of Absolutism 1660-1815*, London, 1954.

Bernhards, H. 'Zur Entwickelung des Postwesens in Braunschweig-Lüneburg, vornehmlich der jüngeren Linie Calenberg-Celle', *Zeitschrift des Historischen Vereins für Niedersachsen*, LXXVII (1912), 1-96.

Bingmann, Karl, *Das rechtliche Verhältnis zwischen Grossbritannien und Hannover, 1714-1837*, Celle, 1925.

Birke, Adolf M., Kurt Kluxen (eds.), *England und Hannover*, Munich, 1986.

Black, Jeremy, *British Foreign Policy in the Age of Walpole*, Edinburgh, 1985.

Black, Jeremy, *Natural and Necessary Enemies: Anglo-French Relations in the Eighteenth Century*, London, 1986.

Blanning, Timothy, C.W., '"That horrid electorate" or "Ma patrie Germanique?" George III, Hanover and the Fürstenbund of 1785', *Historical Journal*, XX, 2 (1977), 311-344.

Borkowsky, Ernst Otto, *Die englische Friedensvermittlung im Jahre 1745*, Berlin, 1884.

Braubach, Max, *Versailles und Wien von Ludwig XIV bis Kaunitz: die Vorstation der diplomatischen Revolution im 18. Jahrhundert*, Bonn, 1952.

Brauer, Gert, *Die hannoversch-englischen Subsidienverträge 1702-1748*, Aalen, 1962.

Brewer, John, *Party Ideology and Popular Politics at the Accession of George III*, Cambridge, 1976.

Broglie, Albert duc de, *La Paix d'Aix la Chapelle*, Paris, 1892.

Brooke, John, *King George III*, London, 1972.

Browning, Reed, *The Duke of Newcastle*, New Haven and London, 1975.

Browning, Reed, 'The Duke of Newcastle and the financial management of the Seven Years War in Germany', *J. of the Society for Army Historical Research*, XLIX (1971), 20-35.

Browning, Reed, 'The Duke of Newcastle and the financing of the Seven Years War', *J. of Economic History*, XXXI (1971), 344-377.

Browning, Reed, 'The Duke of Newcastle and the Imperial election plan, 1749-1754', *J. of British Studies*, VII (1967-68), 28-47.

Campbell, I.B., *The International Legal Relations between Great Britain and Hanover, 1714–1837*, Ph.D. thesis, Cambridge, 1965.

Carswell, John, *The Old Cause: Three Biographical Studies in Whiggism*, London, 1954.

Carter, Alice Clare, *Neutrality or Commitment: The Evolution of Dutch Foreign Policy 1667-1795*, London, 1975.

Charteris, Evan E., *William Augustus Duke of Cumberland and the Seven Years War*, London, n.d. [1925].

Colley, Linda, *In Defiance of Oligarchy: The Tory Party 1714-1760*, Cambridge, 1982.

Conrady, Sigisbert, 'Die Wirksamkeit König Georgs III. für die hannoverschen Kurlande', *Niedersächsisches Jahrbuch fur Landesgeschichte*, XXXIX (1967), 150-191.

Coxe, William, *History of the House of Austria*, London, 1807 (3rd ed. 1847, 3 vols.; vol. III).

Cudmore, Wendy, *Sir Robert Walpole and the Treaty of Vienna, 16 March 1731*, M.A. thesis, London, 1978.

Dann, Uriel, 'Moses Levi of Hanover and King George II', *Jahrbuch des Instituts für Deutsche Geschichte der Universität Tel Aviv*, X (1981), 17-27.

Dann, Uriel, 'Zur Persönlichkeit Gerlach Adolf von Münchhausens - eine Miszelle', *Niedersächsisches Jahrbuch für Landesgeschichte*, LII (1980), 311-316.

Davies, John D. G., *A King in Toils*, London, 1938.

Davis, Garold N., *German Thought and Culture in England 1700-1770*, Chapel Hill, 1969.

Dickson, P. G. M., 'English commercial negotiations with Austria, 1737-1752', in *Statesmen, Scholars and Merchants* (A. Whiteman, P. G. M. Dickson, J. S. Bromley eds.), London, 1973, 81-112.

Dickson, P.G.M., *The Financial Revolution in England*, London, 1967.

Doran, Patrick Francis, *Andrew Mitchell and Anglo-Prussian Diplomatic Relations During the Seven Years War*, New York and London, 1986.

Dorn, Walter L., *Competition for Empire, 1740-1763*, New York, 1940.

Dove, Alfred, *Deutsche Geschichte, 1740-1745*, Gotha, 1883.

Drögereit, Richard, 'Das Testament König Georgs I. und die Frage der Personalunion zwischen England und Hannover', *Niedersächsisches Jahrbuch für Landesgeschichte*, XIV (1937), 94-199.

Droysen, J. G., 'Der Nymphenburger Tractat von 1741', *Zeitschrift für preussische Geschichte*, X (1873), 515-536.

Duchhardt, Heinz, 'England-Hanover und der europäische Friede', *England und Hannover* (Adolf M. Birke, Kurt Kluxen eds.), Munich, 1986, 127-144.

Dunthorne, Hugh Leslie Aldous, *The Alliance of the Maritime Powers 1721-1740*, Ph.D. thesis, London, 1978.

Ebbecke, Otto Karl, *Frankreichs Politik gegenüber dem deutschen Reiche in den Jahren 1748-1756*, Freiburg i. B., 1931.

Ellis, Kenneth, 'The administrative connections between Britain and Hanover', *J. of the Society of Archivists*, III, 10 (October 1969), 546-566.

Ellis, Kenneth, 'British communications and diplomacy in the eighteenth century', *Bulletin of the Institute of Historical Research*, XXI (1958), 159-167.

Ellis, Kenneth, *The Post Office in the 18th Century: A Study in Administrative History*, London, 1958.

Geikie, Roderick, and Montgomery, Isabel A., *The Dutch Barrier 1705-1719*, Cambridge, 1930.

George, M. Dorothy, *English Political Caricature: A Study of Opinion and Propaganda to 1792*, Oxford, 1959.

Geyl, Pieter, 'Holland and England during the War of the Austrian Succession', *History*, X (1925-1926), 46-51.

Gibbs, Graham C., 'English attitudes towards Hanover and the Hanoverian succession in the first half of the eighteenth century', in Adolf M. Birke, Kurt Kluxen (eds.), *England und Hannover*, Munich, 1986, 33-51.

Gmelin, Hans Georg, 'Die Hannoverschen Hofmaler Ziesenis und Ramberg und ihre künstlerischen Beziehungen zu Grossbritannien', in Adolf M. Birke, Kurt Kluxen (eds.), *England und Hannover*, Munich, 1986, 177-194.

Green, V.H.H. *The Hanoverians 1714-1815*, London, 1948.

Grieser, Rudolf, 'Die Deutsche Kanzlei, ihre Entstehung und Anfänge', *Blätter für deutsche Landesgeschichte*, LXXXIX (1952), 153-168.

Grünhagen, Colmar, 'Friedrich der Grosse und seine Umgebung im ersten schlesischen Kriege', *Zeitschrift für preussische Geschichte*, XII (1875), 608-633.

Grünhagen, Colmar, *Geschichte des ersten schlesischen Krieges*, Gotha, 1881, 2 vols.

Guglia, Eugen, *Maria Theresia, ihr Leben und ihre Regierung*, Munich, Berlin, 1917, 2 vols.

Haase, Carl, 'Obrigkeit und öffentliche Meinung in Kurhannover 1789-1803', *Niedersächsisches Jahrbuch für Landesgeschichte*, XXXIX (1967), 192-294.

Hassell, W. von, *Die schlesischen Kriege und das Kurfürstenthum Hannover, insbesondere die Katastrophe von Hastenbeck und Kloster Zeven*, Hanover, 1879.

Hatton, Ragnhild M., *The Anglo-Hanoverian Connection*, London, 1982.

Hatton, Ragnhild M., 'England and Hannover 1714-1837', in Adolf M. Birke, Kurt Kluxen (eds.), *England und Hannover*, Munich, 1986, 17-31.

Hatton, Ragnhild M., *George I, Elector and King*, London, 1978.

Havemann, Wilhelm, *Geschichte der Lande Braunschweig und Lüneburg*, Göttingen, 1857, 3 vols.; vol. III.

Heinemann, O. von, *Geschichte von Braunschweig und Hannover*, Gotha, 1882-1892, 3 vols.; vol. II.
Horn, D. B. *The British Diplomatic Service 1689-1789*, Oxford, 1961.
Horn, D. B., 'The Cabinet controversy on subsidy treaties in time of peace, 1749-50', *EHR*, XLV (1930), 463-466.
Horn, D. B., *Great Britain and Europe in the Eighteenth Century*, Oxford, 1967.
Horn, D. B., 'The origins of the proposed election of a King of the Romans, 1748-1750', *EHR*, XLII (1927), 361-370.
Horn, D. B., *Sir Charles Hanbury Williams and European Diplomacy, 1747-58*, London, 1930.
Hubatsch, Walter, *Friedrich und die preussische Verwaltung*, Cologne, Berlin, 1973.
Hüne, Albert, *Geschichte des Königreichs Hannover und Herzogthums Braunschweig*, Hanover, 1824-30, 2 vols.; vol. I.
Ilchester, Earl of, and Langford-Brooke, Mrs Elizabeth, *The Life of Sir Charles Hanbury-Williams*, London, 1928.
Kaplan, Herbert H., *Russia and the Outbreak of the Seven Years War*, Berkeley and Los Angeles, 1968.
Klopp, Onno, *Geschichte Ostfrieslands unter preussischer Regierung bis zur Abtretung an Hannover, von 1744-1815*, Hanover, 1858.
Klopp, Onno, *Geschichte Ostfrieslands von 1450-1751*, Hanover, 1856.
König, Theo, *Hannover und das Reich, 1740-45*, Düsseldorf, 1938.
Koser, Reinhold, *König Friedrich der Grosse*, Stuttgart, Berlin, 1893, 1903, 2 vols.
Koser, Reinhold, 'Preussen und Russland im Jahrzehnt vor dem siebenjährigen Kriege', *Preussische Jahrbücher*, XLVII (1881), 466-493.
Lampe, Joachim, *Aristokratie, Hofadel und Staatspatriarchat in Kurhannover: Die Lebenskreise der höheren Beamten an den kurhannoverschen Zentral- und Hofbehörden 1714-1760*, Göttingen, 1963, 2 vols.
Langford, Paul, *A Polite and Commercial People: England 1727-1783*, Oxford, 1989.
Langford, Paul, 'William Pitt and Public Opinion 1757', *EHR*, LXXXVIII (1973), 54-80.
Lecky, William E.H., *A History of England in the Eighteenth Century*, London, 1901-03, 7 vols.
Lehzen, W., *Hannover's Staatshaushalt*, Hanover, 1853/54/55; 2 vols.
Lindsay, J.O. (ed.), *The Old Regime 1713-1763*, Cambridge, 1957.
Löb, Abraham, *Die Rechtsverhältnisse der Juden im ehemaligen Königreiche und der jetzigen Provinz Hannover*, Frankfurt a. M., 1908.
Lodge, Sir Richard, 'An episode in Anglo-Russian relations during the war of the Austrian succession', *Transactions of the Royal Historical Society*, 4th series, IX (1926), 63-83.
Lodge, Sir R., 'The first Anglo-Russian treaty, 1739-42', *EHR*, XLIII (1928), 354-375.
Lodge, Sir R., *Great Britain and Prussia in the Eighteenth Century*, Oxford, 1923.
Lodge, Sir R., 'The Hanau controversy in 1744 and the fall of Carteret', *EHR*, XXXVIII (1923), 509-531.
Lodge, Sir R., 'Lord Hyndford's embassy to Russia, 1744-9', *EHR*, XLVI (1931), 48-76, 389-422.
Lodge, Sir R., 'The mission of Henry Legge to Berlin, 1748', *Transactions of the Royal Historical Society*, 4th series (1931), 1-38.
Lodge, Sir R., 'Russia, Prussia and Great Britain, 1742-4', *EHR*, XLV (1930), 579-611.

Lodge, Sir R., 'The so-called "Treaty of Hanau" of 1743', *EHR*, XXXVIII (1923), 384-407.

Lodge, Sir. R., *Studies in Eighteenth Century European Diplomacy 1740-8*, London, 1930.

Lodge, Sir R., 'The Treaty of Worms', *EHR*, XLIV (1929), 220-255.

Mahon, Lord, *History of England from the Peace of Utrecht to the Peace of Versailles 1713-1783*, London, 1853-54, 7 vols.; vols. III-IV.

Marshall, Dorothy, *Eighteenth Century England*, London, 1965.

Mediger, Walther, 'Great Britain, Hanover and the rise of Prussia', in *Studies in Diplomatic History, Essays in Memory of D.B. Horn* (Ragnhild M. Hatton, Matthew S. Anderson eds.), London, 1970, 199-212.

Mediger, Walther, 'Hastenbeck und Zeven: Der Eintritt Hannovers in den Siebenjährigen Krieg', *Niedersächsisches Jahrbuch für Landesgeschichte*, LVI (1984), 137-166.

Mediger, Walther, '... das sogenannte Kriegsgewölbe im Rahmen der hannoverschen Finanzpolitik ... ', introduction to *Findbuch*, Hann. 46 (Kriegsgewölbe), Niedersächsisches Hauptstaatsarchiv, Hanover.

Mediger, Walther, *Mecklenburg, Russland und England – Hannover 1706-1721*, Hildesheim, 1967, 2 vols.

Mediger, Walther, *Moskaus Weg nach Europa: Der Aufstieg Russlands zum europäischen Machtstaat im Zeitalter Friedrichs des Grossen*, Brunswick, 1952.

Meier, Ernst von, *Hannoversche Verfassungs- und Verwaltungsgeschichte 1680-1866*, Leipzig, 1898, 2 vols.

Meyer, Hermann, *Der Plan eines evangelischen Fürstenbundes im siebenjährigen Kriege*, Celle, 1893.

Meyer, Robert, *Die Neutralitätsverhandlungen des Kurfürstentums Hannover beim Ausbruch des siebenjährigen Krieges*, Kiel, 1912.

Michael, Wolfgang, *Englische Geschichte im 18. Jahrhundert*, Leipzig, Basel,1896-1955, 5 vols.

Mini, James Michael, *The Myth of England in the Mind of Germany, 1757-1789: A Study in the Cultural Confrontation of the Enlightenment*. diss., Rutgers University, 1973.

Namier, Sir Lewis B., *England in the Age of the American Revolution*, London, 1930 (1961).

Namier, Sir Lewis B., *The Structure of Politics at the Accession of George III*, London, 1928 (1957).

Newman, Aubrey, N., *The World Turned Inside Out: New Views on George II*, Leicester, 1988.

Niedhart, Gottfried, *Handel und Krieg in der britischen Weltpolitik 1738-1763*, Munich, 1979.

Niemeyer, Joachim, and Ortenburg, Georg, *Die Churbraunschweig-Lüneburgische Armee im Siebenjährigen Kriege*, Beckum, 1976.

Oakley, S. P., 'The Interception of Posts in Celle, 1694-1700', in R. Hatton, J. S. Bromley (eds.), *William III and Louis XIV: Essays in 1680-1720 by and for Mark A. Thomson*, Liverpool, 1968.

Oberschelp, Reinhard, 'Kurhannover im Spiegel von Flugschriften des Jahres 1803', *Niedersächsisches Jahrbuch für Landesgeschichte*, XLIX (1977), 209-247.

Oberschelp, Reinhard, *Politische Geschichte Niedersachsens*, Hildesheim, 1983.

Owen, John B., *The Eighteenth Century 1714-1815*, London, 1974.
Owen, John B., 'George II Reconsidered', *Statesmen, Scholars and Merchants* (A. Whiteman, J. S. Bromley, P. G. M. Dickson eds.), Oxford, 1973.
Owen, John B., *The Rise of the Pelhams*, London, 1957.
Pares, Richard, *King George III and the Politicians*, Oxford, 1953.
Pares, Richard, 'American versus Continental warfare 1739-63', *EHR*, LI (1936), 429-465.
Pemberton, William B., *Carteret: The Brilliant Failure of the Eighteenth Century*, London, 1936.
Plumb, J.H., *England in the Eighteenth Century*, Harmondsworth, 1950.
Plumb, J.H., *Chatham*, London, 1953.
Portzek, Hans, *Friedrich der Grosse und Hannover in ihrem gegenseitigen Urteil*, Hildesheim, 1958.
Press, Volker, 'Kurhannover im System des alten Reiches', *England und Hannover* (Adolf M. Birke, Kurt Kluxen eds.), Munich, 1986, 53-77.
Puster, Klaus, *Möglichkeiten und Verfehlungen merkantiler Politik im Kurfürstentum Hannover unter Berücksichtigung des Einflusses der Personalunion mit dem Königreich Grossbritannien*, Hamburg, 1966.
Ranke, Leopold von, *Zur Geschichte von Oesterreich und Preussen zwischen den Friedensschlüssen zu Aachen und Hubertusburg*, Leipzig, 1875.
Ranke, Leopold von, *Zwölf Bücher preussischer Geschichte*, Leipzig, 1874, books VII-XII.
Reitan, E.A., 'The Civil List in eighteenth-century British politics: parliamentary supremacy versus the independence of the Crown', *Historical Journal*, IX (1966), 318-337.
Richter-Uhlig, Uta, 'Kommunikationsprobleme zwischen London und Hannover: Die Reisen König Georgs II. von England nach Hannover 1727-1740', *Blätter für deutsche Landesgeschichte*, 121 (1985), 207-227.
Röhrbein, Waldemar R., and Rohr, Alheidis von, *Hannover im Glanz und Schatten des britischen Weltreiches: Die Auswirkungen der Personalunion auf Hannover von 1714 bis 1837*, Hanover, 1977.
Rosebery, Lord, *Chatham: His Early Life and Connections*, London, 1910.
Rother, Hermann, *Die Auseinandersetzung zwischen Preussen und Hannover um Ostfriesland von 1690-1744*, diss., Göttingen, 1951.
Runge, Ernst August, *Die Politik Hannovers im deutschen Fürstenbund (1785-1790)*, Erlangen, 1929.
Satow, Sir Ernest M., *The Silesian Loan and Frederick the Great*, Oxford, 1915.
Sautai, Maurice, *Les débuts de la guerre de la Succession d'Autriche*, Paris, 1909.
Sautai, Maurice, *Les préliminaires de la guerre de la Succession d'Autriche*, Paris, 1907.
Savory, Sir Reginald, *His Britannic Majesty's Army in Germany During the Seven Years War*, Oxford, 1966.
Savory, Sir Reginald, 'Jeffery Amherst conducts the Hessians to England, 1756', *J. of the Society for Army Historical Research*, XXIX (1971), 122-181.
Schaefer, Arnold, *Geschichte dès Siebenjährigen Kriegs*, Berlin, 1867-74, 3 vols.
Schlenke, Manfred, 'England blickt nach Europa: Das konfessionelle Argument in der englischen Politik um die Mitte des 18. Jahrhunderts', *Aspekte der deutsch-britischen Beziehungen im Laufe der Jahrhunderte*, London, 1978.
Schlenke, Manfred, *England und das friderizianische Preussen 1740-63*, Freiburg, Munich, 1963.

Schnath, Georg, 'Die Gebietsentwicklung Niedersachsens', *Veröffentlichungen der Wirtschaftswissenschaftlichen Gesellschaft zum Studium Niedersachsens*, Reihe A, Hanover, 1929.

Schnath, Georg, *Geschichte Hannovers ... 1674-1714*, Hildesheim, Leipzig, 1938-1982, 5 vols.

Schnath, Georg (ed.), *Geschichtlicher Atlas Niedersachsens*, Berlin, 1939.

Scott, Hamish Marshall, *Anglo-Austrian Relations after the Seven Years War: Lord Stormont in Vienna, 1763-1772*, Ph.D. thesis, London, 1978.

Sherrard, O.A., *Lord Chatham*, London, 1952-1958, 3 vols.; vols. I-II.

Sichart, L. von, *Geschichte der Königlich Hannoverschen Armee*, Hanover, 1866-71, 5 vols.; vols. II, III.

Sutherland, Lucy, 'The City of London in Eighteenth-Century Politics', in *Lucy Sutherland: Politics and Finance in the Eighteenth Century* (Aubrey Newman ed.), London, 1984.

Thomson, Mark A., *The Secretaries of State 1681-1782*, Oxford, 1932.

Turnstall, Brian, *William Pitt Earl of Chatham*, London, 1938.

Uhle-Wettler, Franz, *Staatsdenken und Englandverehrung bei den frühen Göttinger Historikern*, D.Phil. thesis, Marburg, 1956.

Ulbricht, Otto, *Englische Landwirtschaft in Kurhannover in der zweiten Hälfte des 18. Jahrhunderts*, Berlin, Munich, 1980.

Ulbricht, Otto, '"Im Ealinger Feld habe Turnips gesehen": Landwirtschaftliche Aufzeichnungen Jobst Anton von Hinübers während seines England-Aufenthalts 1766/67', *Jahresheft der Albrecht-Thaer-Gesellschaft*, 19 (1979), 67-109.

Vandal, Albert, *Louis XV et Elisabeth de Russie*, Paris, 1882 (1903).

Vaucher, Paul, *Robert Walpole et la politique de Fleury (1731-42)*, Paris, 1924.

Volz, Gustav Berthold, 'Friedrichs des Grossen Plan einer Losreissung Preussens von Deutschland, *Historische Zeitschrift*, CXXII (1920), 267-277.

Waddington, Richard, *La Guerre de sept ans; histoire diplomatique et militaire*, Paris, 1899-1914, 5 vols.

Waddington, Richard, *Louis XV et le renversement des alliances*, Paris, 1896.

Ward, Sir Adolphus, *Great Britain and Hanover: Some Aspects of the Personal Union*, Oxford, 1899.

Weise, Erich, 'Stader Fernhandelspläne seit den Zeiten der Merchant Adventurers und ihre Beziehungen zu Hamburg', *Hamburger Wirtschaftschronik*, 1950.

Wellenreuther, Hermann, 'Die Bedeutung des Siebenjährigen Krieges für die englisch-hannoveranischen Beziehungen', *England und Hannover* (Adolf M. Birke, Kurt Kluxen eds.), Munich, 1986, 145-175.

Wellenreuther, Hermann, 'Göttingen und England im achtzehnten Jahrhundert', *250 Jahre Vorlesungen an der Georgia-Augusta 1734-1884*, Göttingen, 1985, 30-63.

Wersebe, W. von, *Geschichte der Hannoverschen Armee*, Hanover, 1928.

Wiese, Erwin von, *Die englische parlamentarische Opposition und ihre Stellung zur auswärtigen Politik des britischen Cabinets während des österreichischen Erbfolgekrieges (bezw. der Jahre 1740-1744)*, Waldenburg/Schl., 1883.

Wilkes, John W., *A Whig in Power: The Political Career of Henry Pelham*, New York, 1964.

Williams, Basil, *Carteret and Newcastle: A Contrast in Contemporaries*, Cambridge, 1943.

Williams, Basil, *The Life of William Pitt Earl of Chatham*, London, 1913, 2 vols.

Williams, Basil, *The Whig Supremacy 1714-1760* (rev. C.H. Stuart), Oxford, 1962.
Wilson, Arthur McCandless, *French Foreign Policy during the Administration of Cardinal Fleury 1726-1743*, Cambridge (Mass.), 1936.
Ziekursch, Johannes, *Sachsen und Preussen um die Mitte des 18. Jahrhunderts*, Breslau, 1904.

Subject index